vegetarian entrees

THAT WON'T LEAVE YOU HUNGRY

THE EXPERIMENT BECAUSE EVERY BOOK IS A TEST OF NEW IDEAS

LUKAS VOLGER

VEGETARIAN ENTREES
THAT WON'T LEAVE YOU HUNGRY

NOURISHING, FLAVORFUL MAIN COURSES THAT FILL THE CENTER OF THE PLATE

PHOTOGRAPHS BY CHRISTINA HEASTON

THE EXPERIMENT
NEW YORK

VEGETARIAN ENTRÉES THAT WON'T LEAVE YOU HUNGRY:
Nourishing, Flavorful Main Courses That Fill the Center of the Plate

The Experiment, LLC
260 Fifth Avenue
New York, NY 10001-6408
www.theexperimentpublishing.com

Vegetarian Entrées That Won't Leave You Hungry includes a variety of vegetarian recipes. While care was taken to provide correct and helpful information, the suggestions in this book are not intended as dietary advice or as a substitute for consulting a dietitian or medical professional. We strongly recommend that you check with your doctor before making changes to your diet. The author and publisher disclaim all liability in connection with the use of this book.

Many of the designations used by manufacturers and sellers to distinguish their products are claimed as trademarks. When those designations appear in this book and The Experiment was aware of a trademark claim, the designations have been capitalized.

The Experiment's books are available at special discounts when purchased in bulk for premiums and sales promotions, as well as for fundraising or educational use. For details, contact us at info@theexperimentpublishing.com

Library of Congress Cataloging-in-Publication Data:
Volger, Lukas.
  Vegetarian entrees that won't leave you hungry : nourishing, flavorful main courses that fill the center of the plate / Lukas Volger.
       p. cm.
  Summary: "Includes recipes for filling vegetarian entrees such as salads, soups, rice bowls, risottos, pasta, noodle dishes, dumplings, curries, oven-baked dishes, and eggs every which way"–Provided by publisher.
   ISBN 978-1-61519-033-1 – ISBN 978-1-61519-134-5 (electronic book) 1. Vegetarian cooking. 2. Cookbooks. I. Title.
   TX837.V64 2011
   641.5'636–dc23
                              2011019594

ISBN 978-1-61519-033-1
Ebook ISBN 978-1-61519-134-5

Cover design by Susi Oberhelman
Cover photographs by Christina Heaston
Author photograph by Matt Rebula
Interior design by Pauline Neuwirth, Neuwirth & Associates, Inc.

Manufactured in China
Distributed by Workman Publishing Company, Inc.
Distributed simultaneously in Canada by Thomas Allen and Son Ltd.
First published October 2011

10 9 8 7 6 5 4 3 2 1

✱ **This icon indicates a Group Activity; see page 10.**

4 CURRIES, BRAISED DISHES, AND OVEN-BAKED DISHES   97

VEGETARIAN ENTREES
THAT WON'T LEAVE YOU HUNGRY

WHAT TO PUT IN THE CENTER OF THE PLATE?

SOME TIME AGO, my editor sent me an article by the British writer Rowley Leigh in the *Financial Times* in which he argues that the "vegetarian main course" is some kind of misnomer. "In most households," he writes, the main course is "a chunk of protein with some vegetables beside it. It sort of follows that a hunk of vegetable with some vegetables beside it is a less enticing prospect." He's arguing from a chef's concern for balance, rather than an intent to attack vegetarianism. And to some extent, he has a point.

There's nothing wrong with making a meal of side dishes. After all, in many cuisines, primarily of the East and Middle East, the structure of the meal is such that no single food is meant to steal the spotlight. But if you're not accustomed to such cuisines, and not up for cooking an array of side dishes for dinner every night, determining what to put in the center of the plate can be the hardest part of adapting to and following a vegetarian diet.

If you've picked up this book, you're undoubtedly familiar with the scenario: At a dinner party, or at the Thanksgiving table, or staring into the contents of your refrigerator, you settle for a smattering of nutritionally imbalanced side dishes, overload on bread and cheese, or resort to cooking frozen soy nuggets in the microwave for dinner four nights a week. At run-of-the-mill restaurants, vegetarians don't fare much better. On the menu are one or two "with vegetables" dishes, featuring the vegetables that are otherwise served as sides with everything else on the menu. Maybe you order a "with vegetables" dish, or maybe you just order a salad with a side of French fries. Does that sound appetizing, filling, and nourishing? Not especially.

Thankfully, things are changing. Over the past few years it's become impossible to claim ignorance about the horrors of factory farming—its environmental and health hazards, as well as its ethical implications. In the United States, the USDA recently released new dietary guidelines that put the benefits of plant-based eating front and center. Interest in eating seasonally and locally has spiked to the extent that it's now fodder for satire (I'm thinking in particular of the IFC series *Portlandia*). And restaurants—not only fringe eateries—are beginning to adapt, providing more than just the "with vegetables" options. But what about the home cooks who are skilled at preparing vegetable sides—making salad, steaming broccoli, and grilling corn—but still unsure about how to put together a vegetarian entrée for the center of the plate?

My first book, *Veggie Burgers Every Which Way*, is a deep dive into one kind of filling vegetarian entrée. In fact, I'd long considered veggie burgers the ultimate hearty vegetarian entrée. But looking back over my eating habits, it's clear that I've always favored broader realms. The recipes collected here simply represent the kind of food I'm most inclined to cook and eat. My lazy meal has always been a kitchen-sink salad, eaten directly out of the mixing bowl, but I've discovered that with just a bit of additional effort, hearty yet elegant salads are also easily within reach. Tarts and galettes have always struck me as refined in appearance, fun to make, and universally enjoyed by dinner guests. And then I have a thing for soup, all kinds of soup, though because of the unfortunate state of the air-conditioning in my apartment in New York, hot soup is a decidedly fall through spring meal for me.

One of my first jobs was at a bakery in Idaho, where, in addition to learning how to make bread, I also learned about pastry crust. I had the great pleasure of making quiche in batches of eight. I also had sandwich-making duties, and that's when I learned that a sandwich's most flattering angle is from the center, after it's been cut in half and the fillings are exposed as distinct layers, like strata. I didn't go to culinary arts school for a formal education in food, but that bakery job turned out to be the beginning of my education.

In college I worked part-time in the kitchen of a Manhattan restaurant as a prep cook and a baker. I learned about flavor combinations, discovered what lotus root is, and was taught new ways to make breadsticks and pizza dough and how to properly handle a knife. Ultimately, though, I decided that working in a restaurant kitchen was a little too intense for me, so I found outlets for my curiosity by reading cookbooks and taking classes. While traveling in London, I took a private class on Indian cookery, and in Paris I took one on French cuisine. Here in New York I take classes whenever possible, most recently on kimchi and dim sum. Those motley influences are evident in the breadth of recipes on the pages that follow, which draw on my mix-and-match education and experience. You'll find vegetarian entrées in the form of dumplings and lettuce wraps, burritos and tostadas, curries and noodle bowls, frittatas and gratins, and much, much more.

There seems to be a popular misconception that, unless you're a strict vegetarian or vegan and thus accustomed to following such diets, vegetarian entrées will fail to fill you up. I hear this kind of thing all the time: "I'd love to eat more vegetarian meals, but I'm always hungry afterward" or "I'd love to follow a vegetarian diet, but my husband complains it's not enough food. He doesn't think it's dinner without the meat." I understand where that mentality comes from. Many of us, myself included, grew up believing that vegetables had two basic purposes: to fulfill nutritional requirements (we choked them down because we were promised dessert afterward), and to occupy that circular band of space between the edge of the plate and the hunk of meat in the middle of it. However, the recipes in this book, with their robust textures, bold flavors, and hearty ingredients, challenge that old paradigm.

That said, it seems that everywhere we look we're encouraged to overeat, to the extent that, as a culture, we've developed a distorted sense of what being full means. I probably don't need to provide examples; if you have any familiarity with chain restaurants and fast-food outlets, you know what I mean. The amounts of food served challenge us either to overeat or to waste. The healthiest definition of "full" I ever got was from my seventh-grade English teacher, Mrs. Gratton, who described optimum fullness as "when you've got room for just one more bite." This strikes me as perfect. It's a diplomatic way to describe being properly fed but not feeling sick, and also accommodates our individual appetites and relationships with food. So while I do aim to tempt you with hearty, vegetarian entrées, I don't want to make you sick to your stomach or contribute to an ever-expanding waistline. Therefore, the recipes in this book are not just delicious and fulfilling, they're also sound and sensible.

I've also scattered tutorials throughout the book. Labeled "Vegetarian Kitchen Essentials," these passages are intended to enlighten and embolden you, and to lay the groundwork for you to develop new vegetarian entrées on your own. Dishes like soup, risotto, and noodle bowls can taste just as good—and be more economical—when you know how to make them from whatever ingredients happen to be on hand. Learning to improvise in the kitchen is a thrilling skill to hone, especially if you're just learning how to flex your culinary muscles.

So whether you're a veteran of the vegetarian table or you've just begun participating in the popular online Meatless Monday campaign, you'll find plenty to work with in this book. By combining the entrée recipes with the simple appetizers, salads, and desserts scattered throughout the book, you'll be able to concoct complete weeknight meals for your family and feasts worthy of dinner guests. The only daunting aspect of deciding what to put in the center of your vegetarian plate will be choosing among the many options.

OUTFITTING a VEGETARIAN KITCHEN

MAKING YOUR KITCHEN a place that's conducive to cooking is as important as shopping for groceries. If you face hurdles when you get home from work, exhausted and hungry—when a run to the corner market once you've already kicked off your shoes seems like too much to bear—the most appealing option is likely to be picking up the phone to order in, even if you know that a home-cooked meal will be exponentially more satisfying. Outfitting your kitchen properly will ease the burden and enhance the cooking experience.

Using equipment that you enjoy working with will streamline the process. Invest in one or two knives that work well for you, and keep them sharp. Sometimes a comfortable knife and a spacious, heavy cutting board are all you need to renew your energies in the kitchen. Get rid of disheveled equipment: the rubber spatula that's halfway torn apart, the aluminum stockpot that doesn't sit flat on the burner, the dull vegetable peeler. Aim to eliminate any equipment that makes cooking more difficult than it should be, and replace worn-out items you actually use with higher-quality tools and equipment. You can spruce up your kitchen easily with a quick trip to a restaurant supply store, and it need not be expensive.

A well-stocked pantry is also a must. Keep things like pasta, grains, and canned tomatoes on hand, as well as produce that has a lengthy shelf life, like root vegetables and winter squash. For the types of dishes you make most often, whether egg dishes, sandwiches, or soups, try to have the basic ingredients on hand most of the time. Then, when you can, try to plan ahead. Figure out how much time you'll have to cook over a given period and develop your menus accordingly. If you have more time for cooking on weekends, you might plan to prepare vegetable stock, roast beets or tomatoes, make a batch of pesto, cook a pot of beans, or make a few dishes and store up leftovers. You can also do simpler tasks in advance, such as washing lettuce, making bread crumbs, or slicing a loaf of bread and placing it in the freezer. All will make it easier to put together meals when you have less time and energy for cooking.

This chapter lays the foundation for some kitchen basics, starting with equipment and ending with the importance of finesse. Use it as a reference as you explore the world of satisfying vegetarian entrées.

EQUIPMENT

As far as equipment goes, one can make do with very little in the kitchen. Civilization got us plenty far without food processors, and I recall pulling off all kinds of delicious feasts as a budget-conscious college student. That said, using the right equipment can make the difference between cooking being an absolute pleasure versus being laborious and agonizing. The following list isn't meant to be exhaustive; these are merely tips on a few of the items I believe to be noteworthy.

CUTTING BOARD: A broad, completely flat, heavy cutting board, rather than one that's lightweight, small, or flimsy or has ridges, grooves, handles, or little stilts, makes cooking and prepping an infinitely more relaxing task. My favorite kind is the heavy, all-rubber type used in restaurants. They're more expensive than plastic boards but are less likely to absorb odors and develop mildew and will generally last longer than other types. Mine, which is 18 by 12 inches (45 × 30 cm) and ¾ inch (2 cm) thick, is made by Sani-Tuff, the manufacturer of the most popular rubber cutting boards. They come in many different sizes and shapes and are available online as well as at restaurant supply stores.

FOOD PROCESSOR: I love my 9-cup-capacity food processor. It makes it a breeze to prepare pesto and pie dough and chop large quantities of vegetables. But it is an expensive piece of equipment. I think it's best to acquire a food processor after having first spent a few years making do without one; this way you'll appreciate it for the tasks it streamlines and also be aware of its limitations. A food processor will speed up the steps in several recipes in this book, but it's not a crucial appliance.

GRATIN AND SOUFFLÉ DISHES: There just aren't good substitutes for soufflé dishes and individual gratin dishes, though oven-safe coffee cups can sometimes be used for individual soufflés. French-made porcelain soufflé and gratin dishes can be pricey. Fortunately there are many inexpensive counterparts available at stores, or at garage sales, flea markets, and secondhand stores. For the recipes in this book, I recommend you have the following on hand: a 1½-quart soufflé dish, four individual soufflé dishes, and four individual gratin dishes.

A bonus is that the individual dishes can double up as nibbler bowls at cocktail parties.

IMMERSION BLENDER: Handheld immersion blenders are relatively inexpensive, don't take up counter space, and make pureeing soups and sauces a quick and mess-free job. I use mine all the time and have never regretted purchasing it.

OVEN THERMOMETER: If you've perused many other cookbooks, you've no doubt been proselytized on the merits of oven thermometers. But if this is new information for you, let me begin your indoctrination: You *must* get an oven thermometer! Because ovens are notoriously inaccurate, this relatively inexpensive gadget will improve your baking and roasting many times over. While you can buy a very cheap oven thermometer at a grocery store or hardware store, just a few dollars more will get you one that's a bit more substantial and has an easier-to-read display.

SAUCEPANS AND STOCKPOTS: The best saucepans and stockpots are heavy bottomed. This encourages even heat distribution and also helps prevent burning. Plus, lightweight cookware, such as aluminum, can dent and warp over time, and become wobbly on the burners. Not only is this unsafe, it's also extremely aggravating. Technically the following are all you need as far as saucepans and stockpots go:

- **Stockpot, at least 8-quart capacity**, which can be used to make soups and stocks and to boil pasta. I also have a **6½-quart Dutch oven**, which I prefer to the stockpot for soups, as it's somewhat shallower and wider, granting easier access. It's also ovenproof.

- **Medium saucepan, 3- or 4-quart capacity**, which has a multitude of uses, including cooking rice, beans, and curries and steaming or boiling vegetables. I have a **3-quart saucier** that functions as my medium saucepan. It's essentially a wide, deep skillet that comes with a lid. I don't think it's an essential piece of equipment, but it is one of my favorites for the same reason that I like the Dutch oven so much: It's wider and shallower.

- **Small saucepan, about 1-quart capacity**, which will be your go-to pot for all small-volume needs. You'll find it essential for reheating soups, cooking smaller amounts of rice or other grains, and steaming small amounts of vegetables.

SAUTÉ PANS OR SKILLETS: Two 10-inch (25 cm) sauté pans or skillets, one standard and one nonstick, should suffice, at least for the recipes in this book. I recommend that you reserve the nonstick pan for situations where sticking is an issue, such as cooking eggs and crepes. Otherwise, use the standard pan, including for sautéing or panfrying. Cast-iron skillets are inexpensive, easy to find, excellent conductors of heat, and always ovenproof, but they do require some maintenance. When you purchase a new cast-iron skillet, you'll need to season it, and there are two options:

- Season your skillet all at once: Fill it halfway with oil and put it in a 450°F (225°C) oven for an hour (it will begin to smoke). Then turn off the heat and let it cool. Discard the oil (complying with your city's oil disposal requirements) and wipe the pan dry. Your skillet is now seasoned.

■ Season your skillet gradually as you cook with it: Cook using a generous amount of grease the first few times. If you have reason to shallow-fry anything, that's an excellent way to begin seasoning. With gradual seasoning, wash the skillet immediately after use, using only a small amount of dish soap and a soft sponge. Don't scrub too hard. Dry the skillet thoroughly with a clean towel, then rub in a bit of neutral oil—canola, peanut, or grapeseed— either with your fingers or using a paper towel. As you continue to use your skillet regularly, you'll notice a patina starting to form. This slick film over the cooking surface means you're on your way.

Always wash a seasoned skillet gently, with only a small amount of soap, and dry it thoroughly and immediately. You can even dry it by placing it on the stove over heat for a minute.

SPICE GRINDER: If you're going to primarily stock whole spices (which I recommend), you'll need a spice grinder, which need not be a big investment. I actually own two of them, one for my coffee and one for my spices, but this happened by accident and is indeed excessive. You can wipe your grinder with a damp cloth between uses to collect stray grounds or avoid spicing your coffee, but be sure to let it air-dry completely before using it again. Another way to clean it out is to run a spoonful of rice through the grinder to pick up any residual coffee or spices, then discard.

PASTRY BLENDER AND DOUGH SCRAPER: These tools will come in handy when making tarts and galettes. If you don't have a food processor, an inexpensive pastry blender makes cutting but-ter or shortening into flour a significantly easier job than it is using a fork or two knives, thanks to its metal strips and easy-to-maneuver handle. And a dough scraper—essentially a rectangular slab of metal affixed with a handle—is one of those items that have only one intended use (separating dough from the work surface), but you will probably find, as I have, that it's equally useful for transferring large quantities of chopped vegetables from the cutting board to a pot or a bowl.

Selected Pantry Essentials

Here are a few items that will facilitate convenient home cooking, particularly for the recipes in this book. These are just a few noteworthy items; again, this isn't intended to be an exhaustive list.

▶ SPICES

Whenever possible, buy your spices whole; they hold on to their flavor significantly longer than ground spices do. It also makes a big difference, both in your wallet and in your cooking, to find a spice purveyor that sells in bulk. To use whole spices, toast them briefly in a dry skillet until fragrant, 1 to 3 minutes, then grind with a mortar and pestle or in a spice grinder. In the recipes in this book, and in general, I don't go overboard with dried spices. Too many can clutter up a recipe. For herbs like basil, thyme, dill, and chives, I usually opt for fresh.

CAYENNE PEPPER: Ground cayenne is the simplest way to add heat to a dish that I know of. Cayenne peppers pack a punch, but they still register in the lower half of the Scoville scale, the prevailing system for measuring and ranking the heat units in chile peppers. Cayenne does lose its heat over time, and I find that its heat level varies quite a lot between brands. Be sure to taste as you cook with it, and to refresh your supply frequently.

CHIPOTLE CHILES: Chipotle chiles are dried, smoked jalapeños. Like cayenne peppers, they have a medium heat level on the Scoville scale. Ground chipotles add a distinctive sweet-smoky dimension to soups and chili. Use them as you would ground cayenne. The heat level is marginally lower, but they add a great deal of flavor. Again, taste as you cook and adjust accordingly.

CUMIN: Cumin is a staple of many cuisines, including Indian cuisines, where it's often included in curry powders. To me, it is *the* spice that epitomizes earthiness. Buy the seeds whole, and when recipes call for ground cumin, toast the seeds before grinding them to best bring out their flavor.

GARAM MASALA: Similar to curry powder, garam masala is a spice blend that's a hallmark of Indian and other south Asian cuisines. It's a sweet, peppery blend, with cloves, cinnamon, star anise, cardamom, and other spices varying from region to region, and even from household to household. In addition to its traditional uses, it makes a wonderful addition to your favorite recipe for zucchini bread.

SALT: This may sound excessive, but I keep three types of salt around in my kitchen. I use kosher salt when larger quantities are called for—when boiling pasta or making brines, for example. I use good-quality fine-grain sea salt for most other purposes, such as dressings, baked goods, and eggs, and when the recipes in this book call for just plain salt, this is what I'm referring to. I use fleur de sel as a finishing salt and at the table. I first tried fleur de sel when on vacation in Paris and ended up packing my bag with as much as I could manage to carry home. Fleur de sel is flaky and delicate and has a complex, sea-breeze flavor that I'd never experienced before. It's becoming increasingly available at grocery stores, specialty markets, and, of course, through online retailers.

SMOKED PAPRIKA: Paprika comes in various heat levels. Whatever amount of spiciness you prefer, look for smoked paprika to lend a distinctive flavor to dishes. Good, fresh paprika from Spain or Hungary tastes vastly different from the typical flavorless stuff used as a garnish on deviled eggs.

▶ OILS

It used to be that I cooked almost exclusively with olive oil, but between its low smoke point and how it loses its flavor and takes on an unpleasant odor at higher temperatures, I've begun approaching oil the same way I approach salt. "Neutral oil" is my fine-grain sea salt: I use it most often, particularly when applying heat, such as when sautéing or roasting. With olive oil, on the other hand, I buy a bottle that I love the taste of and use it like a finishing salt, in places where its delicate flavor will shine. Then there are nut and seed oils, such as toasted sesame oil (described below), that have more specific uses. All oils are adversely affected by exposure to air, light, and heat and will eventually go rancid, so it's best to buy them in smaller volumes and store them in a cool, dark place.

NEUTRAL OIL: Neutral oil is used most frequently in this book, and clearly olive oil isn't a neutral oil. The most common neutral oils are canola, grapeseed, peanut, and standard vegetable oil, all available in organic versions. When I refer to "neutral oil" in the recipes here, I'm referring to these.

OLIVE OIL: I am a big fan of olive oil and am willing to splurge on a good bottle of it. These days I mostly use olive oil for finishing drizzles and in delicately flavored salad dressings, instances when I want its delicious flavor to shine. And when I do use it for cooking, it is only at low to medium-low temperatures.

TOASTED SESAME OIL: A prominent ingredient in many Asian cuisines, toasted sesame oil shows up in a lot of the recipes in this book. It's different from plain sesame oil, which is made from raw sesame seeds and has a more delicate flavor. Toasted sesame oil has an unmistakable aroma and flavor that adds a forthright richness to stir-fries and soups, and in small doses can even be used as a finishing oil. But a little goes a *long* way, so use it sparingly.

GROUP ACTIVITY ALERTS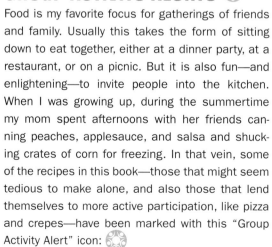

Food is my favorite focus for gatherings of friends and family. Usually this takes the form of sitting down to eat together, either at a dinner party, at a restaurant, or on a picnic. But it is also fun—and enlightening—to invite people into the kitchen. When I was growing up, during the summertime my mom spent afternoons with her friends canning peaches, applesauce, and salsa and shucking crates of corn for freezing. In that vein, some of the recipes in this book—those that might seem tedious to make alone, and also those that lend themselves to more active participation, like pizza and crepes—have been marked with this "Group Activity Alert" icon:

A NOTE ABOUT COOKING TIMES

It's very difficult to calculate how long it will take the average cook to prepare any given recipe. There are so many variables: skill level and dexterity with a knife, functionality of the kitchen and appliances, variations in ingredients (such as the size of vegetables or the age of beans), and so on. In the cooking times noted in the recipes in this book, I've aimed to slightly overestimate. Generally, however, and especially if preparation and cooking time are a major factor, I encourage you to read through a recipe completely and judge its prep time based on your own experience, skills, and situation.

TIPS ON PREPARING a Few Basic Foods

This section first discusses some general cooking methods, for greens, beans, rice, and toasting nuts and seeds, and then includes a few recipes for pantry staples and entrée enhancers like pesto and ginger-scallion sauce.

▶ LEAFY GREENS

Greens, including spinach, arugula, escarole, kale, chard, turnip greens, mustard greens, and collard greens, are a pillar of the vegetarian diet, and of many recipes in this book. They often need to be cooked, both to make their texture complement the dish, and to reduce their bulk to a manageable volume. Blanching, steaming, and sautéing are the three most common methods for cooking greens. Here are some pointers on each method:

❋ **BLANCHING OR PARBOILING** is best when cooking greens in great quantity, or when they'll be used in a pasta dish or alongside it, since this requires bringing a pot of water to a boil anyway. To blanch greens, bring a large pot of salted water to a boil. Add the greens all at once. Cooking time varies depending on the type of green being cooked. For delicate greens like spinach, blanching takes only 10 to 20 seconds. For heartier greens like kale, it can take up to 5 or even 10 minutes. The greens are ready when they're completely wilted (remove a few leaves with tongs or a slotted spoon and taste to check). You may want to reserve the cooking water for other elements of your meal—to cook pasta in, or use as a light stock—in which case use tongs or a slotted spoon to remove the greens. Transfer them immediately to an ice bath to halt the cooking. Once they're cool enough to handle, grab the greens in small fistfuls and squeeze out as much liquid as possible.

❄ STEAMING is, in my opinion, the easiest and most time-efficient method. To steam greens, put 1 inch (3 cm) of water in a soup pot or Dutch oven, then place a steaming basket in it. Bring the water to an active simmer and adjust the heat to maintain the simmer. Add the greens and cover the pot. Again, cooking time varies depending on the type of green being cooked. For delicate greens like spinach, steaming takes no more than 1 minute, while heartier greens like kale require about 5 minutes. The greens are ready when they're completely wilted (again, you can remove a few leaves with tongs or a slotted spoon and taste to check). Discard the cooking water or add it to stock. As with blanching, transfer the greens to an ice bath and, once they're cool enough to handle, squeeze out as much liquid as possible.

❄ SAUTÉING is best for simple dishes where the greens play a starring role. Cooking them in olive oil over low or medium-low heat enriches them and results in a slightly more substantial texture than blanching or steaming. To sauté greens, heat 1 tablespoon or more of oil or butter per 8 ounces (230 g) of greens in a sauté pan over medium heat. Add the greens. If they've just been washed and still have some water clinging to them, no worries; this will just promote their cooking. Use tongs or a spatula to toss the greens until they're uniformly wilted. Don't transfer sautéed greens to an ice bath, as this will rinse off the oil. Press on them lightly with a spatula to extract the liquid and then carefully pour it out from the pan.

▶ **BEANS**

Beans are another pillar of the vegetarian diet, and also play an important role in creating nutritious, filling, center-of-the-plate entrées. Here are the types you'll want to keep on hand for the recipes in this book:

❄ BLACK BEANS: Also known as turtle beans or azuki beans, black beans have shiny black skins and a velvety interior and are naturally high in fiber.

❄ CANNELLINI, NAVY, AND GREAT NORTHERN BEANS: These three beans are often grouped together. Cannellini (sometimes labeled "Italian white kidney beans") are the largest and navy beans are the smallest, but otherwise the three are very similar, with white skins and creamy interiors.

❄ CHICKPEAS: Also known as garbanzo beans, chickpeas are the foundation for hummus. They're higher in protein than many other beans and have an unmistakable eggy flavor.

✳ **KIDNEY BEANS:** Red kidney beans have a mild flavor and are large and starchy. White kidney beans (sometimes labeled "cannellini") are similar in texture and flavor and can be used interchangeably with navy, cannellini, and great northern beans.

✳ **LENTILS:** There are over fifty different types of lentils available worldwide. They come in a rainbow of colors, but the three most commonly available are brown, red, and green. Brown and red lentils are usually split and therefore have shorter cooking times. In some recipes I call for French green lentils, which are sometimes marked as "du puy"— they are a dark green color, and smaller in diameter, but when cooked they retain their structure quite a bit better than other types of lentils.

Canned beans have some advantages, chief among them that they are instantly ready to be used. But home-cooked beans have their advantages, too, including a cleaner taste, better structure, and, potentially, better quality.

You do have to plan ahead if you're going to cook beans from scratch, because, with the exception of lentils, they need to be soaked before cooking. You can soak them overnight, or use the faster soaking method outlined below to reduce the soaking time. Whichever soaking method you use, start by rinsing the beans, then picking through them for disfigured beans or small stones.

OVERNIGHT SOAKING METHOD: Place the beans in a bowl and cover with water, using at least double the volume of the beans. Let rest overnight on the counter.

FASTER SOAKING METHOD: Place the beans in a saucepan or soup pot and cover with water, using at least double the volume of the beans. Bring to a boil and boil for 5 minutes. Cover the pot, remove from the heat, and let stand for 1 hour.

TO COOK THE BEANS: After soaking the beans, drain off the soaking water. Place the beans in a large saucepan or soup pot and cover with water, again using at least double the volume of the beans (which will be greater after soaking). Bring to a boil, then lower the heat, partially cover the pot, and simmer until the beans are tender. Cooking time varies greatly depending on the type of beans and how old they are. The only way to ensure they're properly cooked is to test them along the way. Some beans will take 30 minutes to cook, and some will take a few hours. Don't add salt until the last 10 or 15 minutes of cooking; salting earlier encourages the skins of the beans to seize up, resulting in an unpleasant texture.

▶ RICE

I used to be intimidated by cooking rice. There were so many different methods and cooking times, the question of whether to presoak or not, and the seemingly imprecise method of measuring the amount of water wherein you cover the rice with water to the depth of two knuckles, or something like that. But I've found that rice is more forgiving that we've been led to believe. If there's excess water, just drain it off; if the rice seems too dry, add about 1 tablespoon of water and cook for a few more minutes.

Here's the method that consistently works well for me: Put the rice in a sieve and rinse it. Transfer it to a small saucepan into which the volume of cooked rice will fit snugly. Pour in water, using 2 parts water to 1 part rice. Bring to a boil, then immediately cover the pan and turn the heat down as low as possible. Cook for 25 minutes for white rice, or 30 minutes for brown rice. Remove from the heat and let the rice sit, covered, for 10 minutes. Then fluff with a fork and serve.

My favorite types of rice are the fragrant ones, such as basmati and jasmine, both of which have delicious brown rice counterparts.

▶ NUTS AND SEEDS

Nuts and seeds have significantly more flavor after they've been roasted or toasted, and it's better to handle the task yourself than to buy them pre-roasted or -toasted. A cast-iron skillet is an excellent vessel to use for roasting and toasting nuts, as it can be used interchangeably on the stovetop and in the oven, and is especially good for smaller amounts of nuts and seeds. In general, nuts, like walnuts and cashews, are best roasted in the oven, and small seeds, like sesame seeds, are best toasted on the stovetop.

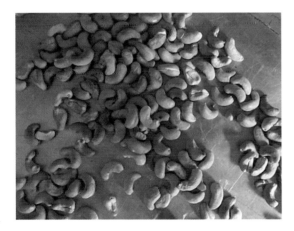

TO ROAST NUTS: Preheat the oven to 325°F (265°C). Spread the nuts in a single layer on a dry baking sheet or in a dry cast-iron skillet. Roast, stirring every 7 minutes or so, for 15 to 20 minutes, until the nuts have darkened a shade and are very aromatic, and, when cut in half, the interior is uniformly browned. Transfer the nuts immediately, as they will continue to roast on the hot baking sheet or skillet even after it's removed from the heat.

TO TOAST SEEDS: Heat a dry cast-iron skillet or sauté pan over medium-low heat. Add the seeds, swirling so that they form an even layer. Toast for about 5 minutes, swirling frequently, until they've darkened a bit and are very aromatic. Transfer the seeds immediately, as they will continue to toast in the hot skillet or pan even after it's removed from the heat.

▶ FRESH GINGER

Fresh ginger lends an unmistakable, bright spiciness to whatever dish it's added to, and it's one of my favorite aromatics to cook with. When purchasing ginger, always choose a root that is as firm as possible—avoid anything that seems even slightly limp. Young ginger root, which has small knobs that are up to ½ inch (1 cm) in diameter, has thin, tender skin, and if you wipe it off with a damp towel, it can be used without peeling first. Mature ginger, with its larger, more bulbous roots that can be 1 inch (3 cm) in diameter, and sometimes more, should be peeled before using. I do this by gently scraping it off with the dull side of a knife. While there are graters available, typically made from porcelain and intended to be used exclusively for ginger, I find it easier to use a Microplane grater. If you don't plan to use up your ginger within two days, it can be frozen whole (peeled first if a larger root) and kept for up to two months. Simply grate it, while still frozen, as needed—it will thaw in 2 or 3 minutes.

▶ LEEKS

Leeks are notorious for having bits of sand and dirt lodged throughout, but there are many ways

to clean them. One popular method is to slice off the roots, and then quarter each leek lengthwise from the root end to a few inches into the dark green part (the leek is still in one piece, connected at the top). Pull the leeks open, blossom-like, and gently rub their insides under running water to rid them of dirt.

My preferred method—which more thoroughly cleans and also alleviates the tedious task of chopping wet vegetables—is to chop them before cleaning, cover them with cold water in a large bowl, and swish them around with your hands to dislodge the dirt. Change the water and repeat. Drain in a sieve or colander.

Recipe Staples, Sauces, and Condiments

IN THIS SECTION I'll outline a few recipes for items like stock and roasted red peppers that you might be more inclined to purchase than to prepare yourself. That's a fine shortcut to take, but hopefully you'll find that some of these items are easier to incorporate into your cooking routines than you thought.

VEGETABLE STOCK

I CAN BE very lackadaisical when it comes to vegetable stock. I know that many chefs consider stock a precise, high art, but I approach it mostly as a way to use up vegetable trimmings that would otherwise go to waste—either trimmings I've saved and frozen or new trimmings from the dish for which I am making the stock (see page 16). This recipe is for my "standard" stock: I make a base from onions, carrots, celery, garlic, bay leaves, and peppercorns and then pick through the trimmings for additional ingredients. And if I don't have the carrots, onions, or celery on hand, I just make do with what's in the freezer.

▶ MAKES ABOUT 6 CUPS (1.5 l)

1 teaspoon neutral oil (canola, grapeseed, peanut, or vegetable oil)

1 onion, coarsely chopped

1 carrot, coarsely chopped

2 celery stalks, coarsely chopped

4 garlic cloves, smashed

6 black peppercorns

1 bay leaf

1 leafy parsley sprig

1 thyme sprig

Vegetable trimmings

7 cups (3.25 l) water

About ½ teaspoon kosher salt

Heat the oil in a stockpot over medium heat. Add the onion, carrot, celery, garlic, and peppercorns and stir until evenly coated. Cover and cook for 5 minutes. Add the bay leaf, parsley, thyme, and any vegetable trimmings you're using, then the water. Bring to a boil, then lower the heat to maintain a gentle but active simmer. Cook, uncovered, for 25 to 35 minutes, tasting and adding salt, a pinch at a time, starting at 15 minutes into the cooking time. Strain the stock using a cheesecloth-lined colander or sieve before cooking with it.

NOTE: To make "light" vegetable stock, as specified in the recipe for Basic Vegetable Risotto (page 63), simply mix two-thirds vegetable stock with one-third water. This is also a nice way to offset the taste of canned or boxed vegetable stock, or even bouillon cubes if that's what you have on hand.

▶ LEFTOVERS: Stored in an airtight container, vegetable stock will keep for up to 3 days in the refrigerator and 1 month in the freezer.

▶ PREPARATION AND COOKING TIME: 1 hour

TIPS ON VEGETABLE STOCK

OVER YEARS OF making stock, I've picked up quite a few pointers. Here's a trick I learned from my editor, Matthew Lore: As I accumulate vegetable trimmings—including stems of Swiss chard or kale, peels and ends from carrots and parsnips, mushroom stems, and the tough ends of asparagus spears—I throw them into a bag I keep in the freezer. When it comes time to make stock, I have a variety of trimmings all ready to go in.

I do sometimes make stock "to order" for a particular dish. When I make soup, for example, I use the trimmings from the vegetables that go into the finished soup to make the stock. This keeps the flavors in line, makes use of as much of the food as possible, and is actually a lot more feasible to pull off than it might sound. After all, stock only takes 30 to 40 minutes to cook, and it sometimes takes that long to prep the ingredients for a dish and get to the point in the recipe where the stock is added. An example is my Basic Vegetable Risotto (page 63), where I include instructions for making a vegetable stock to add to the dish.

Often, stock isn't especially flavorful and needs a bit of salt to bring the flavors into focus. However, too much salt cancels everything out, so it's important, as always, to taste along the way. When cooking and seasoning stock, I find that there's a moment when, subtle as the flavors are, they suddenly become immediate and sharp. That's how I know the stock is done.

Beyond those general pointers, here are a few guidelines in terms of specific ingredients:

* Mushrooms go a long way. Mushroom stems are a terrific addition to stocks, but unless your desired effect is a very mushroomy flavor, use no more than a dozen stems per 8 cups (2 l) of stock.
* Beet trimmings will dye your stock pink. They will also make your stock somewhat sweet, which has a tendency to overwhelm the finished dish. I usually avoid using beet trimmings in stock.
* Too many greens will impart a bitter taste. Hearty greens—which in stock usually take the form of the stems—can definitely brighten up the flavor of stock, but too many will give it an unpleasant, metallic taste. Greens should comprise no more than one-quarter of the volume of the ingredients used in the stock.
* Avoid using onion skins because they, too, will leave a bitter taste.
* Don't use any vegetables that have passed their expiration date. The rule is, if you wouldn't eat it otherwise, don't cook with it. Rubbery or slimy vegetables should never be used in stock.

TOASTED BREAD CRUMBS

CANNED BREAD CRUMBS are easy enough to buy, and in some dishes they are perfectly fine. When using store-bought bread crumbs, I generally I prefer panko, Japanese bread crumbs that are larger and more textured than standard bread crumbs; they're widely available these days in grocery stores. In other dishes, however, homemade bread crumbs will make a huge difference. They're so easy to make; plus, they store well in the freezer and are a great way to use up stale bread.

▶ **MAKES 2 CUPS (240 g)**

8 slices stale but still pliant bread
3 tablespoons olive oil

1. Preheat the oven to 325°F (165°C).
2. Tear the bread into small pieces and place in a food processor. Pulse until the bread is broken down into crumbs. Toss the crumbs with the olive oil, then spread them on a baking sheet.
3. Bake, stirring frequently, for 12 to 15 minutes, until golden brown. Remove from the baking sheet immediately; left on the pan they'll continue to cook and might burn.

▶ LEFTOVERS: Stored in an airtight container, bread crumbs will keep for up to 3 months in the freezer.

▶ PREPARATION AND COOKING TIME: 25 minutes

CROUTONS

CROUTONS ARE A great way to use up bread that's beginning to dry out. They can be made in any number of ways, using any kind of bread you have on hand, though, in general, the better the quality of the bread, the better the croutons will be. I often make crostini-style croutons from a baguette, slicing it into thin rounds, brushing them with olive oil, and baking for 15 minutes at 375°F (190°C) until crisp. But for soups and salads I prefer cubed croutons, and I like them a bit on the salty side.

▶ MAKES 2 CUPS (225 g)

2 cups (200 g) bread, cut or torn into ½-inch (1 cm) cubes

2 to 3 tablespoons olive oil

Generous pinch of salt

Pinch of dried herbs, such as parsley, oregano, thyme, tarragon, or herbes de Provence

1. Preheat the oven to 350°F (180°C).
2. Spread the bread cubes in an even layer on a baking sheet. Drizzle the olive oil over them and toss until the bread is evenly coated. Sprinkle with the salt and herbs.
3. Bake, stirring every 5 minutes, until the croutons are golden brown and crisp. This will take anywhere from 10 to 25 minutes, depending on the density of the bread. Watch them closely, as they can burn easily.

▶ LEFTOVERS: Stored in an airtight container in a cool place, croutons will keep for up to 3 days.

▶ PREPARATION AND COOKING TIME: 30 minutes

ROASTED BELL PEPPERS

SOONER OR LATER, roasted peppers have to be cleaned of seeds, ribs, and skin. I like the following method because it gets the elbow grease over with up front, and because the seeds can be tedious to clean off once the peppers are coated with oil and their juices. Roasted bell peppers are a familiar enough staple nowadays, especially in roasted vegetable panini in which the peppers come from cans or jars. But there's no excuse for this; they're so easy, and so intoxicatingly aromatic, to make at home.

▶ **MAKES 4 ROASTED PEPPERS**

4 bell peppers, any color
2 tablespoons olive oil

1. Preheat the oven to 400°F (200°C).
2. Cut off the tops and bottoms of the peppers. Remove the stems from the tops and set these pieces aside. Make a horizontal slice down the length of each pepper so it can be opened. Carefully cut out the ribs and the seeds. Halve the peppers or cut them into thirds so they lie mostly flat. Toss all the pepper pieces with the olive oil and spread them on a baking sheet.
3. Bake for 45 to 60 minutes, flipping the pieces every 20 minutes; the peppers will be completely tender when done.
4. Allow to cool for at least 20 minutes before removing the skins, which will come off very easily. Just pinch a piece of the skin that has separated from the flesh of the pepper, then gently peel it from the rest of the pepper.

▶ **LEFTOVERS:** Stored in an airtight container, the roasted peppers will keep for up to 5 days in the refrigerator.

▶ **PREPARATION AND COOKING TIME:** 1 hour and 30 minutes

ROASTED GARLIC

ROASTING GARLIC IS a great task to keep on the weekend checklist—having it on hand during the week makes for an easy way to enhance your meals. I find it's best to store the garlic heads whole and break off cloves as needed.

▶ MAKES 4 HEADS OF ROASTED GARLIC

4 heads garlic
1 tablespoon olive oil
¼ cup (60 ml) water

1. Preheat the oven to 375°F (190°C).
2. Turn the garlic heads on their sides and, with a sharp knife, carefully chop off the tops so that most of the cloves are exposed. Arrange the garlic heads in a small, oven-safe dish (a gratin dish or small skillet works well) and drizzle the oil over the top. Pour ¼ cup water into the dish and cover it tightly with foil. Bake for 45 to 60 minutes, until the garlic cloves are completely tender.

3. To remove the roasted garlic, break the heads into cloves as you need them and squeeze out the flesh.

▶ LEFTOVERS: Stored in an airtight container, the roasted garlic will keep for up to 1 week in the refrigerator.

▶ PREPARATION AND COOKING TIME: 1 hour and 15 minutes

ROASTED CHERRY TOMATOES

OVEN-ROASTED TOMATOES LEND a juicy burst of flavor to whatever they're added to: simple pastas, salads, eggs, pizza, and practically any savory dish. Lots of cooks like to drizzle olive oil over the tomatoes before roasting, but I don't think it's necessary; although the skins will be dry and a little bit sticky, the flavor will be sweet and pure.

▶ **MAKES ABOUT 1½ CUPS (225 g)**

2 cups (340 g) cherry tomatoes

1. Preheat the oven to 400°F (200°C). Line a baking sheet with foil.
2. Arrange the tomatoes on the prepared baking sheet and roast for 20 minutes. They will look plump and as if they're about to burst, but they'll begin to shrivel and release some liquid as they cool. Allow to cool before storing.

▶ **LEFTOVERS:** Stored in an airtight container, roasted tomatoes will keep for up to 3 days in the refrigerator.

▶ **PREPARATION AND COOKING TIME:** 25 minutes

caramelized onions

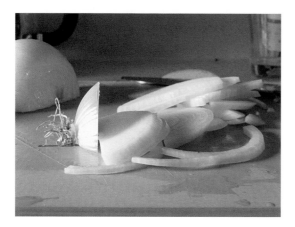

▶ **MAKES ABOUT 1½ CUPS (360 g)**

4 white or yellow onions
3 tablespoons butter or olive oil
Salt
Freshly ground black pepper

1. Cut the onions in half lengthwise and peel them. With the flat side down on the cutting board, cut them crosswise into strips that are about ¼ inch (5 mm) thick.

2. Heat the butter in a wide, heavy-bottomed sauté pan or Dutch oven over low heat. When hot, add the onions. Cook, tossing periodically, until the onions are completely tender, collapsed, richly golden brown, and have absolutely no crunch. This will take anywhere from 35 to 90 minutes; you must be patient. If it seems to be taking too long, turn the heat up slightly—but watch closely to make sure the onions don't burn. Season with salt and pepper to taste.

▶ **LEFTOVERS:** Stored in an airtight container, caramelized onions will keep for up to 3 days in the refrigerator.

▶ **PREPARATION AND COOKING TIME:**
40 minutes to 1 hour and 30 minutes

WHAT A SWEET, cheap indulgence caramelized onions are. The crunchy and astringent raw root vegetable is transformed into a bona fide luxury characterized by a complex, slow-earned sweetness. You can add caramelized onions to practically anything: eggs, tarts, bean salads, crepes, pizzas, casseroles, pasta, sandwiches— whatever you please. In this book you'll see that I call for cooking onions in several different ways: softened but not colored; cooked over medium-high heat until deeply colored and even beginning to burn; cooked over relatively high heat until colored but not soft. What sets caramelizing apart is the low heat and the long, slow cooking time. There simply isn't a shortcut to caramelizing.

onion marmalade

THIS STUFF IS candy. If you can restrain yourself from eating it by the forkful, try it on Onion Crostini (page 32), where it's complemented by a thin smear of soft goat cheese. As a secret ingredient in sandwiches, especially grilled cheese, it really can't be beat, and same goes for crepes, tarts, or any dish where you'd like a sweet kick.

► **MAKES ABOUT 1½ CUPS (400 g)**

2 tablespoons butter or neutral oil (canola, grapeseed, peanut, or vegetable oil)

3 red or white onions

3 garlic cloves, smashed

1 bay leaf

½ cup (80 g) packed brown sugar

¾ cup (180 ml) full-bodied red wine

½ cup (120 ml) red wine vinegar

¼ teaspoon salt

Freshly ground black pepper

1. Cut the onions in half lengthwise and peel them. With the flat side down on the cutting board, cut them crosswise into strips that are about ¼ inch thick.
2. Heat the butter in a deep sauté pan over medium heat. Add the onions, garlic, and bay leaf and cook until the onions are softened, 12 to 15 minutes. Pour in the wine and vinegar, and stir in the sugar, stirring to dissolve. Adjust the heat to maintain a rapid simmer and cook until the mixture is dark and thick with very little liquid pooling around the onions, 35 to 40 minutes. Stir in the salt, then season with pepper to taste. Allow to cool before storing.

► **LEFTOVERS:** Stored in an airtight container, the marmalade will keep for up to 5 days in the refrigerator.

► **PREPARATION AND COOKING TIME:** 1 hour

TWENTY-MINUTE TOMATO SAUCE

THIS BASIC, VERSATILE tomato sauce shows up often in my recipes—in pasta dishes, of course, but also on pizza and pasta bakes, as a base for baked eggs, and as a topping for crepes. I love how the quick cooking time rounds off just enough of the brightness of the tomatoes. With the healthy dose of olive oil this recipe calls for, the result is a vividly red, delectably rich sauce. But one of its greatest merits is that it can be made in the same amount of time it takes to boil a pot of water and cook some pasta.

▶ **MAKES ABOUT 2½ CUPS (600 ml), ENOUGH FOR TOPPING 8 OUNCES OF PASTA**

3 tablespoons olive oil
5 garlic cloves, slivered or coarsely chopped
One 28-ounce (794 g) can whole tomatoes
¼ teaspoon salt
¾ teaspoon red pepper flakes, optional

Warm the olive oil in a medium saucepan or deep sauté pan over medium heat. Add the garlic and sauté until fragrant, about 30 seconds. Add the tomatoes and their juices, along with the salt and red pepper flakes, if using. As you stir, gently break the tomatoes apart by pressing them against the sides of a pan with a wooden spoon. Cook, stirring periodically, for 15 minutes, continuing to crush the tomatoes.

▶ **LEFTOVERS:** Stored in an airtight container, this sauce will keep for up to 3 days in the refrigerator and 1 month in the freezer.

▶ **PREPARATION AND COOKING TIME:** 20 minutes

Pesto variations

TRADITIONALLY, PESTO IS made from basil, garlic, pine nuts, olive oil, Parmesan or Pecorino Romano cheese, and olive oil, laboriously coaxed into a paste using a mortar and pestle. Thanks to food processors, we can now make pesto in about 45 seconds, and thanks to culinary evolution the parameters of pesto have broadened, so it's frequently made with nontraditional ingredients. As you'll see in the following recipes, pesto can be made from almost any combination of nut and herb or leafy green. The trick, as with all cooking, is to taste along the way. Roasted garlic (page 20) can be a delicious addition—either in place of raw garlic or in combination with it. If you don't have a food processor, you can make pesto by mincing the ingredients together as finely as possible and then stirring in the olive oil; it will be a loose approximation, but it will do the job.

BASIL-ALMOND PESTO
▶ MAKES ABOUT ½ CUP (140 g)

¼ cup (30 g) roasted almonds (see page 13)

1 small garlic clove

¼ teaspoon salt

2 cups (80 g) loosely packed fresh basil

About 3 tablespoons olive oil

1 ounce (30 g) Parmesan or Pecorino Romano cheese, grated (¼ cup)

Freshly ground black pepper

Combine the almonds, garlic, and salt in a food processor and pulse until chunky and just combined. Add the basil and pulse until incorporated. With the motor running, add the olive oil in a steady stream, using more or less to achieve the desired consistency. Stir in the Parmesan, pepper to taste, and additional salt if necessary.

▶ LEFTOVERS: Covered tightly and sealed with a piece of plastic placed directly on the surface, pesto will keep for up to 3 days in the refrigerator and 1 month in the freezer.

▶ PREPARATION TIME: 15 minutes

MINT-WALNUT PESTO
▶ **MAKES ABOUT ½ CUP (130 g)**

¼ cup (30 g) roasted walnuts (see page 13)
½ teaspoon fresh lemon juice
¼ teaspoon salt
2 cups (80 g) loosely packed fresh mint
About 3 tablespoons olive oil
Freshly ground black pepper

Combine the walnuts, lemon juice, and salt in a food processor and pulse until just ground. Add the mint and pulse until incorporated. With the motor running, add the olive oil in a steady stream, using more or less to achieve the desired consistency. Stir in pepper to taste, then add additional salt or lemon juice if necessary.

▶ **LEFTOVERS:** Covered tightly and sealed with a piece of plastic placed directly on the surface, pesto will keep for up to 3 days in the refrigerator and 1 month in the freezer.

▶ **PREPARATION TIME:** 5 minutes

KALE-ALMOND PESTO
▶ **MAKES ABOUT 1¼ CUPS (425 g)**

1 bunch kale (about 12 ounces), tough stems removed
⅓ cup (40 g) roasted almonds (see page 13)
1 garlic clove, coarsely chopped
½ teaspoon red wine vinegar
½ teaspoon salt
About ¼ cup (60 ml) olive oil
Freshly ground black pepper

Steam or blanch the kale (see page 10). When cooled, combine the kale, almonds, garlic, vinegar, and salt in a food processor and pulse until just combined. With the motor running, add the olive oil in a steady stream, using more or less to achieve the desired consistency. Stir in pepper to taste, then add additional salt or lemon juice if necessary.

▶ **LEFTOVERS:** Covered tightly and sealed with a piece of plastic placed directly on the surface, pesto will keep for up to 3 days in the refrigerator and 1 month in the freezer.

▶ **PREPARATION TIME:** 25 minutes

OLIVe TaPenaDe

FRUITY, GOOD-QUALITY OLIVES and nothing else—except perhaps a bit of oil to get the mixture moving in the food processor—are all you need to make a great tapenade. Use your favorite type of olive, or a variety. I like buying olives from the olive bars that are increasingly common at grocery stores and specialty stores. That way I can buy only what I need. Tapenade is a flavorful addition to pasta or sandwiches, and is also great dabbed on top of baked eggs.

▶ **MAKES ABOUT** ⅔ **CUP (300 g)**

1 cup olives
1 tablespoon olive oil, optional

1. If the olives have pits, smash them with the flat side of a knife and slip the pits out.
2. Place the pitted olives in a food processor and puree until smooth. If you prefer tapenade with a thinner consistency, add the oil in a steady stream with the motor running.

▶ **LEFTOVERS:** Stored in an airtight container, the tapenade will keep for up to 2 weeks in the refrigerator.

▶ **PREPARATION TIME:** 5 minutes

GINGER-SCALLION SAUCE

THIS SAUCE IS a staple of Korean and Asian cuisine. After you make it once, you will always keep it on hand. It's delicious on any kind of grilled vegetable, on rice, with scrambled eggs, or stirred into noodle bowls, and extremely versatile as a marinade. This is my adaptation of a version made popular by New York City's Momofuku restaurant and in their cookbook.

▶ **MAKES ABOUT ¾ CUP (180 ml)**

1 bunch scallions, white and green parts, thinly sliced

2 heaping tablespoons freshly grated ginger (see page 13)

1 small garlic clove, minced

3 tablespoons neutral oil (canola, grapeseed, peanut, or vegetable oil)

1 teaspoon soy sauce

¾ teaspoon sherry vinegar

½ teaspoon salt

½ teaspoon toasted sesame oil

Combine all the ingredients and stir together. Taste and adjust the seasonings if necessary. Let stand for at least 1 hour before serving.

▶ **LEFTOVERS:** Stored in an airtight container, this sauce will keep for up to 1 week in the refrigerator.

▶ **PREPARATION TIME:** 10 minutes

VEGETARIAN NAPA CABBAGE KIMCHI

KIMCHI, "KOREA'S NATIONAL dish," is in vogue these days both because of the increasing stateside interest in Korean cuisine, and because people are more interested in the heath benefits of fermented foods. Kimchi is made up from all kinds of different vegetables, but the most familiar kind is made from cabbage. If your city has a Koreatown, you can easily find delicious prepared kimchi (though check the ingredients, as many include fish sauce or salted shrimp). If not, it may be best to make it yourself. I learned the following technique in a class devoted to the subject at Purple Yam, a remarkable restaurant in Ditmas Park, Brooklyn. The instructor recommended tracking down Korean sea salt—which is soft and light and similar to fleur de sel—but I figure you'll have enough trouble finding the red pepper powder (*gochugaru*), which, sadly, doesn't have a good substitute. Perhaps the best bet is to purchase it online (see Resources, page 231).

MAKING KIMCHI CAN be a fun thing to organize a gathering around. You can begin soaking the cabbage in the brine the night before, or even in the morning, then invite a few friends over to help you whip up a few batches; everyone will learn from the experience, and you can all share the fruits of your labor. A last note: This recipe makes a substantial batch of kimchi, so you'll need to use an extra-large mixing bowl to combine the ingredients.

▶ **MAKES ABOUT 2 QUARTS (2 l)**

9 cups (2.25 l) water

¼ cup (65 g) plus 1 tablespoon kosher or other coarse salt

1 small head Napa cabbage

¼ cup (30 g) all-purpose flour

5 plump garlic cloves

2-inch (6 cm) piece of ginger (one plump knob), peeled (see page 13)

1 daikon radish, peeled and julienned or finely diced

1 carrot, peeled and julienned or finely diced

6 scallions, white and green parts, cut into 1-inch pieces

¼ cup chopped fresh chives, cut into 1- to 2-inch (3–5 cm) pieces

5 tablespoons Korean red pepper powder, or more as needed

2 teaspoons sugar

1. Combine the ¼ cup kosher salt into 8 cups (2 l) of the water in a large mixing bowl and whisk until the salt dissolves. Taste for balance. It should taste like seawater; you don't want the saltiness to be too faint, or the cabbage won't ferment properly.

2. Core the cabbage and cut it into 1-inch (3 cm) pieces. Place it in the salt water and put a plate directly on top of the cabbage to keep it submerged. Allow to sit in the refrigerator for at least 6 hours or overnight.

3. Combine the flour and the remaining 1 cup (240 ml) water in a small saucepan over medium-high heat. Cook, whisking constantly, until the mixture thickens and has the consistency of glue, 3 to 5 minutes. Allow to cool, then refrigerate until ready to proceed with the recipe. (The flour mixture can be made in advance, while soaking the cabbage.)

4. Mince the garlic and ginger, either by hand or in a mini food processor (which in this case does a better job than a standard food processor). Drain the cabbage, then add the daikon, carrot, scallions, chives, and ginger-garlic mixture. Stir in 3 tablespoons of the flour paste, 5 tablespoons of the red pepper powder, the sugar, and 1 tablespoon of salt. Toss well. Taste and adjust, adding more pepper powder or salt if necessary. Also assess the texture—it should be a gloppy mess—and add additional flour paste if the kimchi seems too dry.

5. Pack the kimchi into clean jars, pressing down to pack tightly. Seal the jars and leave them at room temperature for 2 days, then transfer to the refrigerator. Once a day, turn the jars on one side and then on end to moisten the kimchi at the top with some of the liquid that collects. The kimchi can be eaten at any point, but it will be best after at least 1 week of fermenting.

▶ LEFTOVERS: Stored in its jar in the refrigerator, kimchi can be eaten as long as it tastes good to you—and as long as no mold develops.

▶ PREPARATION TIME: 3 days, but only about 30 minutes of hands-on time

THE IMPORTANCE OF FINESSE

GOOD COOKING, INCLUDING simple cooking, requires patience, awareness, and skill. Simple cooking doesn't necessarily mean easy or fast. Recipes oriented toward home cooks, whether those recipes appear in cookbooks or other media, tend to overstate the "easy" factor. Great food certainly can be easy and fast to make, or include only three ingredients or less. And as a person who spends a lot of the day in the kitchen, I understand the appeal of such recipes. But the thing that has most transformed my confidence as a cook doesn't have anything to do with unlocking the secret of how to make cooking easy.

Writing about the kitchen ethic of Thomas Keller and his staff in *The Elements of Cooking*, Michael Ruhlman defines finesse as "a conviction that paying attention to a few small details in any given preparation has an enormous impact on the finished dish." Adopting this ethic will do wonders for your capabilities in the kitchen. For me, patience, awareness, and skill start with reading through the recipe before beginning to cook. Are you going to make any changes or substitutions? If so, consider what effect this will have on the finished dish and whether you need to modify any steps in the method.

Whenever you are cooking, taste, smell, and scrutinize as you proceed. The more you do this, the more adept you'll become at knowing what to look for. Does everything appear as it should, or as the recipe claims it should? If not, take a deep breath. There's no need to fret. Most mishaps can be rescued, and again, the more attentively you cook, the more adept you'll become at troubleshooting. As you finish preparing a dish or a meal, restrain yourself from rushing the food to the table. The last few minutes of careful attention can make a good dish great. Do a final taste test and adjust the seasonings if necessary, tasting not just for salt and pepper, but also the balance of flavors, including sweetness and acidity. Make sure the food is at its optimum serving temperature. Apply any herb garnishes that you're using.

Above all, take pleasure in your culinary creation. If it's not exactly how you envisioned it, don't agonize or apologize. (That was Julia Child's rule, after all: Don't ever apologize for your cooking.) Always look at cooking as a learning experience and take note of what you might do differently next time. Your efforts and attention will reward you, and those you cook for, with a multitude of enticing meals in the years to come.

FIVE APPETIZERS

AN APPETIZER only needs to tingle the taste buds. If you overload diners with a smorgasbord of heavy appetizers, they'll have no appetite for the main course that follows. The nibbler portion of the evening can easily be procured from an Italian grocer: a cheese platter, a selection of olives, or some antipasti should suffice. Of course, you may want to offer something you've put together yourself. So here are a few of my favorite hors d'oeuvres that won't distract from the entrée.

ONION CROSTINI

CROSTINI WORK WELL as bite-size passed hors d'oeuvres, meaning you can assemble them individually just before serving, or you can lay out the makings and let your guests assemble them on their own. A ficelle is similar to a baguette, but thinner—usually about 1½ inches in girth. Your neighborhood bakery may be able to make a ficelle on request.

▶ **SERVES 5 OR 6**

1 recipe Onion Marmalade (page 23)
6 ounces (170 g) creamy goat cheese, at room temperature
1 baguette or ficelle, thinly sliced

1. If desired, bake the baguette slices in a 375°F (190°C) oven for about 15 minutes, until crisp. Store in an airtight bag or container until ready to serve.
2. To assemble, spread the goat cheese on the bread, then top with a spoonful of Onion Marmalade.

warm olives

THIS IS ONE of the easiest kinds of recipes—dressing up already prepared food, in this case mix-and-match olives from your grocery store that are warmed with aromatics, then drizzled with olive oil for a fruity finish. Don't skip the step of rinsing away the brine or oil that the olives are sold in; rinsing completely freshens their flavor.

► **MAKES 1 CUP (300 g)**

1 cup (300 g) mixed olives, preferably with pits
3 teaspoons olive oil
1 bay leaf
One strip of lemon or orange zest, ½ inch (1 cm) wide
1 dried chile pepper

1. Rinse the olives under cold running water, then pat them dry with a tea towel or paper towel.
2. Heat 1½ teaspoons of the olive oil in a small sauté pan over low heat. Add the olives and swirl the pan to coat them with the oil. Add the bay leaf, zest, and chile pepper. Cook until heated through, about 10 minutes. Transfer to a serving bowl and toss with the remaining 1½ teaspoons of olive oil.

Dates stuffed with blue cheese and arugula

THESE STUFFED DATES could almost count as savory dessert. They showcase a simple but spectacular combination of sweet, salty, and spicy (the spice coming from the arugula). They're easy to put together and can be assembled hours in advance. Just be sure not to buy dates that have already been pitted; they'll be mushy and difficult to fill.

► **MAKES 16 STUFFED DATES**

16 Medjool dates
3 ounces (85 g) creamy blue cheese, such as Fourme d'Ambert
1 handful of arugula

Use a paring knife to make a lengthwise slit in each date. Gently open the date and remove the pit. Pit all of the dates in this way, then place a small knob of the blue cheese in each hollow. Press a few arugula leaves into the cheese, then close the date back up. If desired, spear each date with a toothpick to keep it sealed.

WHITE Bean DIP FOR CRUDITÉS

THIS DIP IS excellent with crackers or on a crudités platter with radishes, cucumber sliced into thick rounds, cherry tomatoes, chilled asparagus spears, quartered endive, cold, parboiled fingerling potatoes halved or quartered into bite-size pieces, and red, orange, and yellow bell peppers sliced into thick strips. However, it's also great on sandwiches, so you'll probably want to make an extra batch expressly for that purpose.

► **MAKES ABOUT 1½ CUPS (325 g)**

2 cups cooked white beans, or one 15-ounce (425 g) can, drained and rinsed

Pulp or flesh from 2 heads roasted garlic, skins discarded (page 20)

2 tablespoons olive oil

1 tablespoon minced fresh rosemary

½ teaspoon salt

¼ teaspoon freshly ground black pepper

1 tablespoon pesto, preferably homemade (see pages 25 and 26)

1. Combine the beans and roasted garlic in a food processor and process until blended. With the motor running, add the olive oil and process until smooth. If the mixture is too thick, add hot water or bean cooking liquid, 1 tablespoon at a time, to achieve the desired consistency. Stir in the rosemary, salt, and pepper, then taste and adjust the seasonings if necessary.

2. When ready to serve, transfer to a serving dish and make a hollow in the middle of the dip with the back of a spoon. Place the pesto in the hollow, then quickly swirl it in using a couple of short motions.

Mango-Watercress Spring ROLLS WITH Peanut-HOISIN sauce

AT CATERING EVENTS I'm always amazed at people's enthusiasm for miniature foods. I assure you that your guests will think these diminutive spring rolls are "soooo cute," making them well worth the effort involved in the assembly. These are so light and refreshing, you could consider them a palate cleanser. When cutting the mango and cucumber, bear in mind that you'll need 20 pieces of each.

► **MAKES 20 MINI SPRING ROLLS AND ABOUT ⅓ CUP (80 ml) SAUCE—JUST ENOUGH TO ACCOMPANY THE SPRING ROLLS**

FOR THE SPRING ROLLS

5 round spring roll wrappers

1 mango, cut into thick matchsticks

1 Kirby or pickling cucumber, peeled if desired, seeded, and cut into thick matchsticks

20 watercress sprigs

FOR THE SAUCE

3 tablespoons hoisin sauce

2 tablespoons creamy natural peanut butter

1 tablespoon soy sauce

1 teaspoon sriracha sauce

1 teaspoon rice wine vinegar

1. Use clean kitchen shears to cut the spring roll wrappers into quarters.

2. Fill a shallow pan with hot water (hot tap water is fine). Working with two spring roll

wrappers at a time, submerge them in the water just until pliant, 20 to 30 seconds. Transfer to a clean tea towel and quickly blot off excess moisture. Then arrange a piece each of mango, cucumber, and watercress across the wide end of each quartered wrapper. Fold the corners over the center, then roll into a mini cigar shape. Store finished rolls between lightly moistened tea towels to prevent them from drying out as you continue to assemble the remaining rolls.

3. To make the sauce, whisk together all the ingredients, then taste and adjust the seasonings if necessary, adding more sriracha sauce if you'd like more heat. Serve the sauce alongside the spring rolls.

2

HEARTY BEAN- AND GRAIN-BASED SALADS, SOUPS, RICE BOWLS, AND RISOTTOS

THERE'S SO MUCH to like about dishes that incorporate beans and grains: the flavors and textures, the endless ways to improvise, the health benefits, and, of course, how economical they are. Few foods give you more nutritional bang for the buck than beans and grains. The cupboards and shelves that serve as a pantry in my studio apartment are jam-packed with beans and grains in a variety of colors, shapes, and sizes, stored in various bags, jars, and other containers to create an edible mosaic. I never would have gotten very far in vegetarian cuisine without having a few solid bean- and grain-based recipes under my belt.

Recent years have been great for beans, and particularly heirloom varieties, which often have a striking appearance and distinctive flavor and texture. Look for dried beans, both common and heirloom varieties, at farmers' markets, where they'll be at the peak of freshness. For unusual beans, online retailers may be your best bet (see Resources, page 231). In this book I've aimed to use beans that are more widely available, but I encourage you to try a new one every now and then. As long as you have beans in your cupboard, you're only a few steps away from dinner.

Lentils, which require no presoaking, can be ready in about half an hour. As for beans, you'll find detailed cooking instructions in chapter 1 (see page 11). But in short, all you need to do is set a bowl of dried beans to soak before you head to work and then start them cooking when you get home. This bit of advanced planning will allow you to put together a hearty, nutritious meal with minimal labor at the end of the day. And if even that seems too much, canned beans are, of course, instantly ready to eat; just give them a quick rinse before cooking them or combining with other ingredients.

Much of what I've said about beans is also true for grains. Sometimes the stages of my culinary history seem defined by discovering new grains to try: rugged ones like bulgur, shapely little beads of farro, and the increasingly colorful varieties of quinoa. Whole grains adapt themselves so easily to whatever's cooking, contributing bulk, texture, nutrition, and flavor. I like to keep several varieties of rice on hand, particularly brown basmati and brown jasmine rice. It's exciting that these and other whole-grain versions of exotic rices are becoming more widely available, especially since they have a better nutritional profile than white rice. (As with wheat, the white rice varieties are simply processed a few steps further than their brown counterparts, with the hull and bran being removed and the grain being whittled down to its starchy center.)

For optimum freshness, it's best to buy beans and grains in smaller amounts, so you'll use them up in a shorter time. However, if stored in airtight containers rather than plastic bags, which insects and other critters can eat through, beans and whole grains will keep for months and sometimes years—typically the only adverse effect of aging is a longer cooking time.

BLACK-EYED PEA SALAD WITH ROASTED SQUASH AND RADICCHIO

BLACK-EYED PEAS, THOSE beans that promise prosperity at the turn of the year, make this my go-to New Year's Day salad. It's bright with citrus flavor, easy to make, clean on the palate, and made from ingredients that are readily available during the winter—the perfect way to kick off a new year. If you're unfamiliar with kabocha squash, I recommend seeking it out. It's quickly becoming a favorite among fans of winter squash, due to being slightly sweeter than butternut squash and a bit starchier in texture. When you cut it in half, take a whiff; the fragrance is fruity and intoxicating. Kabocha squash has skin that is thin and tender enough that it's edible, though not everyone likes to eat it. One final note: You'll need to soak the black-eyed peas in advance, so plan ahead.

▶ **SERVES 3 OR 4**

1 kabocha squash or small butternut squash (about 1½ to 2 pounds, 675 g to 1 kg)

3 tablespoons olive oil

1 cup (180 g) black-eyed peas, soaked for at least 4 hours or overnight

Kosher salt

3 tablespoons fresh lime juice (from 2 or 3 limes)

1 tablespoon Dijon mustard

1 tablespoon honey, or 2 teaspoons agave syrup

1 small head radicchio, cut into thin strips

½ cup (15 g) coarsely chopped fresh cilantro leaves

1. Preheat the oven to 400°F (200°C).

2. If using kabocha squash, trim the ends from the squash with a heavy, sharp knife or a cleaver, then halve the squash lengthwise. Scoop out the seeds. Cut the squash lengthwise into ¾-inch (2 cm) wedges, then carefully trim off the peel, just as you would for cantaloupe. Cut the wedges crosswise into ¾-inch (2 cm) cubes. If using butternut squash, trim the ends and cut the squash in half at the point where the skinny top transitions into the bulbous bottom. With the flat surface on the cutting board, carefully cut the skin off in thin strips from top to bottom. Cut each piece of squash in half lengthwise and scoop out the seeds. Cut the squash as described for kabocha, first lengthwise into ¾-inch (2 cm) wedges, then crosswise into ¾-inch (2 cm) cubes.

3. Arrange the squash on a baking sheet. Drizzle with 1 tablespoon of the olive oil and roast for 20 to 30 minutes, until tender and slightly caramelized.

4. Meanwhile, drain the soaked beans, put them in a medium saucepan, and add water to cover by 2 inches (5 cm). Bring to a boil over high heat, then turn the heat down to maintain a gentle simmer. Cook, uncovered, for 30 minutes. Stir in ½ teaspoon salt and continue cooking until the beans are tender, up to 30 more minutes, adding more salt or water if necessary. Drain and transfer to a mixing bowl to cool.

5. Whisk together the lime juice, mustard, honey, a big pinch of salt, and the remaining 2 tablespoons of olive oil to make a dressing. Taste for balance.

**BLACK-EYED PEA SALAD WITH ROASTED SQUASH
AND RADICCHIO**

6. Combine the squash, beans, radicchio, and cilantro. Add the dressing in increments, gently tossing it with the squash mixture and tasting along the way until it's to your liking. Serve at room temperature or chilled.

▶ LEFTOVERS: Stored in an airtight container, this salad will keep for up to 3 days in the refrigerator.

▶ PREPARATION AND COOKING TIME: About 1 hour

BULGUR SALAD WITH KALE AND FETA

BULGUR SALAD WITH KALE AND FETA

THIS ROBUST, BOLDLY flavored salad can be served warm, at room temperature, or chilled, which makes it perfect on-the-go food. The prep time is fairly brief and efficient—if you start cooking the bulgur before chopping or cooking any of the other ingredients, all of the elements will come together at the same time. A note about the kale: In this recipe, the cooking time is fairly brief, so it's somewhat chewy. It you prefer it to be more tender, I recommend following the instructions on page 10 for steaming or parboiling the kale before stirring it into the peppers and onion. This salad also makes an excellent stuffing for red, yellow, or orange peppers, as described in the variation on page 44.

▶ **SERVES 3 OR 4**

1 cup (180 g) bulgur

2 cups (475 ml) water

1 tablespoon neutral oil (canola, grapeseed, peanut, or vegetable oil)

2 teaspoons cumin seeds

1 small red onion, or ½ large red onion, sliced into strips

2 jalapeño peppers, minced (seeded for a milder heat level)

2 garlic cloves, minced

½ teaspoon salt

¼ cup (60 ml) dry white wine or water

½ bunch kale (about 6 ounces, 170 g), cut into thin strips

3 scallions, white and green parts, thinly sliced

½ cup (15 g) coarsely chopped fresh cilantro

3 ounces (85 g) feta cheese, crumbled

1 tablespoon olive oil

1. Combine the bulgur and water in a small saucepan over high heat. Bring to a boil, then lower the heat, cover, and simmer for 15 minutes, until tender. Strain off any water that hasn't been absorbed.

2. Heat 1 tablespoon of the neutral oil in a sauté pan over medium-high heat. Add the cumin seeds and let sizzle until fragrant, about 30 seconds. Add the onion and cook until it's browned around the edges, about 6 minutes. Stir in the jalapeños, garlic, and salt. Pour in the wine to deglaze the pan, scraping up any browned bits with a wooden spoon or spatula. Add the kale and cook, tossing from time to time, until wilted, about 4 minutes. Transfer to a mixing bowl and allow to cool slightly. Stir in the scallions, cilantro, feta, cooked bulgur, and olive oil. Taste and adjust the seasonings. Serve warm, at room temperature, or cold.

▶ **LEFTOVERS:** Stored in an airtight container, this salad will keep for up to 3 days in the refrigerator.

▶ **PREPARATION AND COOKING TIME:** 30 minutes

variation

STUFFeD PePPeRS
▶ SERVES 4

Preheat the oven to 400°F (200°C). Prepare
Bulgur Salad with Kale and Feta according to
the recipe on page 43. While the bulgur is cooking, steam 4 yellow or red bell peppers until
tender but not completely soft, 6 to 8 minutes.
Transfer to a baking sheet or plate and, once
cool enough to handle, slice in half lengthwise
and carefully remove the seeds and ribs. Divide
the salad among the peppers, then place them
in a greased roasting dish into which they will
all fit snugly. Cover tightly with foil and bake
for 20 minutes. Remove the foil and bake for 5
to 10 more minutes, until the filling is heated
through and browned on the top. Serve warm,
2 pepper halves per person.

WARM LENTIL AND WHEAT BERRY SALAD WITH EGGPLANT AND ONION

THE LITTLE MEDITERRANEAN restaurant near where I live serves *mujaddara*, a side dish of bulgur and lentils topped with fried onion and a plop of yogurt. It inspired me to formulate this similar but more substantial salad. Here wheat berries replace the bulgur and are cooked in the same pot with the lentils. A medley of vegetables round out the dish: smoky panfried eggplant, sweet grilled onion, barely wilted baby spinach, and cucumber for a welcome fresh crunch. The smaller Japanese eggplants typically have a sturdier structure when cooked than the conventional "globe" ones, and therefore I prefer to use them in salads like this. You can also try adding raisins, dried cranberries, sliced radishes, cubes of apple, or diced dried apricots. This salad uses only a simple, light dressing of olive oil, a bit of vinegar, and earthy cumin, allowing the flavors of the other elements to fully shine.

▶ SERVES 3 OR 4

1½ teaspoons salt

¾ cup (165 g) wheat berries, hard or soft

¾ cup (180 g) green lentils

4 tablespoons olive oil

2 teaspoons sherry vinegar or red wine vinegar

¼ teaspoon freshly ground black pepper

1 teaspoon cumin seeds

1 sweet yellow or white onion, sliced into ½-inch-thick rings

3 garlic cloves, smashed and coarsely chopped

1 Japanese eggplant, quartered lengthwise and cut crosswise into ½-inch-thick slices

4 cups (170 g) loosely packed baby spinach

1 English (seedless) cucumber, peeled if desired and diced

Fresh lemon juice for spritzing

1. Put at least 2 quarts (2 l) of water in a saucepan over high heat and bring to a boil. Add 1 teaspoon of the salt and then the wheat berries. Turn the heat down to maintain an active simmer), cover, and cook for 50 minutes.

2. Add the lentils, cover, and cook until the lentils are tender, 30 to 40 minutes.

3. Drain (hopefully reserving the liquid, which makes a fortifying addition to stocks and soups). Return the lentils and wheat berries to the pot. Stir in 1 tablespoon of the olive oil, 1 teaspoon of the vinegar, the remaining ½ teaspoon salt, and the pepper, then cover to keep the mixture hot.

4. Heat 2 more tablespoons of the olive oil in a sauté pan over medium-high heat. Add the cumin seeds and let sizzle until fragrant, about 30 seconds. Add the onion and toss quickly, then cook, stirring and shaking the pan only occasionally, until tender, 8 to 10 minutes. Add the garlic and cook, stirring occasionally, until fragrant, about 1 minute. Transfer the onion to the pot with the lentils and wheat berries and cover the pot.

5. Using the same sauté pan, heat the remaining 1 tablespoon of olive oil and lower the heat to medium. Add the eggplant and cook, stirring and scraping occasionally, until just tender, 4 to 6 minutes. Deglaze the pan with the

remaining 1 teaspoon of vinegar and 2 table-spoons of water, scraping up any browned bits with a wooden spoon or spatula. Once most of the liquid has boiled off, transfer the eggplant mixture to the pot with the lentils.

6. Add the spinach to the warm lentils and wheat berries. Toss until the ingredients are evenly distributed and the spinach is slightly wilted. Stir in the cucumber and divide among plates or transfer to a serving bowl. Garnish with a spritz of lemon juice and serve immediately.

NOTE: This salad is meant to be served warm, with the spinach stirred into the warm lentils and wheat berries so that it wilts slightly. If you need to cook the lentils and wheat berries beforehand, I recommend assembling the salad as follows: Place a pile of the lentil and wheat berry mixture on each plate, followed by a handful of spinach. Then portion the hot onion and eggplant on top of the spinach, which will encourage it to wilt a bit.

▶ LEFTOVERS: Stored in an airtight container, this salad will keep for up to 3 days in the refrigerator.

▶ PREPARATION AND COOKING TIME:
About 1 hour and 45 minutes

**WARM LENTIL AND WHEAT BERRY SALAD WITH
EGGPLANT AND ONION**

RICE BOWLS

RICE BOWLS are so versatile. They can be adapted to suit your preferences and mood, and also to make use of what you have on hand or what's in season. They typically aren't soups, but rather vehicles for a rich variety of vegetables, beans, nuts, and more, with a scoop of perfectly cooked rice acting as a base. I've had a difficult time determining the exact origin of what now constitutes a rice bowl. In Korea there's *bibimbap*, in Japan there's *oyakodon* and *gyudon*, and then there's Rice, a small restaurant chain in New York that boasts rice bowls of Asian, European, African, South American, Indian, and Caribbean influence. Given the simplicity and versatility of the dish, it seems clear that any cuisine that depends heavily on rice can stake a claim to the rice bowl.

In any case, a rice bowl is a wonderful single-dish meal for hungry vegetarians. The advantages are many: clean flavors, simple assembly, a great backdrop for a variety of vegetables, and an excellent way to use leftovers. When I make rice bowls, they are a single-dish meal, boasting copious amounts of vegetables, either raw or cooked, crunchy nuts and seeds, and an appealing array of simple ingredients. Here are a few guidelines for concocting your own creations:

- **USE FRESHLY COOKED RICE THAT IS SOMEWHAT STICKY:** Unfortunately, leftover rice tends to be dry—not what you want in a rice bowl. I recommend that you cook fresh rice (see page 12 for instructions), and that you use a fragrant, somewhat delicate rice that has an appealing flavor on its own. I like brown basmati and jasmine rices, and I also like black and red rices. But feel free to experiment with whatever you have on hand. I allot 1 cup (150 g) of cooked rice per serving.

- **USE VEGETABLES FOR TEXTURAL CONTRAST:** Any vegetables that require cooking, such as eggplants and potatoes, need to be fully cooked beforehand. Others may be at their best for rice bowls when raw, and maybe tossed with a bit of salt and vinegar, such as thinly sliced cabbage or cucumbers. Raw, crunchy vegetables, such as carrots, radishes, should be sliced thinly or julienned. Eggplant can be panfried, in the same method, for example, as in the Warm Lentil and Wheat Berry Salad on page 45. Asparagus or broccoli should be steamed just until tender. Greens, such as spinach, arugula, or even kale, are delicious either sautéed or raw, depending on your preference.

- **ADD A LIQUID ELEMENT THAT WILL PER-MEATE THE RICE:** This could be just a drizzle of soy sauce or toasted sesame oil, or it could mean tossing or cooking your vegetables in some kind of marinade, your favorite curry paste, kimchi, or a simple sauce such as a mixture of chili paste, rice vinegar, and soy sauce.

- **PROVIDE A PROTEIN BOOST:** A poached or fried egg will not only provide protein, it will also add a bit of cohesion to a rice bowl. Eggs should be added just before serving. Other high-protein additions include cubes of tofu or tempeh. If using tempeh, it's best to brown it first. If using tofu (preferably firm), brown it in a bit of oil or simply dice it up, then pile it on top. Another possibility is cooking it along with any vegetables you're cooking, and for added flavor, consider marinating it in one of the tofu marinades on page 157.

Here are a few suggested pairings to give you an idea of how you might put these principles to work, followed by guidelines for creating rice bowls of your own. As you consider what toppings to put over the rice, think about how you envision the finished dish, especially with regard to texture. For vegetables, would you rather eat them cooked or raw? If raw, what about quick pickling them in salt and a bit of rice vinegar for a more zippy flavor? If cooked, should some flavoring agents be added, like chili paste, soy sauce, or toasted sesame oil?

Japanese Rice Bowl

Divide 4 cups (600 g) cooked medium-grain brown or white rice among 4 bowls. Divide 4 avocado halves, 1 pound (450 g) steamed asparagus, 2 cups (380 g) cooked and shelled edamame, and 1 sheet of nori sliced into thin strips, among the bowls, scattering them over the rice. Whisk together 1 tablespoon wasabi powder and ¼ cup (60 ml) soy sauce, then drizzle 1 tablespoon of the sauce over each serving. Garnish with toasted sesame seeds and thinly sliced scallions.

Tofu and Cashew Rice Bowl

Slice a 14-ounce (380 g) block of tofu into thin rectangles, keeping the rectangles the same thickness. Line a baking sheet with paper towels and transfer the tofu to the pan in a single layer. Top with more paper towels and a second baking sheet, then place some weight (such as cans or a heavy pot) on top. Let sit for 15 minutes to squeeze out some of the moisture. Panfry the tofu slices in oil until lightly browned. Divide 4 cups (600 g) cooked medium-grain brown or white rice among 4 bowls. Divide the fried tofu over the rice, along with 1 cup (150 g) roasted cashews, 2 minced shallots, and ¼ cup (10 g) coarsely chopped fresh cilantro or parsley. Whisk together 3 tablespoons soy sauce, 2 teaspoons chili paste, and 2 teaspoons rice vinegar, and drizzle the sauce over each serving.

TOPPINGS FOR BODY AND TEXTURE

- Sautéed or steamed spinach, chard, or kale (see page 10), cut into bite-size pieces
- Tender fresh greens, such as mâche, watercress, or baby spinach
- Panfried or roasted eggplant
- Sautéed zucchini or yellow squash
- Sliced or cubed avocado
- Roasted, steamed, or boiled potato or sweet potato
- Raw carrots

TOPPINGS FOR PROTEIN

- Fried or poached egg
- Browned or uncooked tofu
- Panfried tempeh cubes
- Panfried seitan strips or small pieces
- Cooked beans, such as edamame, black beans, red beans, or chickpeas

TOPPINGS FOR MOISTURE AND FLAVOR

- Twenty-Minute Tomato Sauce (page 24) or other simple tomato sauce
- Carrot-Ginger Dressing (page 136)
- Wasabi powder whisked into soy sauce
- Soy sauce or tamari
- Chili paste, soy sauce, and rice vinegar whisked together
- Curry paste
- Kimchi, preferably homemade (page 29)

GARNISHES

- Minced fresh herbs, such as parsley, cilantro, or chives
- Roasted nuts, such as almonds or cashews (see page 13)
- Toasted sesame oil
- Julienned ginger (see page 13)
- Minced shallots
- Thinly sliced scallions
- Mung bean sprouts
- Thinly sliced nori
- Slivered garlic

BROWN RICE BOWL WITH BOK CHOY AND KIMCHI

**THIS IS SIMPLE, sloppy comfort food—
and a way to stretch kimchi into a
substantial dish. It's a riff on Kimchi
Stew (page 57), and like that dish it's
best made with kimchi that is quite
fermented. Depending on the spiciness
of the kimchi, you may want to add a bit
of heat to the dish in the form of chili
paste or sriracha sauce. And depending
on the saltiness of the kimchi, you may
want to add a bit of salt to the finished
dish. I've included options for tofu and
fried eggs, two interpretations that
take this rice bowl in quite different
directions.**

▶ **SERVES 4**

1½ cups (330 g) short-grain or medium-grain
  brown rice

3 cups (750 ml) water

1 to 2 tablespoons neutral oil (canola, grapeseed,
  peanut, or vegetable oil)

2 teaspoons toasted sesame oil

8 scallions, white and green parts, cut into 1-inch
  pieces

8 ounces (230 g) bok choy, large bok choy cut into
  1-inch pieces, or baby bok choy separated into
  leaves

2 cups (320 g) kimchi, preferably homemade
  (page 29), partially drained

1 to 2 teaspoons chili paste, such as sambal oelek,
  or sriracha sauce

8 ounces (230 g) firm tofu, cut into cubes, or 4 eggs

Salt

2 tablespoons minced fresh chives for garnish

1. Combine the rice and water in a small saucepan
   over medium-high heat. Bring to a boil, then
   lower the heat, cover, and simmer over the low-
   est possible heat for 30 minutes. Remove from
   the heat and, leaving the lid on, let the rice sit
   for 10 minutes. Alternatively, you can use a rice
   cooker, following manufacturer's instructions.

2. Meanwhile, heat 1 tablespoon of the neutral
   oil and the sesame oil in a sauté pan over
   medium heat. Add the scallions and bok choy
   and sauté until the bok choy is just softened,
   5 to 7 minutes. Add the kimchi and cook, stirring occasionally, until the kimchi and the bok
   choy are tender, 6 to 8 minutes. Stir in the
   chili paste, if using, and taste for salt. If using
   tofu, add it now and cook, stirring gently from
   time to time, until heated through.

3. If using eggs, heat 1 tablespoon of neutral
   oil in a clean sauté pan. Fry the eggs, 2 at a
   time, until the whites are set and the yolks are
   cooked to the desired doneness.

4. To assemble, divide the rice among 4 serving
   bowls. Top with the kimchi mixture and then
   the fried egg, if using. Garnish with the chives
   and serve hot.

▶ **LEFTOVERS:** Stored in an airtight container,
the kimchi mixture will keep for 1 day in
the refrigerator. When assembling the dish,
use freshly cooked rice and fry the eggs
immediately before serving.

▶ **PREPARATION AND COOKING TIME:**
45 minutes

SOUPS

IS THERE anything better on a chilly evening than hot soup? When cold weather comes gusting in, soup is one of the few things that allows me to bear it.

My soups aren't fussy or complicated. Rather, they're simple expressions of a vegetable or bean. I build them the same way I engineer my veggie burgers: by focusing on a single ingredient or a couple of complementary ones. Then I gently add a few things here and there so the primary ingredient remains the star of the show. Here are a few guidelines that will help you create a soup from whatever ingredients you choose.

- **BROWN SOME ONIONS:** Cook chopped or sliced onions until softened, typically over medium or medium-high heat. Or you can take this a step further and let them begin to color or even burn at the edges (this is different from caramelizing, which is done over low heat and takes a great deal longer). Onions provide a somewhat sweet, complex base to soups. You can also begin with a mirepoix, which is a sautéed mixture of vegetables, usually carrots, celery, and onions.

- **ADD AROMATICS:** After the onions are cooked to your liking, add aromatic ingredients, such as minced garlic, ginger, bay leaves, or fresh or dried herbs, or a combination. These will continue to perfume the soup as it cooks and more ingredients are added.

- **DEGLAZE THE PAN:** Deglazing is adding a small amount of liquid (usually something acidic, like wine) to a hot pan, then cooking off the liquid. This adds a concentrated, bright flavor that infuses the onions and, more importantly, allows you to scrape the flavorful browned bits off the bottom of the pan. I like to deglaze with wine (red or white) or vermouth, or a small amount of vinegar plus water (usually 1 tablespoon vinegar with 2 to 3 tablespoons water). To avoid scratching the pot, use a wooden spoon or another utensil that won't damage the pot.

- **ADD SLOW-COOKING OR MAIN INGREDIENTS:** This is the stage at which I add my headlining ingredients, like squash, beans, or combinations of vegetables. Squash can be roasted beforehand, which imparts a sweeter flavor to the finished dish. If you're adding a combination of vegetables, be sure to add them sequentially, in the order of longest cooking time to shortest. For vegetables (but not dried beans), you can add them to the pot and sauté for a few minutes to brown them slightly and jump-start the cooking, or you can forgo this and move on to the next step.

- **POUR IN THE STOCK:** Pour in some vegetable stock, being sure to cover the ingredients in the pot completely. For a pureed soup, don't cover them by too much, or the finished soup will be very thin. (See page 15 for my basic recipe for vegetable stock.) When I don't have homemade stock, I prefer to use water over canned, boxed, or concentrated vegetable stock, which always taste stale and salty to me. Bring the soup to a boil, then lower the heat and simmer until the all of the ingredients are cooked. When making pureed soups, I like to add one potato along with the stock; it gives the finished soup a little bit of body and a slightly creamy texture. If the soup doesn't contain dried beans, add some salt at the beginning of the simmering stage, and then continue tasting and adjusting as the soup cooks. For soups with beans, wait until the last 10 to 15 minutes of cooking time to add salt.

- **ASSESS THE BODY AND ADJUST AS NEEDED:** If the soup is too thick, thin it with additional stock or water. If it's too thin, simmer, uncovered, for 10 to 15 minutes. Another option if the soup is too thin is to combine a few ladlefuls of soup with 1 tablespoon of potato starch or cornstarch. Whisk the mixture into the soup and simmer for about 5 minutes.

- **MAKE LAST-MINUTE ADDITIONS:** I add greens to most savory dishes I cook, but I especially enjoy adding them to soups. They should be cleaned and trimmed of any tough or fibrous parts. Cut them up into bite-size pieces, then simply stir them in. Heartier greens, such as kale or collard greens, should be cooked for a final few minutes; tender greens like spinach can be stirred in once the pot is removed from the heat; and some greens fall in between. For pureed soups, if you'd like your greens to stay intact, stir them in after pureeing the soup. When the pot is removed from the heat, stir in any tender fresh herbs you're using.

- **TASTE AND ADJUST THE SEASONINGS:** As always, taste for salt and acid. The latter can be adjusted by adding a few drops of fresh lemon juice, for example. For a more luxurious mouthfeel, you can stir in a few tablespoons of heavy cream.

- **STORE LEFTOVERS:** Most soups keep exceptionally well, and some even improve overnight, as this gives their flavors the chance to meld. After the soup has cooled to room temperature, place it in an airtight container. It will keep for about 3 days in the refrigerator and 1 month in the freezer.

ROASTED CARROT AND GOLDEN BEET SOUP

ROASTED CARROT AND GOLDEN BEET SOUP

THIS SIMPLE ROASTED vegetable soup has a rounded, mature sweetness, thanks to the carrots' neutralizing effect on the more forthright sugars in the beets. It's also very fortifying, and, like all dishes that involve roasted vegetables, it's a good thing to make on evenings when your home is chilly, since the oven needs to be on for over an hour. The garlic, which is added to the beets and carrots for the last twenty minutes of the roasting time, adds a welcome jolt of richness and transforms the soup into a savory affair. You can substitute standard red beets if golden beets aren't available, but be aware that the color of the soup may seem unappealing, even if it tastes great. This is a robust pureed soup, more filling than it might sound, but one way to bulk it up further is to stir in 10 ounces of fresh baby spinach along with the dill in step 5, and allow it to just wilt.

▶ **SERVES 4**

2 pounds (1 kg) carrots, chopped into 1-inch (3 cm) pieces

1 pound (450 g) golden beets, trimmed and cut into quarters if large

3 tablespoons canola or grapeseed oil

Salt

Freshly ground black pepper

2 heads garlic, broken into cloves and peeled

1 tablespoon butter

1 onion, or 2 medium leeks (well cleaned; see page 13), minced

2 teaspoons grated fresh ginger (see page 13)

About 6 cups (1.5 l) vegetable stock (page 15), water, or a combination

1 tablespoon chopped fresh dill

1. Preheat the oven to 400°F (200°C).
2. Spread the carrots and beets on a baking sheet. Drizzle with 2 tablespoons of the oil, a big pinch of salt, and several grinds of black pepper, then mix with your hands to ensure that the vegetables are evenly coated.
3. Roast the vegetables, stirring every 15 minutes, for 1 hour. Add the garlic, tossing it with the vegetables until it's evenly coated in the oil. Continue baking for about 20 minutes, until the vegetables are completely tender. When cool enough to handle, peel the beets and coarsely chop them.
4. Heat the remaining 1 tablespoon of oil and the butter in a soup pot over medium heat. Add the onion and sauté until softened but not colored, 6 to 8 minutes. Add the ginger and the roasted vegetables and stir to combine. Pour in the stock, adding enough to cover the vegetables by about 1 inch (3 cm). Bring to a boil, then stir in ½ teaspoon of salt. Lower the heat, cover, and simmer for 20 minutes.
5. Remove from the heat and puree until very smooth, using an immersion blender or working in batches and using a food processor or regular blender. If the soup is too thick, stir in a ladleful of stock or water. Stir in the dill and additional salt and pepper to taste. Serve hot. If you'd to make this soup a tad richer, put a pat of butter in the bottom of each bowl just before ladling in the soup.

▶ **LEFTOVERS:** Stored in an airtight container, this soup will keep for up to 3 days in the refrigerator and 1 month in the freezer.

▶ **PREPARATION AND COOKING TIME:**
2 hours

SPINACH-POTATO SOUP

THIS SOUP HAS a bit of an Asian flair, with a base of sautéed scallions, ginger, and garlic, and toasted sesame oil and miso to add a nutty, savory sheen. As you make it, a heavenly aroma will fill your kitchen and environs. Because it's a smooth pureed soup, it might not seem all that filling. One way to make it more substantial is to ladle the hot soup over a scoop of freshly cooked jasmine rice; or you could serve it with one of the classic soup accompaniments: a salad or sandwich. But there's a generous helping of spinach here, made somewhat meaty by the potatoes, so this soup is actually quite fortifying.

► SERVES 4

1 tablespoon neutral oil (canola, grapeseed, peanut, or vegetable oil)

2 teaspoons toasted sesame oil

4 scallions, white and light green parts, thinly sliced

3 garlic cloves, minced

2 teaspoons grated fresh ginger (see page 13)

1 bunch spinach (about 14 ounces, 380 g), tough stems removed

2 medium russet potatoes (about 1 pound, 450 g), peeled and roughly chopped into 1-inch pieces

5 cups (1.25 l) vegetable stock (page 15)

2 tablespoons miso paste

Squeeze of lemon juice

2 cups cooked jasmine rice (see page 12), optional

1. Heat the neutral oil and sesame oil in a soup pot over medium heat. Add the scallions and sauté just until softened, about 1 minute. Add the garlic and ginger and sauté for another minute. Add the spinach and potatoes, cover the pot, and cook until the spinach is softened and wilted, 3 to 4 minutes, tossing periodically with tongs. Pour in the stock and bring to a boil, then lower the heat, cover, and simmer until the potatoes are completely cooked, 10 to 15 minutes.

2. Remove from the heat and puree until smooth, using an immersion blender or working in batches and using a food processor or regular blender.

3. Bring the soup back to a simmer. Ladle about ½ cup (120 ml) of the soup into a small bowl, add the miso, and whisk until smooth. Stir the miso mixture back into the soup and simmer for 5 to 10 minutes.

4. Add lemon juice to taste. If using the rice, divide it evenly among the serving bowls, then ladle the soup over the rice just before serving.

► LEFTOVERS: Stored in an airtight container, this soup will keep for up to 3 days in the refrigerator and 1 month in the freezer.

► PREPARATION AND COOKING TIME: 45 minutes

KIMCHI STEW

KIMCHI STEW (*kimchi jigae*) is traditionally made in a stone pot called a *dolsot*, which is attractive enough to go from the stovetop to the dinner table with the stew still bubbling away in it. Of course you can make it in whatever kind of soup pot you own, but it's a worthwhile and fun excursion to track down a *dolsot* at a Korean kitchen supply store (and it would make an excellent gift for a friend or loved one with culinary leanings).

THIS STEW IS extraordinarily easy. Traditionally, it provided a way to use up kimchi that was on the verge of overfermenting, giving the soup a distinctive somewhat sour taste. Making it with "younger," or less fermented, kimchi gives it a crispier, brighter taste that is also very good, though less complex. I recommend that you try your hand at making your own kimchi to use in this dish (see page 29 for a recipe), but store-bought will also do; just be sure to check the ingredients, as prepared kimchi often contains fish sauce or salted shrimp. Regarding the chili paste, you may not need it if you're using kimchi that's spicy on its own.

▶ SERVES 4

1 tablespoon neutral oil (canola, grapeseed, peanut, or vegetable oil)

1 tablespoon toasted sesame oil

1 bunch scallions, green and white parts, thinly sliced

2 garlic cloves, minced

1 teaspoon grated fresh ginger (see page 13)

4 cups (640 g) kimchi with its juices, preferably homemade (page 29)

1 tablespoon chili paste, such as sambal oelek

About 4 cups (1 l) vegetable stock (page 15) or water

14 ounces (380 g) firm tofu, cubed

Chives for garnish

Heat the neutral oil and sesame oil in a soup pot over medium heat. Add the scallions and sauté until softened, 2 to 3 minutes. Add the garlic and ginger and sauté until fragrant, about 1 minute. Add the kimchi and chili paste, if using. Pour in the vegetable stock, using just enough to cover the vegetables. Bring to a boil, then partially cover and simmer for 1 hour. Stir in the tofu and continue cooking until it's warmed through. Garnish with the chives and serve hot.

▶ LEFTOVERS: Stored in an airtight container, this soup will keep for up to 3 days in the refrigerator.

▶ PREPARATION AND COOKING TIME: 1 hour and 20 minutes

BARLEY SOUP WITH MUSHROOMS AND PARSNIPS

THE BEER IN this soup gives it a surprise kick and mellows the sweetness of the carrot and parsnip. Thick and textured, and practically a stew, it's a hugely filling, nutritionally sound soup that's also a snap to put together. Parsnips are so compatible with the mushrooms and barley and enrich the soup in a bold, surprising way, but if you prefer not to use them, you can substitute potatoes or celery root. For a brighter, slightly more acidic soup, swap a crisp, dry white wine for the beer.

▶ SERVES 4

2 tablespoons neutral oil (canola, grapeseed, peanut, or vegetable oil)

2 leeks, white and pale green parts only, thinly sliced and cleaned (see page 13)

8 ounces (230 g) cremini mushrooms, thinly sliced

1 large carrot, peeled and cut into ¼-inch (5 mm) cubes

1 medium parsnip, peeled and cut into ¼-inch (5 mm) cubes

3 garlic cloves, minced

2 thyme sprigs

1 bay leaf

¾ cup (165 g) pearl barley

¾ cup (180 ml) light-flavored beer

6 cups (1.5 l) vegetable stock (page 15) or water

¾ teaspoon salt

¼ teaspoon freshly ground black pepper

Heat the oil in a soup pot over medium heat. Add the leek and sauté until just softened, about 5 minutes. Add the mushrooms and sauté until just beginning to brown and release their liquid, 4 to 6 minutes. Stir in the carrot and parsnip. Turn the heat up to medium-high, cover, and cook for 5 minutes. Add the garlic, thyme, and bay leaf and sauté just until fragrant, about 1 minute. Stir in the barley, then pour in the beer and cook, stirring constantly, until the liquid is reduced by half. Add the vegetable stock. Bring to a boil, then stir in the salt. Lower the heat and simmer, partially covered, until the barley is tender, 35 to 45 minutes. Stir in the pepper and adjust the seasonings if necessary. Serve hot.

▶ LEFTOVERS: Stored in an airtight container, this soup will keep for up to 3 days in the refrigerator and 1 month in the freezer.

▶ PREPARATION AND COOKING TIME: 1 hour and 20 minutes

SPICED LENTIL SOUP

OH, LENTIL SOUP—What an inexpensive, nutritious, delicious dinner. Plus, I find a steaming bowl of lentil soup to be exactly the fortification my brain needs after a grueling day. I feel like I've been making lentil soup my entire adult life for exactly these reasons. The version here is my standard recipe, the result of an accident I once made in mistaking cinnamon for cumin. Cinnamon adds a mysterious sweetness and manages to teach an old, familiar pot of soup some new tricks. I prefer the dark French green lentils here, but you can substitute any green or brown lentil. However, I wouldn't recommend using red lentils; once cooked, they have too little body to support a soup like this.

▶ SERVES 4

1 tablespoon olive oil

1 carrot, diced

1 onion, diced

8 ounces (230 g) cremini or white button mushrooms, thinly sliced

1 large turnip, peeled and cut into ½-inch (1 cm) cubes

3 garlic cloves, minced

1 tablespoon tomato paste

½ cup (120 ml) dry red wine

1½ cups (300 g) French green lentils

6 cups (1.5 ml) vegetable stock, preferably homemade (page 15), or water

1 teaspoon ground cumin

½ teaspoon ground cinnamon

½ teaspoon freshly ground black pepper

1½ teaspoons salt

Croutons, preferably homemade (page 18), for garnish

Coarsely chopped fresh parsley for garnish

1. Heat the oil in a soup pot over medium heat. Add the carrot and onion and sauté until softened, 8 to 10 minutes. Add the mushrooms and sauté until they release their liquid and it cooks off, about 10 minutes. Add the turnip, followed by the garlic and tomato paste, and stir until the vegetables are evenly coated. Turn the heat up to high and pour in the wine to deglaze the pan, scraping up any browned bits with a wooden spoon or spatula.

2. Add the lentils and stock and bring to a boil. Stir in the cumin, cinnamon, and pepper, then lower the heat, partially cover, and simmer for 20 minutes. Stir in the salt and continue to simmer until the lentils are tender, about 10 minutes more. Puree half of the soup with an immersion blender or working in batches and using a food processor or regular blender. Stir the puree back into the soup, taste, and adjust the seasonings if necessary. Garnish with the croutons and parsley and serve hot.

▶ LEFTOVERS: Stored in an airtight container, this soup will keep for up to 3 days in the refrigerator and 1 month in the freezer.

▶ PREPARATION AND COOKING TIME: 1 hour and 15 minutes

Delicata Squash Soup

WHEN I FIRST made this soup, I took one slurp, looked outside, and in that instant was finally willing to resign myself to the fact of summer being over. Delicata, a winter squash that starts to show up early in the fall, is shaped like a giant cucumber and has pale yellow, striped skin and flesh that's also pale yellow, with a sweet, nutty flavor. Its skin is thinner than that of other varieties of winter squash, so it's much easier to peel. In fact, the skin is edible, though for this soup it's better to remove it. In this recipe, apple cider brings a bit of tartness to balance the squash's sweetness, and there's a tingle of heat from the jalapeño and ginger. I often have beet or turnip greens in the crisper of my refrigerator, and I enjoy slicing them into thin strips and mixing them into the soup at the end, but this isn't a mandatory component, so I've marked that step as optional.

▶ **SERVES 3 OR 4**

2 pounds (1 kg) delicata squash

3 tablespoons butter or neutral oil (canola, grapeseed, peanut, or vegetable oil)

1 medium onion, diced

3 garlic cloves, minced

1½ teaspoons grated fresh ginger (see page 13)

1 jalapeño pepper, minced (seeded for a milder heat level)

1 cup (240 ml) apple juice or apple cider

5½ cups (1.3 l) water

¾ teaspoon salt

1 large Yukon Gold or red bliss potato (about 8 ounces, 230 g), peeled and coarsely chopped

2 cups (200 g) thinly sliced turnip greens, beet greens, or Swiss chard, optional

Fresh lemon juice

Croutons, preferably homemade (page 18), for garnish

Coarsely chopped fresh cilantro for garnish

1. Peel the squash with a vegetable peeler. Cut it in half lengthwise and scoop out the seeds. Cut the squash lengthwise into 1-inch (3 cm) strips, then cut the strips crosswise into 1-inch (3 cm) cubes.

2. Heat the butter in a soup pot or Dutch oven over medium heat. Add the onion and sauté until softened, about 6 minutes. Add the garlic, ginger, and jalapeño and sauté until fragrant, about 1 minute. Add the squash, mixing it in thoroughly. Turn the heat up to medium-high, pour in the juice, and cook, stirring occasionally, until the liquid is reduced by half. Add the water, potato, and salt. Bring to a boil, then lower the heat, cover, and simmer for 20 to 30 minutes, until the squash and potato are completely tender.

3. Remove from the heat and puree until smooth, using an immersion blender or working in batches and using a food processor or regular blender. Return the puree to a simmer. If using the greens, stir them in and, after they've wilted, about 2 minutes, add lemon juice to taste. Adjust the seasonings if necessary. Garnish with the croutons and cilantro and serve hot.

▶ **LEFTOVERS:** Stored in an airtight container, this soup will keep for up to 3 days in the refrigerator and 1 month in the freezer.

▶ **PREPARATION AND COOKING TIME:** 45 minutes

Red Bean CHILI

WHILE MY FRIEND Lesley was living in London, she sent me a recipe for a nonvegetarian chili that called for a healthy dose of red wine and a cinnamon stick. It sounded so unique and tasty that it became the inspiration for this recipe. This chili isn't the chunky kind you could eat with a fork; it's more of a hearty, luxurious soup. The deeply aromatic warm spice from the garam masala and ginger is unexpected, the serrano brings just the right amount of heat, and the red wine lends a bright and sophisticated flavor. Cocoa powder may seem like an unconventional ingredient, but think of it along the lines of a mole twist. Note that the kidney beans must be soaked in advance, so plan ahead. Once your chili has simmered to perfection, you can serve it over white or brown rice, and garnished with anything from sour cream or grated Cheddar or Monterey Jack cheese to pickled jalapeño peppers and guacamole.

▶ **SERVES 5 OR 6**

2 tablespoons olive oil

2 onions, chopped

3 garlic cloves, minced

2 teaspoons grated fresh ginger, peeled (see page 13)

1 or 2 serrano chiles, seeded and minced

1 tablespoon ground cumin

1 tablespoon garam masala

1 teaspoon unsweetened cocoa powder

1 cup (240 ml) full-bodied red wine

One 28-ounce (794 g) can whole tomatoes

2 tablespoons tomato paste

2 cups (400 g) red kidney beans, soaked for at least 4 hours or overnight

3 cups (750 ml) water, plus more as needed

1 teaspoon salt

¼ teaspoon freshly ground black pepper

1 cup (25 g) coarsely chopped fresh cilantro or parsley

1. Heat the oil in a soup pot over medium heat. Add the onions and sauté until softened, 6 to 8 minutes. Add the garlic, ginger, serranos, cumin, and garam masala, and sauté until very fragrant, 2 to 3 minutes.

2. Turn the heat up to high, pour in the wine, and cook until the liquid is reduced by half, about 3 minutes. Stir in the tomatoes with their juices and the tomato paste and cook until thick and the tomatoes have softened, 10 to 15 minutes.

3. Smash the tomatoes against the side of the pan with a wooden spoon, then stir in the beans and water. Bring to a boil, then lower the heat, cover, and simmer for 1 hour. Stir in the salt and pepper, then continue to simmer, covered, until the beans are tender and the stewy liquid is velvety—at least 30 minutes. The chili shouldn't be too thick; add up to 2 cups (475 ml) additional hot water if the beans rise above the surface of the liquid. Continue to taste and season as needed.

4. Stir in the cilantro and serve hot.

▶ **LEFTOVERS:** Stored in an airtight container, this chili will keep for up to 4 days in the refrigerator and 1 month in the freezer.

▶ **PREPARATION AND COOKING TIME:** About 2 hours

RISOTTOS

IF YOU'VE never tried making risotto because you think it's too complicated, you're in for a welcome surprise. There is nothing complicated about it: it's simply a way of cooking rice in which the liquid is added as the rice absorbs it. Yes, you need to be stirring most of the time, but if you approach the task with the right frame of mind, that aspect can actually be a pleasure. In making risotto, I've found a few tips to be helpful:

- Don't use an overly salty or heavily flavored vegetable stock. The rice has a delicate flavor that you don't want to muddy up. And as with soups, I find water preferable to canned, boxed, or concentrated vegetable stock in risotto. In the recipe for Basic Vegetable Risotto, I include a recipe for risotto broth—technically a riff on court-bouillon, which is a quick method for making broth or poaching liquid—made from the vegetable trimmings. I like to make the broth right alongside the risotto. As soon as the broth starts simmering, you can begin to cook the onions. I view this as an economical and efficient solution when I'm making risotto, and because the stock is fresh and already simmering, it results in the absolute best flavor.

- Pay attention to the amount of liquid in the pan as you stir in the broth. Don't wait for the rice to absorb all of the liquid before adding another ladleful; there should always be a bit of extra liquid pooling in the bottom of the pan. This ensures that the finished risotto is light and loose, not heavy and gummy.

- In risotto, as in so many other dishes, textural contrast is key. But it can be tricky to achieve since the cooking time for the risotto is determined by that of the rice, rather than that of the accompanying vegetables. When adding vegetables, the most important thing to keep in mind is their cooking times. Forgiving vegetables, such as carrots or parsnips, can be first sautéed and then cooked along with the rice and will still retain a pleasant texture at the end of the cooking time. Tender leafy greens, such as baby spinach, should be stirred into the rice in the last minute or two of cooking; otherwise they'll turn to mush in the finished dish. Slow-cooking vegetables like winter squash or quick-cooking but temperamental ones like asparagus should be cooked separately and then stirred in towards the end, with enough just time left to be heated through.

- As for wine, I like to add it mostly in the beginning, to deglaze the vegetables, and then add a bit more at the end to ensure that some of the bright wine flavor remains in the dish.

For a fun alternate way to use any leftovers, be sure to check out the recipe for Panko-Crusted Risotto Cakes (page 145).

Basic Vegetable Risotto

THIS IS HANDS-DOWN my favorite way to make risotto. The flavors are perfectly aligned, with just the right amount of sweet, bitter, and rich, and the dish is dotted with perfectly tender vegetables. While risotto is sometimes too light to qualify as a main course, I find this one to be substantial and filling as a centerpiece dish. I recommend making this risotto with the Risotto Broth given here, but if you are short on time you can substitute light vegetable stock or water.

▶ **SERVES 3 OR 4**

FOR THE RISOTTO BROTH

1 teaspoon butter

2 garlic cloves, smashed

1 bay leaf

Peel and ends from the carrot for the risotto

Peel and ends from the parsnip for the risotto

¼ white onion, coarsely chopped (use the rest of the onion for the risotto)

3 black peppercorns

1 parsley sprig

6 cups (1.5 l) water

½ teaspoon kosher salt

FOR THE RISOTTO

1 large carrot, peel and ends reserved for the risotto broth

1 medium parsnip, peel and ends reserved for the risotto broth

1 head radicchio

3 tablespoons butter

¾ white onion, diced

1 cup (220 g) Arborio or Carnaroli rice

1 cup (240 ml) dry white wine

1 recipe Risotto Broth (above), or 5 cups (1.25 l) light vegetable stock (see note, page 16) or water

¼ teaspoon salt

¼ teaspoon freshly ground black pepper

1½ ounces (45 g) Parmesan cheese, grated (⅓ cup), plus more for the table

Minced fresh flat-leaf parsley for garnish

1. To make the broth, melt the butter in a medium saucepan over medium heat. Add the garlic, bay leaf, vegetable trimmings, onion, peppercorns, and parsley and sauté just until fragrant, about 1 minute. Pour in the water and bring to a gentle boil. Stir in the salt, then lower the heat, cover partially, and simmer for 25 to 30 minutes. Strain out the vegetables and discard them. Return the broth to its pot and keep warm over low heat while you proceed with the risotto recipe.

2. While the broth is simmering, start making the risotto. Cut the carrot and parsnip into ½-inch (1 cm) cubes. Cut the radicchio in half lengthwise, remove the core, then slice into thin strips.

3. If you aren't making the risotto broth recipe, put the 5 cups (1.25 ml) of vegetable stock or water in a saucepan and bring it to a simmer.

4. Melt 2 tablespoons of the butter in a deep sauté pan or Dutch oven over medium heat. Add the onion and sauté until just softened, about 5 minutes, lowering the heat if it begins to burn. Add the carrot and parsnip and continue sautéing until the onion is translucent but not browned, 8 to 10 more minutes. Turn the heat up to medium-high, add the rice, and stir constantly until the rice grains appear translucent through to their centers, 2 to 3 minutes.

5. Pour in ¾ cup (180 ml) of the wine. Cook and stir until most but not all of the liquid

BASIC VEGETABLE RISOTTO

is absorbed. Lower the heat to medium-low and ladle in about ½ cup (120 ml) of the simmering broth. Once again cook and stir until most but not all of the liquid is absorbed. Continue periodically ladling in the broth as the rice absorbs it, stirring leisurely. The goal is to maintain a light, loose consistency and not let the risotto become heavy or gluey. After 15 minutes of adding the broth, stir in the radicchio, salt, and pepper along with another ladleful of broth. Keep stirring and adding broth by the ladleful until the rice is tender but not mushy, beginning to test for doneness after about 25 minutes. If you fear running out of broth before the risotto is done, add hot water to the broth.

6. Stir in the remaining ¼ cup (70 ml) of wine, then remove from the heat. Stir in the cheese and the remaining 1 tablespoon of butter. Cover and let sit for 5 minutes. Then give the risotto a stir and serve immediately, garnishing with the parsley and passing additional Parmesan cheese and a pepper mill at the table.

▶ LEFTOVERS: Risotto is best eaten freshly cooked, but stored in an airtight container, it will keep for 1 day in the refrigerator.

▶ PREPARATION AND COOKING TIME: 1 hour and 15 minutes

VARIATIONS

VEGAN RISOTTO: Substitute olive oil for the butter and omit the Parmesan cheese. A very light drizzle of truffle oil or a sprinkling of truffle salt just before serving is an excellent enrichment.

BARLEY RISOTTO: Substitute 1 cup (220 g) pearl barley for the Arborio rice. It will take a bit longer for the barley to cook until tender, and the broth can be added in larger increments. One way to speed its cooking time is to soak the barley as you would beans, for 4 hours or more, prior to making the risotto.

MUSHROOM RISOTTO WITH SPINACH: Use 8 ounces (230 g) of cremini or white button mushrooms and omit the parsnip and radicchio. Stem the mushrooms, thinly slice the caps, and add the stems to the risotto broth. After sautéing the onion for 5 minutes in step 4, add the sliced mushrooms and sauté until they release their liquid, 4 to 6 minutes. Then add the rice and proceed with the recipe, stirring in 5 ounces of fresh baby spinach during the last 1 or 2 minutes of cooking.

RISOTTO WITH PEAS, FENNEL, AND CHERRY TOMATOES: Substitute a basic light vegetable stock or water for the risotto broth and omit the onion, carrot, parsnip, and radicchio. In place of the onion, sauté 1 large fennel bulb, thinly sliced, in step 4 and cook until completely softened, 10 to 12 minutes. Add the rice and proceed with the recipe. During the last 5 minutes of cooking time, stir in 1 recipe of roasted cherry tomatoes (page 21) and 1 cup (180 g) fresh, shelled English peas.

PUMPKIN RISOTTO WITH SPINACH AND CHESTNUTS

THIS RECIPE FEATURES an alternate method for risotto in which pumpkin is cooked in vegetable stock and then pureed, so in effect you're making a thin pumpkin soup and ladling it into the risotto. Another alternative would be roasting the pumpkin as the squash is prepared in the Black-Eyed Pea Salad with Roasted Squash and Radicchio (page 39) and then folding it in at the end of the risotto's cooking time. Regarding the roasted chestnuts in this recipe, you can certainly roast your own (see note), but I usually look for the ones that come in vacuum-packed pouches or in dry-packed jars, and I prefer using those rather than chestnuts submerged in liquid. They're always available around Thanksgiving and Christmas, which makes this an obvious dish for the holiday table, and they bring a sweet and distinctive textural contrast that pairs beautifully with the autumnal flavors of the pumpkin.

▶ **SERVES 3 OR 4**

1 small baking pumpkin (about 2 pounds, 1 kg)

5 cups (1.25 l) light vegetable stock or water

3 tablespoons butter

1 white onion, diced

2 garlic cloves, minced

1 bay leaf

2 teaspoons minced fresh thyme, or ¾ teaspoon dried

1 cup (220 g) Arborio or Carnaroli rice

1 cup (240 ml) dry white wine

¼ teaspoon salt

¼ teaspoon freshly ground black pepper

½ cup (190 g) roasted chestnuts, coarsely chopped

5 ounces (140 g) baby spinach

1½ ounces Parmesan cheese, grated (⅓ cup), plus more for the table

Minced fresh flat-leaf parsley for garnish

Toasted pumpkin seeds (see page 13) for garnish

1. To prepare the pumpkin, trim off the ends so as to make flat surfaces. With a flat side on the cutting board, peel the pumpkin with either a sharp, sturdy knife or a vegetable peeler, cutting off the skin in strips from top to bottom. Cut the pumpkin in half and scoop out the seeds. Cut it into strips 1 inch (3 cm) thick, then cut the strips into 1-inch (3 cm) cubes. You should have about 3 cups (340 g) chopped pumpkin.

2. Combine the pumpkin and the stock in a saucepan. Bring to a boil, then lower the heat, cover and simmer until the pumpkin is tender, 25 to 35 minutes. Remove from the heat and puree until very smooth, using an immersion blender or working in batches and using a food processor or regular blender. It should be relatively thin—no thicker than the consistency of heavy cream. If necessary, stir in additional hot water. Return the puree to a simmer.

3. Melt 2 tablespoons of the butter in a deep sauté pan or Dutch oven over medium heat. Add the onion and sauté until translucent, 10 to 12 minutes. Add the garlic, bay leaf, and thyme and sauté until fragrant, about 1 minute. Turn the heat up to medium-high, add the rice, and stir constantly until the rice grains appear translucent through to their centers, 1 to 2 minutes.

4. Pour in ¾ cup (180 ml) of the wine. Cook and stir until most but not all of the liquid is absorbed. Lower the heat to medium-low and ladle in about ½ cup (120 ml) of the simmering pumpkin broth. Once again cook and stir until most but not all of the liquid is absorbed. Continue periodically ladling in the broth as the rice absorbs it, stirring leisurely. The goal is to maintain a light, loose consistency and not let the risotto become heavy or gluey. Keep stirring and adding broth by the ladleful until the rice is tender but not mushy, beginning to test for doneness after about 25 minutes, and stirring in the salt and pepper at this point as well. If you fear running out of broth before the risotto is done, add hot water to the broth.

5. Stir in the remaining ¼ cup (70 ml) of wine, then remove from the heat. Stir in the chestnuts, spinach, cheese, and the remaining 1 tablespoon of butter. Cover and let sit for 5 minutes. Then give the risotto a stir and serve immediately, garnishing with the parsley and pumpkin seeds and passing additional cheese and a pepper mill at the table.

NOTE: To roast your own chestnuts, preheat the oven to 400°F (200°C). With a sharp paring knife, cut an "X" into the flat side of each chestnut, ensuring that you've cut through the shell. Roast for 20 to 30 minutes, until the skins have curled back and are dark in color. Cool until safe to handle, then remove the skins using a paring knife.

► LEFTOVERS: Risotto is best eaten freshly cooked, but stored in an airtight container; it will keep for 1 day in the refrigerator.

► PREPARATION AND COOKING TIME: 1 hour and 30 minutes

REUSING DISPOSABLE ITEMS

I experience a twinge of guilt about relying on disposable kitchen items like plastic wrap and resealable bags, to the extent that I've gone through periods of not using them at all. This is very difficult to do, so I've never been able to stick with it for very long. I have, however, learned that many "disposable" items can in fact be reused a few times before being recycled or discarded. Plus, reusing these kinds of items even once makes your supply last twice as long and will therefore save you money. In all cases be observant and discard or recycle anything that's exceeded its useful life—especially if you detect obvious signs, like mold developing or something smelling odd.

- **ALUMINUM FOIL:** Heavy-duty foil is one of the easiest things to reuse. Wipe it off with a sponge or damp cloth, fold it up, and store it for future use.
- **CHEESECLOTH:** My primary uses for cheesecloth are for lining a colander to strain out the vegetables from vegetable stock and for squeezing the liquid from blanched, steamed, or sautéed greens. For these purposes, you can reuse it over and over. Just rinse it thoroughly under running water and then drape it over a rack to dry completely.
- **PARCHMENT PAPER:** Parchment paper is best reused when reserved for a specific use. For example, you might have a few sheets you use to line baking sheets for cookies and others you use to line pans for roasted vegetables. Whatever the use, let the parchment paper dry completely, gently wipe it down with a clean towel or paper towel, then fold or roll it up to store for future reuse.
- **PLASTIC BAGS AND PLASTIC WRAP:** Simply rinse out plastic bags and drape them over a dish rack or a countertop plastic bag dryer (a little stand with several dowels sticking out of it) to air-dry. Though it's a little trickier, you can do the same thing with plastic wrap. Bag dryers are available at natural food stores and other environmentally conscious stores, as well as from online retailers.
- **PLASTIC FOOD CONTAINERS AND TAKEOUT CONTAINERS:** This one is a no-brainer for anyone who's ever scoffed at the prices of Tupperware, disposable or otherwise. The plastic containers that yogurt, sour cream, and other foods come in can be washed and reused over and over again, and this is also true of some takeout containers.

3

Pasta, Asian Noodle Dishes, and Dumplings

NOODLES ARE ALWAYS happy to fill the center of the vegetarian plate. In fact, pasta with vegetables is so familiar a vegetarian option that it's practically ubiquitous. But pasta is open to learning new tricks, and as with beans and whole grains, as long as you've got some noodles in your cupboard, you're only a pot of boiling water away from dinner. Sauces can often be thrown together from a handful of standard pantry items, and usually in the amount of time it takes for pasta to boil. This is a big reason why pasta is such an ideal weeknight food.

Dried pasta keeps well, so I recommend that you always have some on hand. I find most dried pastas are good, but I especially like the Italian organic brand Bionaturae for Italian-inspired dishes. For Asian dishes it's fun to seek out new varieties of noodles at ethnic markets, but again, the varieties available at typical grocery stores is also very good. Buy a few different types to keep on hand; this may provide unexpected inspiration later on down the line. While fresh pasta is also widely available, it's best to seek out stores that make the pasta on the premises. The little airtight pouches of "fresh" pasta sold at grocery stores are rarely, if ever, better than dry pasta.

The trick of pairing pasta with toppings is to find a balance in body. Hearty sauces need to be matched with a hearty pasta. Most of the Italian-style sauces in the following recipes are robust, and therefore aren't paired with dainty pastas. Asian noodle dishes invite a different approach altogether. With noodle bowls, a crucial element of the dish is a flavorful broth, and with stir-fried noodles it's essential to have snappy fresh vegetables, sauces based on flavor profiles of the East, and perhaps some nuts.

WHOLE WHEAT SPAGHETTI WITH CREAMED KALE AND CHICKPEAS

WHEN I HEAR the word *supper*, this type of dish is exactly what comes to mind, in large part because I associate supper with cool weather, when the best place to be in the house is huddled over the stove. Creamed spinach has long been a guilty pleasure of mine, but I've always regarded it a calorie-laden side dish. Then I started experimenting with heartier greens like kale and chard (and you should feel free to substitute chard below) and made further progress by lightening up the béchamel sauce with vegetable stock, which also contributes a more nuanced vegetal flavor. I'd be happy to forgo the pasta and the chickpeas in this recipe and just serve the kale on toast. But as far as dinner goes, you can't get more filling than this. If you're averse to whole wheat pasta, consider using half standard, semolina spaghetti and half whole wheat. Check the cooking times on the packages, and add the pastas sequentially, adding the one with the longest cooking time first.

▶ SERVES 4

1 bunch kale (about 12 ounces, 325 g)

1 pound (450 g) whole wheat spaghetti

3 tablespoons butter

2 shallots, minced

3 tablespoons all-purpose flour

1½ cups (360 ml) reduced-fat milk (1% or 2%)

1½ cups (360 ml) vegetable stock, preferably homemade (page 15)

¼ teaspoon salt

Pinch of freshly grated nutmeg

Freshly ground black pepper

Pulp or flesh from 2 heads roasted garlic, skins discarded (page 20)

2 cups (425 g) cooked chickpeas, or one 15-ounce can, drained and rinsed

1 teaspoon grated lemon zest, plus more for garnish

Parmesan cheese for garnish

1. Blanch the kale (see page 10) in a large pot of salted water until tender, removing it from its cooking water with tongs or a slotted spoon, rather than pouring it into a colander, so as to reserve the cooking water. Finely chop the kale.

2. Return the pot of water to a boil. Add the pasta and cook until al dente. When you drain the pasta, reserve at least 1 cup (240 ml) of the cooking water.

3. Meanwhile, melt the butter in a medium saucepan or Dutch oven over medium heat. Add the shallots and sauté until fragrant and slightly softened, 2 to 3 minutes. Sprinkle the flour over the shallots, whisking constantly to evenly distribute the flour, and cook still whisking constantly, until the mixture is a shade darker and smells nutty, 2 to 3 minutes. Gradually add the milk and stock, whisking constantly to break up any lumps. Bring to a boil, then lower the heat to medium-low and simmer until the mixture thickens slightly, 6 to 8 minutes total.

4. Stir in the salt and nutmeg and season with pepper. Taste and adjust the seasonings if necessary. Stir in the kale, roasted garlic, chickpeas, and lemon zest, being careful to break

**WHOLE WHEAT SPAGHETTI WITH CREAMED KALE
AND CHICKPEAS**

up the kale so the leaves are as evenly coated as possible. Cook, stirring occasionally, until the kale and chickpeas are heated through, 2 to 3 minutes.

5. Combine the cooked pasta and kale mixture, tossing well with tongs. If the sauce is too thick, loosen the dish with a bit of the reserved cooking water, adding it in small increments. Garnish with more lemon zest and pass freshly grated Parmesan at the table.

▶ LEFTOVERS: Stored in an airtight container, this pasta will keep for 1 day in the refrigerator.

▶ PREPARATION AND COOKING TIME: 45 minutes

TOMATO AND WHITE BEAN SAUCE OVER RIGATONI

I MAKE THIS hearty pasta dish fairly often because it's such an easy meal to pull together from standard pantry ingredients. It's also great for feeding a crowd on short notice. The white beans lend a robust, meatlike quality to the sauce; the white wine gives it a bright, zippy profile on the palate; and the toasted bread crumbs on top offer a welcome crunch. You can substitute any shape of pasta you'd like; I prefer rigatoni because it's sturdy enough to carry the sauce, but whatever you have on hand will do the job just fine.

▶ **SERVES 5 TO 6**

3 tablespoons olive oil

1 medium onion, minced

5 garlic cloves, minced

1 cup (250 ml) dry white wine

Two 28-ounce (794 g) cans whole tomatoes

4 cups (850 g) cooked white beans, or two 15-ounce cans, drained and rinsed

1 teaspoon salt

½ teaspoon red pepper flakes

1 pound (450 g) rigatoni

½ cup (60 g) toasted bread crumbs, preferably homemade (page 17) for garnish

1. Heat the oil in a Dutch oven or deep sauté pan over medium heat. Add the onion and sauté until softened but not browned, 6 to 8 minutes. Add the garlic and sauté until fragrant, about 1 minute. Turn the heat up slightly and pour in the wine. Cook, scraping up any browned bits from the bottom of the pot, until the liquid is reduced by half. Add the tomatoes and their juices and bring to a boil. Lower the heat and simmer, uncovered, until the tomatoes are slightly softened, about 10 minutes. Using or the back of a wooden spoon, coarsely crush the tomatoes against the side of the pan. Stir in the beans, salt, and pepper flakes and simmer until the tomatoes are tender, 8 to 10 minutes.

2. Meanwhile, bring a large pot of salted water to a boil. Add the rigatoni and cook until al dente. Drain the pasta.

3. Either toss the sauce with the rigatoni or divide the pasta among serving plates and ladle the sauce over it. Just before serving, sprinkle with the bread crumbs, 1 tablespoon per serving.

▶ **LEFTOVERS:** Stored in an airtight container, this pasta will keep for 1 day in the refrigerator.

▶ **PREPARATION AND COOKING TIME:** 30 minutes

SPINACH LINGUINE WITH CORN, PESTO, ROASTED TOMATOES, AND POACHED EGG

THIS HAS GOT to be the easiest kind of pasta dish there is, and yet it's scrumptious and beautiful enough to serve at a dinner party. It's a perfect meal for late summer, when bouquets of basil, piles of corn, and pints of sweet cherry tomatoes are all at peak freshness. I strongly urge you to use homemade pesto, as it is a primary element here. Basil-Almond Pesto (page 25) is my favorite for this, and the final garnish with roasted almonds echoes the theme. The eggs can be poached up to 30 minutes in advance; just store them in room-temperature water, and then reheat in simmering water for 30 seconds just before serving.

▶ **SERVES 4**

1 pound (450 g) spinach linguine or spaghetti

1½ cups (180 g) fresh corn kernels (from about 3 ears)

2 teaspoons vinegar

4 eggs

1 cup (240 ml) pesto, preferably Basil-Almond Pesto (page 25; a double batch)

4 cups (340 g) baby spinach or arugula

1 recipe Roasted Cherry Tomatoes (page 21)

¼ cup (30 g) roasted almonds (see page 13), coarsely chopped

2 ounces (60 g) Parmesan cheese, grated (½ cup), plus more for the table

Freshly ground black pepper

1. Bring a large pot of salted water to a boil. Add the pasta and cook until al dente. About 1 minute before the end of the cooking time, add the corn. When you drain the pasta, reserve at least 1 cup of the cooking water.

2. Put at least 3 inches (8 cm) of water in a small saucepan over high heat. Bring to a boil, add the vinegar, then lower the heat to maintain a very gentle simmer. Crack one egg into a small bowl, being careful not to break the yolk. Lower the bowl into the simmering water and gently transfer the egg into the saucepan, then do the same with second egg, cooking no more than 2 eggs at a time. Cook until the whites are set and the yolks are cooked to the desired doneness, about 2½ minutes for a yolk that's runny, 4 minutes for partially set, and 5 minutes for hard. To check doneness, lift the egg up from the water using a slotted spoon and gently touch the yolk with your finger. When the eggs are cooked, remove with the slotted spoon, and transfer to a bowl of room temperature water. Poach the remaining 2 eggs in the same fashion. Remove from the heat, but reserve the cooking water. Before assembling the finished dish, warm the poached eggs in simmering water for about 30 seconds.

3. Combine the hot pasta with the pesto, spinach, tomatoes, almonds, and Parmesan, tossing until the spinach is wilted. Add the reserved pasta water in small increments to loosen the consistency if necessary. Divide the pasta among 4 serving plates or bowls, and top each serving with a poached egg. Serve right away, garnishing with additional Parmesan and passing a pepper mill at the table.

▶ **LEFTOVERS:** Minus the poached eggs and stored in an airtight container, this pasta will keep for 2 days in the refrigerator.

▶ **PREPARATION AND COOKING TIME:** 20 minutes

MUSHROOMS AND ARTICHOKES WITH FARFALLE

MUSHROOMS AND ARTICHOKES are a stellar combination, offering a unique pairing of texture and flavor. I'm not above using frozen artichoke hearts, especially in this dish. When I worked as a prep cook, I had the task of cleaning crates of artichokes at a time, and some residual dread of the chore still sits with me. If you wish to use fresh, I've included instructions for how to clean artichokes in the sidebar. The crème fraîche—basically France's version of sour cream—enriches this dish, giving it body as well as tang.

► SERVES 4

2 tablespoons butter

2 leeks, white and light green parts, halved lengthwise, sliced into thin half-moons, and cleaned (see page 13)

8 ounces (230 g) cremini mushrooms, stemmed and thinly sliced

One 10-ounce (280 g) package frozen artichoke hearts, thawed, or 5 fresh artichoke hearts, quartered

One 14-ounce (380 g) can whole tomatoes, drained and coarsely chopped

4 garlic cloves, slivered

¾ cup (180 ml) dry white wine

¾ cup (180 ml) crème fraîche or sour cream

1½ ounces (45 g) Parmesan cheese, grated (⅓ cup), plus more for garnish

1 pound (450 g) farfalle

Coarsely chopped fresh parsley for garnish

1. Melt the butter in a deep sauté pan or Dutch oven over medium heat. Add the leeks and sauté until just beginning to soften, 4 to 6 minutes.

Add the mushrooms and sauté until they release their liquid and it cooks off, 5 to 7 minutes. Add the artichoke hearts and tomatoes and cook, stirring occasionally, for 5 minutes. Add the garlic and sauté until fragrant, 2 to 3 minutes. Turn the heat up to high, pour in the wine, and cook until the liquid is reduced by half, 5 or 6 minutes. If using fresh artichokes, continue cooking until they're tender. Remove from the heat and stir in the crème fraîche and Parmesan.

2. Meanwhile, bring a large pot of salted water to a boil. Add the pasta and cook until al dente. When you drain the pasta, reserve at least 1 cup of the cooking water.

3. Toss the sauce with the hot pasta, thinning it out with some of the reserved pasta water if necessary. Dust with Parmesan cheese and parsley and serve hot.

► LEFTOVERS: Stored in an airtight container, this pasta will keep for 1 day in the refrigerator.

► PREPARATION AND COOKING TIME: 35 minutes

HOW TO TRIM an ARTICHOKE

I FIND that the best way to get to the heart of an artichoke is by steaming them whole one day, eating away at the leaves, and reserving the heart for future dishes. (And in case you don't know, only the tender part of the leaves is edible, and usually eaten by scraping it off with your teeth.) But if you don't have time for a two-day approach, use the following instructions to clean and trim uncooked artichokes.

Cut off and discard the top inch or two of leaves from the artichoke. Put the artichoke on a cutting board upside down, so the flat, trimmed face is flat on the cutting board. Cutting downward, trim off the outer layers of leaves, then switch to a paring knife to trim off the entire outer layer of skin from the stem and the base of the stem until the heart is revealed. Chop the heart in half lengthwise, then scoop out the choke. Quarter the hearts and store them in water that has a few drops of lemon juice in it.

ONE-POT ORZO WITH SPRING VEGETABLES, GREEN OLIVES, AND FETA

I LOVE A good one-pot pasta dish, and this one is inspired by a light pasta dish I had at a dinner party. It's terrific in the spring, when snappy, thin asparagus spears are available at farmers' markets, alongside bunches of knobby little carrots. Orzo, which is the pasta that looks like rice, makes this dish somewhat similar to risotto, but lighter and easier to make, and with a clean flavor tinged a tangy-salty Mediterranean dimension from the olives and feta. Grocery stores often have olive bars where you can purchase only the amount you need, and that's where I like to get my olives. Here I like plump, bright green Manzanilla olives, which have a slightly nutty flavor and firm texture. I smash them with a knife, which loosens the pit and makes it easy to slip out, and then chop the flesh. You could also use a spoonful of olive tapenade per plate, either purchased or homemade (page 27).

▶ SERVES 4

1 tablespoon olive oil

1 medium white onion, minced

8 ounces (230 g) carrots cut into ¼-inch (5 mm) pieces

3 cups (750 ml) water

1½ cups (330 g) orzo

¼ teaspoon salt

8 ounces (230 g) asparagus, tough ends snapped off, cut into 1-inch (3 cm) pieces

8 ounces (230 g) spinach, cleaned and tough stems removed

½ cup green olives, pitted and finely chopped

3 ounces feta cheese, crumbled

Pinch of grated lemon zest

Freshly ground black pepper

Heat the oil in a deep sauté pan or medium saucepan over medium-low heat. Add the onion and carrots and stir until evenly coated. Cover and cook for 7 minutes. Pour in the water and bring to a boil. Add the orzo and the salt, and turn the heat down to maintain an active simmer. Cook, uncovered and stirring periodically, for 5 minutes. Add the asparagus, cover, and cook until the orzo and asparagus are almost tender, about 3 minutes. Add the spinach—don't bother stirring it in, just place it on top of the pasta—and cover the pot to let it steam for 1 or 2 minutes, after which the vegetables and orzo should be tender. Remove from the heat and fold in the olives and feta. Stir in the lemon zest and season with pepper and additional salt if necessary. Serve hot, warm, or at room temperature.

▶ LEFTOVERS: Stored in an airtight container, this pasta will keep for 2 days in the refrigerator.

▶ PREPARATION AND COOKING TIME: 25 minutes

NOODLE BOWLS

NOODLE BOWLS and rice bowls have a lot in common. The biggest difference—besides being based on noodles rather than rice—is the added component of a flavorful, nutritious hot broth that encompasses the dish. In vegetarian versions of the dish, an enhanced vegetable stock is typically what's used. Two of my favorite broths for noodle bowls are based on miso and kombu—ingredients that are increasingly available at natural food stores and well-stocked grocery stores, as well as Asian markets. Miso is a paste usually made by fermenting soybeans, sometimes along with other beans, grains, or ingredients. It comes in many different varieties, and it keeps for a long time. Lighter-colored misos tend to have a somewhat sweet flavor; those that are more darkly colored are typically saltier and more robustly flavored. Kombu, a sea vegetable that's a type of kelp, can be used to flavor the Japanese broth known as dashi, and the kombu itself can be eaten after it's been used to infuse the broth. Here are some pointers on making miso broth and dashi:

MISO BROTH: Prepare 1 recipe of vegetable stock (page 15). Remove a few ladlefuls of vegetable stock from a simmering pot into a small mixing bowl. Whisk in the miso, using about ¼ cup of miso (or 2 tablespoons of miso per 3 cups [750 ml] of vegetable stock). When smooth, pour the mixture back into the pot and whisk to combine.

DASHI: Prepare 1 recipe of vegetable stock (page 15). At the end of the broth's cooking time, add one 10-inch (25 cm) piece of kombu seaweed (or one 5-inch [12 cm] piece per 3 cups [750 ml] of vegetable stock). Remove from the heat and let stand for 1 hour. Strain out the kombu and the vegetables. If desired, you can stir in a bit of miso into the dashi.

Next, you'll have to determine which type of noodle to use. Here are my favorite varieties for noodle bowls; all three are commonly available:

RAMEN is a Chinese wheat noodle (the name also refers to the finished noodle bowl, not just the noodles). Hand-cut ramen noodles, if you ever have the chance to try them, elevate ramen into something far more special than the plastic pouches college students subsist on.

SOBA is a Japanese noodle made from buckwheat noodles. Soba is slightly skinnier than spaghetti and is cut so that the noodle's shape is square, not round. Soba has a somewhat nutty flavor and a tender structure.

UDON is a Japanese wheat noodle that varies in thickness, but in general it's quite thick and chewy when cooked.

The noodles should be cooked separately from the broth, in unsalted water, until al dente. For soba noodles, you don't want a rapid boil, because they are somewhat delicate. For all varieties, once they're cooked, rinse them under cold water to wash off the starch. Combine the noodles with the broth just before serving.

After combining the noodles and broth, the dish can be flavored with soy sauce or tamari, sriracha sauce, toasted sesame oil, or a combination of these. Ginger-Scallion Sauce (page 28) is also an excellent addition, even on plain noodles minus the broth.

As for toppings, the simple combination of noodles and broth makes for a satisfying meal, but textural contrast is nice, and additional ingredients will also round out the dish nutritionally. Here are a few suggestions:

■ Tofu, panfried until golden or stirred in uncooked
■ Hard-boiled egg, halved lengthwise
■ Sautéed, steamed, or blanched hearty greens, such as chard or kale (see page 10)
■ Tender greens, such as baby spinach or watercress, added raw, to wilt in the hot broth

■ Fresh mushrooms, thinly sliced and lightly sautéed
■ Dried mushrooms, reconstituted and coarsely chopped (as well as the soaking water, which can be strained and added to the broth)
■ Mung bean sprouts
■ Radishes, sliced into thin rounds
■ Scallions, thinly sliced on the diagonal
■ Pickled ginger

I tend to go light on the toppings, as I prefer not to have much in the way of noisily slurping up the noodles, but it's also fine to add a lot of toppings and embellishments. Experiment as you see fit. The beauty of noodle bowls is that they're endlessly variable and can be adapted to suit your preferences or whims.

SOBA NOODLES IN MUSHROOM-GINGER BROTH

HERE'S A VARIATION on a noodle bowl that features a custom-made vegetable broth. I love the bright, fragrant broth, which features sweet spice from the ginger, and a rounded acidity thanks to the wine. In the broth, feel free to substitute mushroom stems for the fresh mushrooms. When I cook, I collect fresh mushroom stems and keep them in the freezer specifically for purposes like this; you'll want about 2 cups of mushroom pieces total. Although the noodle bowl itself may seem to have a paltry array of toppings, that simplicity belies how flavorful this dish is.

▶ **SERVES 4**

FOR THE MUSHROOM-GINGER BROTH

1 tablespoon neutral oil (canola, grapeseed, peanut, or vegetable oil)

8 ounces (230 g) mushrooms, coarsely chopped, or 2 cups mushroom pieces

½ onion, diced

½ cup (120 ml) white wine

5 dried shiitake mushrooms

One 1-inch (3 cm) piece of ginger, sliced into long, thin strips (see page 13)

2 garlic cloves, smashed

4½ cups (1 l) water

¼ teaspoon salt

3 to 4 tablespoons miso

FOR THE NOODLE BOWLS

One 8 to 10-ounce (230–280 g) package soba

1 recipe mushroom-ginger broth (above)

¼ cup (65 ml) Ginger-Scallion Sauce (page 28)

Coarsely chopped roasted, unsalted peanuts (see page 13) for garnish

1. To make the broth, heat the oil in a 2-quart saucepan over medium-high heat. Add the fresh mushrooms and onion and stir until evenly coated. Cover and cook until the vegetables have released some of their moisture, about 5 minutes. Pour in the wine, scrape up any browned bits, then stir in the dried mushrooms, ginger, garlic, and water. Bring to a boil, then stir in the salt. Lower the heat and simmer until reduced by about 1 cup (240 ml), 35 to 45 minutes, tasting along the way, until the flavors come into focus. You should be able to taste every element of the broth in perfect balance. Strain out and discard the solids and return the broth to the saucepan. Transfer a few ladlefuls of the broth to a small mixing bowl and whisk in 3 tablespoons miso paste. Transfer this mixture back to the saucepan, stirring to combine. If you'd like a more prominent miso flavor, add up to 1 tablespoon more, adding it in the same fashion. Cover and keep the broth at a simmer until you're ready to serve.

2. Meanwhile, cook the soba. Bring a large pot of unsalted water to a boil, then lower the heat to maintain a gentle boil. Add the soba and cook until al dente. Drain and rinse well under cold running water.

3. To assemble the noodle bowls, divide the soba among 4 wide, shallow serving bowls. Pour the simmering broth over them, then garnish each serving with 1 tablespoon of the scallion sauce and a scattering of peanuts. Serve hot.

▶ LEFTOVERS: This dish is best eaten freshly cooked, but the broth can be made up to 2 days in advance.

▶ PREPARATION AND COOKING TIME: 1 hour

MUSHROOM, SPINACH, and TOFU DUMPLING BOWL

THESE ARE PLUMP, filling dumplings that capitalize on a whole host of boldly flavored ingredients. The recipe makes a lot of dumplings, and while it might be too much work for a weeknight, the upside is that that they freeze really well. Just arrange the filled dumplings on a baking sheet, being careful to ensure that they aren't touching. When the sheet is full, lightly cover it with plastic wrap and freeze for 2 hours. At that point, the dumplings will be firm enough to transfer to an airtight container or resealable bag. You'll have ready-to-go dumplings in your freezer for the weeknights ahead—just drop them, still frozen, into simmering broth and cook for 8 to 10 minutes.

▶ **MAKES ABOUT 48 DUMPLINGS; SERVES 8**

6 dried shiitake mushrooms

8 ounces (230 g) fresh spinach, or 5 ounces fresh or frozen spinach

8 ounces (230 g) cremini or white button mushrooms, coarsely chopped

5 ounces (140 g) extra-firm tofu

1 tablespoon olive oil

1 teaspoon grated fresh ginger (see page 13)

3 garlic cloves, minced

1 teaspoon soy sauce

1 teaspoon rice vinegar

1 teaspoon toasted sesame oil

½ teaspoon salt

3 scallions, white and pale green parts and 1 inch (3 cm) of the dark green part, thinly sliced

2 tablespoons minced fresh cilantro or parsley

48 wonton or gyoza wrappers

Dashi or miso broth (see page 79), made from 1 recipe vegetable stock (page 15)

Mung bean sprouts for garnish

Soy sauce for the table

Sriracha sauce for the table

1. Put the dried mushrooms in a small bowl and cover with boiling water. Let stand for 20 minutes, until softened. Remove the mushrooms and squeeze them to remove excess water. Chop off and discard the stems and coarsely chop the caps. (You can save the soaking water to add to the broth if you like.)

2. If using fresh spinach, steam or blanch it until tender (see page 10). If using frozen spinach, cook it in the microwave, cooking at 2 minute intervals on medium heat, stirring at each interval with a fork. Continue to cook until thawed, then drain. Once cool enough to handle, squeeze out as much liquid as possible, then finely chop it.

3. In a food processor, combine the reconstituted mushrooms, fresh mushrooms, and tofu. Pulse until uniformly combined and coarsely ground.

4. Heat the olive oil in a deep sauté pan over medium heat. Add the mushroom mixture and sauté until the mushrooms release their liquid and it cooks off, 10 to 12 minutes. Stir in the spinach, then the ginger and garlic, and sauté until fragrant, about 1 minute. Stir in the soy sauce, vinegar, sesame oil, and salt and cook until the moisture has cooked off, about 5 minutes. Remove from the heat and stir in the scallions and cilantro. Allow to stand until cool enough to handle before assembling the dumplings.

5. Prepare a clean work surface and create a dumpling assembly station by arranging the

following in that area: the wonton wrappers, still stacked together, with a lightly moistened tea towel or paper towel draped over them to prevent them from drying out; a small bowl of water; the mushroom mixture; and a baking sheet or platter for the finished dumplings, with another moistened tea towel or paper towel for draping over them.

6. Place about 2 heaping teaspoons of filling in the center of a wrapper. Dip your finger in the bowl of water and use it to moisten one half of the perimeter of the wrapper. Beginning at opposite corners, seal the dumplings from each end so that your fingers meet in the center, and you can tuck inside any filling that might be poking out. Place the finished dumplings on the baking sheet and cover with the moistened towel to protect them from drying out. Continue with the remaining wrappers and filling. As you arrange the finished dumplings on the baking sheet, make sure they don't touch each other.

7. Just before serving, bring the dashi or miso broth to simmer in a saucepan.

8. Lower the dumplings into the stock, working in batches to avoid crowding, and cook until heated through, about 2 minutes. With a slotted spoon, transfer the cooked dumplings to serving bowls, 6 dumplings per serving. Ladle the hot broth over the dumplings. Garnish with the bean sprouts and serve immediately. Pass soy sauce and sriracha sauce at the table.

▶ **LEFTOVERS:** Stored in an airtight container, the assembled dumplings will keep for 1 day in the refrigerator and up to 2 weeks in the freezer.

▶ **PREPARATION AND COOKING TIME:** 1 hour and 15 minutes

Sweet potato and cabbage dumpling bowl

THESE DUMPLINGS ARE sweet, a little bit crunchy, super healthy, and easy to make. And served in miso broth, as in this recipe, they're fantastically filling and satisfying. Served warm or cold, the filling is a delicious salad on its own, especially as part of a picnic basket or bag lunch. I recommend doubling the recipe if you opt for the salad, or double the recipe, make the dumplings one night, and have the remaining filling for lunch the next day.

YOU CAN TAKE this dumpling bowl in any direction you choose. My version is very straightforward—miso soup with baby spinach and tofu—but you could add a different kind of greens, thin rice or wheat noodles such as vermicelli, a handful of bean sprouts, sautéed mushrooms, and so forth. The dumplings—steamed, boiled, or deep-fried—are also great on their own without the soup, as an appetizer or a lighter meal.

▶ **MAKES ABOUT 24 DUMPLINGS; SERVES 4**

1 tablespoon neutral oil (canola, grapeseed, peanut, or vegetable oil)

1 teaspoon toasted sesame oil

½ red onion, diced

¼ teaspoon cayenne pepper

1 cup (170 g) grated sweet potato (about ½ medium potato)

1 cup (85 g) thinly sliced and chopped Savoy, Napa, or red cabbage

2 teaspoons soy sauce

½ teaspoon rice wine vinegar

Pinch of salt

1 teaspoon toasted sesame seeds (see page 13)

2 tablespoons minced fresh parsley

24 wonton or gyoza wrappers

Dashi or miso broth (see page 79), made from 1 recipe vegetable stock (page 15)

7 ounces (205 g) tofu, cut into small cubes

4 handfuls of baby spinach

1. Heat the neutral oil and sesame oil in a sauté pan over medium heat. Add the onion and cayenne and sauté until softened and beginning to brown, about 10 minutes. Stir in the sweet potato, cabbage, soy sauce, vinegar, and salt. Cook, stirring occasionally, until the vegetables are slightly softened but still retain a bit of crunch, 12 to 15 minutes. Remove from the heat and stir in the sesame seeds and parsley. Allow to stand until cool enough to handle before assembling the dumplings.

2. Prepare a clean work surface and create a dumpling assembly station by arranging the following in that area: the wonton wrappers, still stacked together, with a lightly moistened tea towel or paper towel draped over them to prevent them from drying out; a small bowl of water; the sweet potato mixture; and a baking sheet for the finished dumplings, with another moistened tea towel or paper towel for draping over them.

3. Place about 2 heaping teaspoons of filling in the center of a wrapper. Dip your finger in the bowl of water and use it to moisten one half of the perimeter of the wrapper. Beginning at opposite corners, seal the dumplings from each end so that your fingers meet in the center, and you can tuck inside any filling that might be poking out before sealing it up

completely. Place the finished dumplings on the baking sheet and cover with the moistened towel to protect them from drying out. Continue with the remaining wrappers and filling. As you arrange the finished dumplings on the baking sheet, make sure they don't touch each other.

4. Just before serving, bring the dashi or miso broth to simmer in a saucepan.

5. Lower the dumplings into the stock, working in batches to avoid crowding, and cook until heated through, about 2 minutes. With a slotted spoon, transfer the cooked dumplings to serving bowls, 6 dumplings per serving, then distribute the tofu and then the spinach among the bowls. Ladle the hot broth over, taking care to submerge the spinach so that it wilts. Serve immediately.

▶ LEFTOVERS: Stored in an airtight container, the dumplings will keep for 1 day in the refrigerator and up to 2 weeks in the freezer.

▶ PREPARATION AND COOKING TIME:
45 minutes

STEAMING DUMPLINGS

A BAMBOO steaming basket is really the best device for steaming dumplings. This inexpensive kitchen gadget allows you to steam multiple layers of dumplings at a time, and unlike a metal, collapsible steaming basket, it features a flat surface. If using a brand-new bamboo steaming basket, rub the inside with vegetable oil, which will both soften the bamboo and prevent the dumplings from sticking to it.

To use the basket, put about 1 inch of water in a sauté pan or wok and bring it to a simmer. Meanwhile, arrange the dumplings inside the basket, making sure that they aren't touching one another. Place the steaming basket directly in the water and steam the dumplings until the skin is translucent and the filling heated through. This will take about 5 minutes for unfrozen dumplings, and 8 to 10 for frozen ones.

Classic Pad Thai

I LOVE PAD THAI, but for a long time I had trouble making it. It's easy to dirty every dish you own only for it to turn out bland and the noodles to form a gummy mass. Yet pad thai is street food in Thailand, so it shouldn't be so difficult! Things got better when I began to simplify the process. Many recipes call for presoaking the noodles, but I prefer the method below. It requires a bit of arm power, but the noodles will be packed with flavor and not the least bit gummy. I've also worked to create an authentic flavor profile without using tamarind paste, which is traditional but difficult to track down.

▶ SERVES 3 OR 4

3 tablespoons neutral oil (canola, grapeseed, peanut, or vegetable oil)

2 eggs

3 tablespoons soy sauce

1 tablespoon white vinegar

2 teaspoons chili paste, such as sambal oelek, or more for a spicier dish

Juice of 1 lime

2 tablespoons packed brown sugar

2 medium shallots, minced

3 garlic cloves, minced

About 2½ cups (600 ml) water

8 ounces (230 g) narrow rice noodles, about ⅛-inch (5 mm) thick

7 ounces (205 g) firm tofu, cut into small cubes

1½ cups (115 g) mung bean sprouts

½ cup (75 g) coarsely chopped roasted, unsalted peanuts (see page 13), plus more for garnish

½ cup (15 g) chopped fresh cilantro, plus more for garnish

Lime wedges for garnish

1. Heat 1 tablespoon of the oil in a deep sauté pan or wok over medium-high heat. Crack the eggs into the pan. Using a rubber spatula, flatten the yolks and scramble the eggs. They should cook in less than 1 minute. Remove from the heat and transfer to a small bowl or plate.

2. Whisk together the soy sauce, vinegar, chili paste, lime juice, sugar, and ½ cup (120 ml) water in a small bowl or measuring cup.

3. Put the remaining 2 tablespoons of oil in the pan, again over medium-high heat. Add the shallots and garlic and sauté until fragrant, about 1 minute. Pour in the soy sauce mixture, then add the uncooked noodles. Using a spatula, press the noodles into the sauce. Let them sit for about 2 minutes, pressing on them with the spatula to encourage them to soak up the sauce, and then carefully flip. Pour in ½ cup (120 ml) water and let sit again, pressing with the spatula. Repeat flipping and pressing, adding more water (up to 2 cups, or 480 ml, total) as the noodles soak up the liquid, until the noodles become pliant and can be tossed with tongs. After 10 minutes, begin tasting the noodles. Continue cooking, tossing often, until tender, up to 5 or 8 minutes more.

4. Stir in the tofu, 1 cup (80 g) of the bean sprouts, and the peanuts, cilantro, and scrambled egg. Taste and adjust the seasonings if necessary, adding additional soy sauce if needed. Serve hot, garnished with more peanuts and cilantro, the remaining bean sprouts, and lime wedges.

Variation

It's tempting to add a good dose of greens to this Pad Thai. My favorite is baby spinach, which can be added in the last minute or two of cooking. Just toss it with tongs until wilted and combined. It's best to cook heartier greens like broccoli rabe or kale separately—after the eggs, for example—and then add them to the noodles at the end.

▶ **LEFTOVERS:** This dish is best eaten freshly cooked, but stored in an airtight container, it will keep for up to 2 days in the refrigerator.

▶ **PREPARATION AND COOKING TIME:**
35 minutes

SWEET AND SPICY UDON NOODLES

UDON IS MY favorite member of the Asian noodle family. They're substantial and chewy, and whatever sauce they're cooked in completely permeates them. At Asian grocery stores you can usually find fresh or frozen udon, both of which are more delicate than dried. Since dried udon is easiest to find, that's what I've called for here. If you use fresh or frozen udon, just skip the boiling step. This is an easy meal to throw together—basically just udon, a pile of veggies, and a sauce based on hoisin sauce, a readily available jarred sauce usually used for dipping spring rolls and egg rolls. This dish is also an excellent way to use leftover veggies; if they're already cooked, just stir them in with the noodles until heated through.

▶ SERVES 4

8 ounces (230 g) udon

3 tablespoons neutral oil (canola, grapeseed, peanut, or vegetable oil)

3 garlic cloves, minced

8 ounces (230 g) broccoli, cut into small florets (about 3 cups), stem reserved for another use

¼ cup (60 ml) water

1 teaspoon grated fresh ginger (see page 13)

½ head Savoy cabbage, cut into thin strips

1 carrot, thinly sliced on the diagonal

1 red bell pepper, cut into thin strips

2 tablespoons hoisin sauce

1 tablespoon soy sauce

2 teaspoons chili paste, such as sambal oelek

1 tablespoon packed brown sugar

2 tablespoons toasted sesame seeds (see page 13)

Chopped fresh cilantro, basil, or mint leaves for garnish

1. Bring a large pot of water to a boil. Add the udon and cook until al dente. Drain and rinse under cold running water to stop the cooking.

2. Meanwhile, heat 1 tablespoon of the oil in a deep sauté pan or wok over medium-high heat. Add one-third of the garlic and then the broccoli. Cook until the garlic begins to color, 1 to 2 minutes, then pour in the water. Continue to cook until the broccoli is tender and most of the water has cooked off, 3 to 5 minutes. Transfer to a mixing bowl.

3. Wipe out the sauté pan. Heat the remaining 2 tablespoons of oil in the same pan over medium heat. Add the ginger and the remaining garlic and sauté until fragrant, about 1 minute. Add the cabbage and cook, stirring, until it begins to wilt, 4 or 5 minutes. Add the carrot and bell pepper and cook, tossing occasionally, until the cabbage is tender and the carrot and pepper still have a bit of crispness, 6 to 8 minutes. Transfer the vegetables to the bowl with the broccoli.

4. Stir together the hoisin sauce, soy sauce, chili paste, and sugar in a small bowl or measuring cup. Pour the mixture into the pan, still over medium heat. When it begins to bubble, add the cooked noodles and toss quickly with tongs to coat the noodles with sauce. Then add the vegetables and toss to

combine. If the dish seems too dry, add a bit of water, 1 tablespoon at a time. Cook until the noodles and vegetables are thoroughly coated with sauce and everything is beginning to caramelize, 4 or 5 minutes. Stir in the sesame seeds, then garnish with the cilantro and serve hot.

▶ LEFTOVERS: Stored in an airtight container, this dish will keep for up to 2 days in the refrigerator.

▶ PREPARATION AND COOKING TIME: 40 minutes

SESAME NOODLES WITH ARUGULA

SESAME NOODLES WITH ARUGULA

COLD SESAME NOODLES have long been one of my favorite Chinese take-out items. This is a fairly straightforward recipe—easy, filling, and boldly flavored. It's inspired by a classic version of the dish in a cookbook by Madhur Jaffrey, an expert in Asian cuisines. This version is brightened up a bit with arugula, but feel free to take your own liberties with the veggies. Anything that brings textural contrast, such as snap peas, carrots, or even bean sprouts, will taste great here. It also makes great leftovers or an excellent picnic dish. Be sure to pack chopsticks!

▶ SERVES 3 OR 4

8 to 10 ounces (230–280 g) soba or udon

2½ tablespoons tahini

2½ tablespoons soy sauce

1 tablespoon neutral oil (canola, grapeseed, peanut, or vegetable oil)

1 teaspoon toasted sesame oil

1 teaspoon sherry vinegar

¼ teaspoon salt

¼ teaspoon freshly ground black pepper

Pinch of cayenne pepper

1 bell pepper (red, orange, or yellow), julienned

5 ounces (140 g) baby arugula

3 scallions, white part and 1 inch of the dark green part, thinly sliced

2 teaspoons toasted sesame seeds (see page 13)

2 tablespoons coarsely chopped fresh cilantro or mint

1. Bring a large pot of unsalted water to a boil. Add the noodles. If using soba, which is a more delicate noodle, lower the heat to medium to maintain an active simmer. Cook the noodles until just tender. Drain and rinse well under cold running water until cooled.

2. Meanwhile, combine the tahini, soy sauce, oils, vinegar, salt, pepper, and cayenne in a large bowl and whisk until smooth. Taste for seasonings, bearing in mind that without the noodles the sauce should be quite assertive; it will be milder when mixed with other ingredients in the finished dish. Add the noodles, bell pepper, and arugula directly to the sauce and toss thoroughly with tongs. If necessary to thin out the sauce, add hot tap water 1 tablespoon at a time. Add the scallions, sesame seeds, and cilantro, give the noodles a final toss, and serve. The noodles can be served at room temperature, or chilled and served cold.

▶ LEFTOVERS: Stored in an airtight container, these noodles will keep for up to 2 days in the refrigerator. They may need to be loosened up with 1 to 2 tablespoons of hot water.

▶ PREPARATION AND COOKING TIME:
20 minutes

HOSTING a DINNER PARTY

IF YOU'RE new to playing host or hostess, there's nothing to be afraid of. Entertaining doesn't have to be stressful or complicated. Having people over for a home-cooked meal is an act of appreciation—a way to get to know others better or an opportunity to catch up with friends. I've been inviting friends and loved ones over for dinner for a long time, and I also continue to work occasionally as a caterer, so along the way I've learned a few tips that you might find helpful.

DETERMINE YOUR SCOPE: You *could* prepare an eight-course dinner, straight from the latest issue of *Saveur*. Or you could serve pizza, salad, and ice pops, and it would probably be just as much fun. Decide up front what you want the scope of your dinner party to be and plan accordingly. If you're going to try an elaborate new recipe for your guests (after all, it's very tempting to make something that will impress), I strongly recommend that you practice it once in advance to work out the kinks. In general, it's wise to stick with dishes you feel confident with and are guaranteed to excel at.

MAKE A GAME PLAN: Always be sure to read completely through the recipes well in advance so you can plan ahead. For example, crusts for tarts and galettes need to be refrigerated at various stages; many recipes call for precooked rice and beans; and nuts may need to be roasted. Also consider what cookware and appliances you'll need to use. This is important, because it's impossible to throw a dinner party in which all dishes must be finished in the oven but won't all fit. For warm dishes, divide them among the stovetop and the oven, and remember that cold or room-temperature dishes can help alleviate last-minute hassles.

PLAN AHEAD: There are always a few things you can do beforehand. I take great pleasure in setting my table early in the process. Wash salad greens and fresh herbs early on. You can also prep some vegetables in advance: washing, trimming, peeling, and possibly chopping them. Similarly, you can prepare salad dressings. If you're using serving platters, dig them out from the cupboards or closets so that you won't have to hunt for them later.

DIVVY UP THE WORK: Let your guests help you out. This could mean splitting up the meal potluck style, so that someone brings a side dish or salad and another brings bread and wine. Or it might simply be letting someone into your kitchen to mince garlic and pick the leaves off thyme sprigs. In any case, be willing to let other people participate. For small gatherings, I usually let others bring wine, appetizers, or dessert. When I'm having a party for a larger group, I ask the guest who's most skilled at cooking to arrive a little early and help out. Even if it's just to help dry dishes, a second pair of hands in the kitchen can be a big help.

REMEMBER THE LITTLE TOUCHES: One reason I like to entertain is because a dinner party can be a departure from my day-to-day cooking. In addition to selecting recipes that are more special, I like to add little finishing touches like garnishes and put extra care into plating and serving the food. Beyond the food preparation, there are some easy and inexpensive ways to spruce things up. Having candles on the table will, of course, amp up the romance level. But even if it's not a romantic evening, candles have a way of making everyone feel more comfortable. Similarly, fresh flowers provide a burst of color and convey to your guests that you value their company. And, of course, cloth napkins are always a nice addition to the "tablescape," and a way to bring a bit of your personality to the fore.

CREATE A THEME: Assigning a theme to your dinner party can give it the power of purpose. However, taking it to an extreme can be off-putting, especially for guests who, like me, don't like to be strong-armed into "having fun." I like themes that provide opportunities for enlightenment, such as selecting a wine region and having everyone bring a bottle from that region to share. Dinner parties can also be organized around cookbooks or specific food writers. I have a group of friends with whom I meet once a month to cook recipes from Laurie Colwin's *Home Cooking* books. The recipes provide great talking points, and the resulting discussions enrich what otherwise tends to be a more private experience. A more obvious theme is a dinner party organized around a specific cuisine or type of food. Interactive foods, such as tapas, dumplings, pizza, or sushi, are particularly good choices that can be fun for everyone.

SHOW FINESSE AT THE FINISH LINE: It can be anxiety inducing to present anyone—and especially someone whose approval you care about—with a plate of food you've cooked. It's easy to get distracted with guests over, but try to steal a couple minutes to fine-tune your dishes. If things aren't going the way you think they ought to, just take a deep breath, think through your plan of action, and work deliberately. This is not *Top Chef*; there's no clock ticking. Taste. Adjust the seasonings. Assess. Those final five minutes can make or break a dish. Take them as your chance to fiddle, transform the dish into how you envisioned it, and make the difference between something that's just fine and something that's *great*. And in the end, remember, the ultimate purpose of the dinner party is gathering and connecting with others—something best done when you're in a calm, relaxed mood and free of self-recriminations!

4

CURRIES, BRAISED DISHES, AND OVEN-BAKED DISHES

THERE'S NOTHING DAINTY about the dishes in this chapter; they're some of the most filling dishes in the book. All are the kind of slow-cooked dishes that will perfume your home or apartment and have anyone within reach of the aroma woozy with anticipation. With these entrées, the act of cooking—and smelling—can offer satisfaction on par with that of eating the finished dish.

Curries are a very broad category of food, and they're some of my favorite dishes to make. I encourage you to further explore this area—there are some excellent Indian cookbooks, particularly by Madhur Jaffrey and Raghavan Iyer. This is a great way to learn new ways to use familiar spices, like cinnamon and cumin. You might be struck, as I was at first, by how small things that characterize Indian cuisine—or any regional cuisine—can have big impacts on an otherwise familiar set of ingredients. The flavor profile associated with Indian cuisine tends to be complex, with warmth and sweetness from spices like cinnamon and cardamom, astringency from turmeric, earthiness from cumin, and heat from ingredients like cayenne, chiles, and ginger. One of its other hallmarks is applying heat to the point of near ruin. Onions, for example, aren't sautéed over medium-low heat, making sure they soften without coloring, as in braised dishes in the Italian or French style; rather, they're cooked over higher heat and intended to color deeply. This forms a crucial base in the finished dish: sweet and bitter and complicated.

Braising, at core, is the method of cooking in a covered vessel, with a small amount of liquid, over an extended period of time in order to maximize the flavor penetration and tenderness of the finished dish. Some curries fall into this category. Aromatics make braises ripe with flavor, and braising vegetables like celery or carrots can transform an everyday ingredient into an unexpected delicacy. Braises almost always improve in flavor as they sit, either on the stovetop with the heat off as you prepare accompaniments, or in the refrigerator overnight. For that reason they are excellent make-ahead meals.

And last but not least, this chapter offers a variety of oven-baked pasta dishes. I consider these my important contributions to the field of macaroni and cheese, in which I incorporate a bigger helping of vegetables and a smaller helping of dairy than in traditional recipes (though not so small that you'll be left wanting cheese). Among their many merits, they freeze and transport beautifully, making them a favorite of mine for informal gatherings like open houses or game day spreads. These are some of the most robust, filling dishes in the entire book—they definitely won't leave you hungry.

Easy Tomato Curry

I MAKE THIS kind of easy, basic curry all the time. It can be made quickly and uses standard pantry items. It's also very versatile; view it as a base and follow one of the variations to turn it into a more substantial meal. Start cooking the rice before you begin the curry, and everything will come together at the same time. This recipe relies on a creamy element, with options for using either coconut milk or yogurt. As with most curries, Indian flatbread makes a nice accompaniment.

▶ **SERVES 4**

3 tablespoons neutral oil (canola, grapeseed, peanut, or vegetable oil)

1½ teaspoons cumin seeds

1 large onion, diced

3 garlic cloves, minced

2 teaspoons grated fresh ginger (see page 13)

2 teaspoons curry powder, preferably homemade (page 229)

¼ teaspoon cayenne pepper (omit if using a hot curry powder)

One 28-ounce (794 g) can diced tomatoes

½ cup (120 ml) coconut milk, or 2 tablespoons plain, unsweetened yogurt

½ teaspoon salt

½ teaspoon sugar

1½ teaspoons garam masala

3 cups (450 g) cooked rice (see page 12), preferably Fragrant Jasmine Rice (page 107)

½ cup (15 g) coarsely chopped fresh cilantro for garnish

1. Heat the oil in a deep sauté pan or medium saucepan over medium-high heat. Add the cumin seeds, let them sizzle for about 10 seconds, then add the onion. Cook, stirring occasionally, until deeply colored and even beginning to burn, 12 to 15 minutes. Add the garlic, ginger, curry powder, and cayenne and sauté until fragrant, about 30 seconds. Stir in the tomatoes, and if using coconut milk, stir it in at this point as well. Bring to a boil and cook until the liquid is slightly reduced and the flavors have come into focus, 15 to 20 minutes.

2. Stir in the salt, sugar, and garam masala. Remove from the heat and, if desired, puree the curry using an immersion blender, food processor, or regular blender. If using yogurt, stir it in at this point. Divide the rice among 4 plates or bowls, ladle the curry over the rice. Garnish with the cilantro and serve.

▶ **LEFTOVERS:** Stored in an airtight container, this dish will keep for up to 2 days in the refrigerator and 1 month in the freezer.

▶ **PREPARATION AND COOKING TIME:** 35 minutes

Variations

TOMATO CURRY WITH TEMPEH: Before preparing the curry, cut 8 ounces (230 g) of tempeh into thin rectangles, then sauté in a deep sauté pan or medium saucepan in 1 tablespoon of oil over medium-high heat until golden brown on each side, about 3 to 5 minutes per side. Remove with a slotted spoon and set aside, then make the curry as described above in the same pan, adding only 2 tablespoons of oil to the pan before adding the cumin seeds. Stir in the tempeh when you add the salt.

TOMATO CURRY WITH TOFU: Before preparing the curry, cube 10 ounces (280 g) of tofu and pat dry with a paper towel. Sauté the tofu in a deep sauté pan or medium saucepan in 1 to 2 tablespoons of oil over medium-high heat. Remove with a slotted spoon and set aside, then make the curry as described on page 99, using the same pan. Stir in the tofu when you add the salt.

TOMATO CURRY WITH LENTILS: While preparing the curry, combine ¾ cup (150 g) green lentils and 2 cups (480 ml) water in a small saucepan. Bring to a boil, then lower the heat, cover, and simmer until the lentils are tender, 25 to 35 minutes. Puree the cooked curry with an immersion blender or in batches in a food processor. Drain the lentils and stir them into the pureed curry.

TOMATO CURRY WITH CHICKPEAS: When adding the salt and sugar, stir in 2 cups of cooked chickpeas, or one 15-ounce (425 g) can of chickpeas, drained and rinsed.

TOMATO CURRY WITH POTATOES AND BROCCOLI: Peel 1 large russet potato and cut it into ¾-inch (2 cm) cubes. Cut a small bunch of broccoli into small florets. Add the potatoes to the pan when you stir in the tomatoes and cook for 10 minutes. Stir in the broccoli and continue cooking until the broccoli and potatoes are tender, about 8 to 10 minutes more.

TOMATO CURRY WITH EGGPLANT: Dice 1 medium or 2 small eggplants and add to the pan along with the garlic and ginger. Check the eggplant for doneness before removing from the heat.

saag paneer

SAAG PANEER, ONE of my favorite dishes, is an Indian counterpart to creamed spinach. The first recipe I learned called for heavy cream, which is indulgent and delicious, but I've come to prefer the tang and relative lightness of yogurt in this version. You can also forgo the dairy completely; it will still be a winning dish, though the spices may be sharp on your palate. Green cayenne chiles are common in Indian cuisine, but they can be tricky to come by at grocery stores; I've had the best luck finding them at Indian groceries and farmers' markets. Paneer can also be hard to come by; luckily it's easy to make at home (see page 104 for a recipe), but for vegan versions tofu can be substituted (or you could go a totally different direction and stir in 3 cups of cooked chickpeas with the spinach, in which case this becomes *chana saag*). Lastly, I recommend using mature spinach, the kind sold in bunches, rather than prepackaged baby spinach, which is too delicate for this dish.

▶ SERVES 4

8 ounces (230 g) paneer (1 recipe, see page 104) or firm tofu

2 bunches of spinach (about 1½ pounds, 675 g), washed thoroughly and tough stems removed

3 tablespoons neutral oil (canola, grapeseed, peanut, or vegetable oil)

1¼ teaspoons cumin seeds

1 onion, diced

2 or 3 green cayenne chiles, finely chopped, or 1 serrano pepper, seeded and finely chopped

4 garlic cloves, minced

2 teaspoons grated fresh ginger (see page 13)

¾ teaspoon salt

1 teaspoon garam masala

½ teaspoon ground coriander

2 heaping tablespoons plain, unsweetened Greek-style yogurt, optional

¼ cup (6 g) fresh chopped cilantro for garnish

3 cups (450 g) cooked Fragrant Jasmine Rice (page 107)

1. If using tofu, cut it into ¾-inch (2 cm) slices, layer the slices between clean towels or paper towels, and place under a weight for 15 minutes to squeeze out some of the moisture. Cut the slices into ¾-inch (2 cm) cubes.

2. Steam or blanch the spinach until tender (see page 10). Put the cooked spinach in a clean tea towel or cheesecloth and squeeze out as much liquid as possible, then coarsely chop the spinach.

3. Cut the paneer into ¾-inch (2 cm) cubes. Heat 1 tablespoon of the oil in a large saucepan or deep sauté pan over medium heat. Working in two batches, sauté the paneer or tofu until golden on all sides, about 10 minutes. Using a slotted spoon or spatula, transfer to a plate lined with a paper towel or a clean paper bag.

4. Put the remaining 2 tablespoons of oil in the pan and turn the heat up to medium-high. Add the cumin seeds and let sizzle just until fragrant, about 10 seconds, then add the onion and sauté until richly colored and even burned on the edges, 12 to 15 minutes.

5. Meanwhile, put the chiles, garlic, and ginger on a cutting board and mince them together until they resemble a paste. Alternatively, puree them in a blender or mini food processor, adding about 1 tablespoon of water if necessary.

SAAG PANEER

6. Add the chile mixture, salt, garam masala, and coriander to the onion and cook for about 5 minutes, stirring constantly to prevent the garlic from burning. Lower the heat to medium, add the spinach and then the paneer, and cook, stirring gently, until fully combined and heated through. Remove from the heat and stir in the yogurt, if desired. Garnish with the cilantro and serve immediately, over the rice.

variation

For a smoother sauce, before adding the paneer, puree the spinach mixture in a food processor or blender. Transfer it back to the same pot and stir in the paneer and yogurt.

▶ **LEFTOVERS:** Stored in an airtight container, this dish will keep for up to 2 days in the refrigerator.

▶ **PREPARATION AND COOKING TIME:** 45 minutes

HOMEMADE PANEER

Paneer can be difficult to track down. One day I decided to make *saag paneer* at my dad's house in Charlotte, North Carolina, but I couldn't find a store that sold paneer. So I decided to look into what might be involved in making it, and was happy to learn that it's easy to do at home. I've never looked back. In fact, I take special pride in being able to make organic paneer from whatever milk I choose.

▶ **MAKES ABOUT 1½ CUPS (360 ml), ENOUGH FOR ONE RECIPE SAAG PANEER**

8 cups (2 l) milk (whole or 2%)
2 to 4 tablespoons fresh lemon juice or white vinegar

1. Place a colander in the sink and line it generously with at least 3 layers of cheesecloth, using enough that the cheesecloth drapes over the edges of the colander.

2. Pour the milk into a 2-quart (2 l) saucepan and bring to a boil over medium-high heat. As soon as it begins to boil, remove from the heat and stir in 2 tablespoons of the lemon juice. Watch for the curds to begin separating from the whey; within a few minutes, you'll notice a clear distinction between the thick, lumpy, snow white curds and off-yellow liquid whey. If the curds don't appear to be separating, add up to 2 more tablespoons of lemon juice.

3. Pour the contents of the saucepan into the colander, allowing the whey to drain down the sink. Let the curds drain for at least 10 minutes, until cool enough to handle.

4. Wrap the cheesecloth securely around the curds, press the bundle into a flat disk, and place it on a cutting board or other work surface. Set a baking sheet or flat-bottomed dish on top of the disk and weigh it down with a few heavy items, such as cans or another heavy cutting board. Let stand for at least 15 minutes to press out some of the moisture.

5. Remove the paneer from the cheesecloth. Wrapped tightly, the paneer will keep for up to 3 days in the refrigerator.

cashew and cauliflower curry

TO GIVE THIS dish its curry flavors, I've used an approach I first learned in an Indian cooking class I took several years ago at Ren's Kitchen in London. Called *tarka* or *chaunk*, it's a method that forgoes curry powder in favor of whole spices, which sizzle in the oil before other ingredients are added. You may need to outfit your spice cupboard or drawer (which is easy and cheap if you can find a spice shop that sells in bulk), or you could just substitute 2 teaspoons of your favorite curry powder, adding it along with the onion. But the clean, sharp flavors this method produces make it worth the additional effort, including that of fishing out the spices while you're eating. Here, cashews enhance the nuttiness of cauliflower and make for a rich and textured flavor combination.

▶ SERVES 4

2 medium white potatoes (8 ounces, 230 g)

1 small cauliflower (about 1 pound, 450 g)

3 tablespoons neutral oil (canola, grapeseed, peanut, or vegetable oil)

8 black peppercorns

5 whole cloves

3 cardamom pods, smashed

1 cinnamon stick

1 bay leaf

1 dried chile pepper

2 teaspoons cumin seeds

1 large onion, minced

3 garlic cloves, minced

2 teaspoons grated fresh ginger (see page 13)

1½ teaspoons turmeric

½ cup (120 ml) water

2 teaspoons garam masala

½ teaspoon salt

2 tablespoons plain, unsweetened yogurt

½ cup (75 g) roasted, unsalted whole cashews (see page 13)

⅓ cup (10 g) fresh chopped cilantro, plus additional for garnish

3 cups (450 g) cooked Fragrant Jasmine Rice (page 107)

1. Peel the potatoes, then quarter them lengthwise, then cut crosswise into pieces ¼ inch (5 mm) thick. Cut the cauliflower into small florets.

2. Heat the oil in a deep sauté pan or medium saucepan over medium heat. Add the peppercorns, cloves, cardamom, cinnamon, bay leaf, and chile and let sizzle just until fragrant, about 30 seconds. Add the cumin seeds, let sizzle for 10 seconds, then add the onion. Cook, stirring frequently, until the onion is deeply colored and even beginning to burn, 10 to 12 minutes.

3. Add the garlic and ginger and sauté until fragrant, about 1 minute. Add the cauliflower and potatoes and cook, stirring just a few times, until the cauliflower begins to show some color, 3 to 5 minutes. Add the turmeric and water, cover, and cook until the cauliflower and potatoes are tender, 10 to 15 minutes. Uncover and continue cooking until most of the liquid bubbles off, 1 to 2 minutes. Stir in the garam masala and salt. Remove from heat, then stir in the yogurt, cashews, and cilantro. Garnish with additional cilantro and serve hot, over cooked rice.

▶ LEFTOVERS: Stored in an airtight container, this dish will keep for up to 2 days in the refrigerator and 1 month in the freezer.

▶ PREPARATION AND COOKING TIME: 30 minutes

CASHEW AND CAULIFLOWER CURRY

FRAGRANT Jasmine RICE

▶ **MAKES ABOUT 3 CUPS (750 ml), ENOUGH FOR 4 SERVINGS**

1 cup (220 g) jasmine rice

1 cinnamon stick

1 star anise

3 cardamom seeds, smashed

5 black peppercorns

2 cups (475 ml) water

Combine all the ingredients in a small saucepan over medium-high heat. Just as the mixture begins to boil, cover, turn the heat down as low as possible, and cook for 25 minutes. Remove from the heat and let stand for 10 minutes without removing the lid. Remove the whole spices if desired, fluff with a fork, and serve.

Lentil and Kabocha Squash Curry

KABOCHA SQUASH IS a gem of a winter squash that grows all year round and is increasingly available at grocery stores and farmers' markets, and this curry is a terrific vehicle for it. Its mellow sweetness, framed by the curry spices, plays off the earthiness of the lentils, and the end result is an incredibly substantial dish. Kabocha squash doesn't need to be peeled, but not everyone likes the skin. If you wish to peel it, I find it easiest to do once the squash has been cut into wedges, as one would do with a cantaloupe. If you can't find kabocha squash, substitute a similar quantity (by weight) of sweet potatoes or butternut squash.

▶ SERVES 4

1 kabocha squash (2 to 2½ pounds, 1 kg)

2 tablespoons neutral oil (canola, grapeseed, peanut, or vegetable oil)

1 tablespoon butter or neutral oil

1½ teaspoons cumin seeds

1 onion, minced

4 garlic cloves, minced

2 teaspoons grated fresh ginger (see page 13)

2 teaspoons curry powder, preferably homemade (page 229)

Pinch of cayenne pepper (omit if using a hot curry powder)

1 cup (220 g) red lentils, green lentils, or a combination

3 cups (750 ml) vegetable stock (page 15) or water

1½ teaspoons garam masala

½ teaspoon salt

½ teaspoon sugar

2 scallions, chopped, for garnish

¼ cup (15 g) fresh chopped cilantro for garnish

3 cups (450 g) Fragrant Jasmine Rice (page 107)

Lemon wedges for garnish

1. Using a heavy, sharp knife or a cleaver, trim the ends from the squash, then halve the squash lengthwise. Scoop out the seeds. Cut the squash lengthwise into ¾-inch (2 cm) wedges, carefully trim off the peel if you wish, then cut the wedges crosswise into ¾-inch (2 cm) cubes.

2. Heat the oil and butter in a deep sauté pan or Dutch oven over medium-high heat. Add the cumin seeds, let them sizzle for 10 seconds, then add the onion. Cook, stirring frequently, until the onion is deeply colored and even beginning to burn, 10 to 12 minutes. Add the garlic, ginger, curry powder, and cayenne and sauté until fragrant, about 1 minute. Stir in the squash and let sizzle for 3 to 5 minutes. Stir in the lentils and stock. Bring to a boil, then lower the heat, cover, and simmer for 25 minutes, until the lentils and squash are tender and the curry has thickened. Stir in the garam masala and salt, taste, and adjust the seasonings if necessary. Garnish with the scallions, cilantro, and lemon wedges. Serve hot, over the rice.

▶ LEFTOVERS: Stored in an airtight container, this dish will keep for up to 2 days in the refrigerator and 1 month in the freezer.

▶ PREPARATION AND COOKING TIME: 1 hour

SPRING VEGETABLE PAELLA WITH ENDIVE

PAELLA, A SPANISH rice dish traditionally made with seafood, can be an excellent and hearty vegetarian entrée when the vegetables are cooked with care and the seasonings are kept in check. While there is some heat in it, it shouldn't be overwhelmingly spicy, and the flavor should be well-rounded, with no one thing in particular overwhelming the taste buds. Saffron is a standard paella seasoning, but if you can't find it or wish to omit it, substitute ½ teaspoon turmeric. Though this won't replicate the flavor of saffron, it will lend the dish the saffron color. The rice should be relatively dry, even slightly toasted on the bottom. You can achieve this by turning up the heat for the last minute of cooking, until the rice smells toasty. The endive, which is seared and then added back to the pan to braise with the rice, is silky and tender and adds a perfect amount of bulk.

▶ SERVES 4

2 tablespoons neutral oil (canola, grapeseed, peanut, or vegetable oil)

2 endive, halved lengthwise

1 white or yellow onion, minced

2 bell peppers (any color), diced large

4 garlic cloves, minced

1 tablespoon seafood seasoning, such as Old Bay

2 bay leaves

1 teaspoon sugar

1 teaspoon smoked paprika

¼ teaspoon cayenne pepper

¼ teaspoon crushed saffron threads, or ½ teaspoon turmeric

1 cup (200 g) jasmine or basmati rice, white or brown

One 15-ounce (425 g) can whole tomatoes, drained and chopped

1½ cups (360 ml) vegetable stock (page 15) or water

½ teaspoon salt

1 bunch asparagus, tough ends snapped off, cut into 1-inch (3 cm) pieces

1 cup (180 g) fresh or frozen peas

Lemon wedges for garnish

1. Heat the oil in a deep sauté pan or Dutch oven (something that has a lid) over medium-high heat. Add the endive, cut side down, and cook until beginning to brown on the bottom, about 5 minutes. Carefully remove with a spatula or tongs and set aside.

2. Lower the heat to medium. Add the onion and sauté until just softened, 4 to 6 minutes. Add the bell peppers and sauté for 3 minutes, until just beginning to soften. Add the garlic and sauté until fragrant, about 1 minute. Stir in the seafood seasoning, bay leaves, sugar, paprika, cayenne, and saffron. Add the rice and stir until evenly coated with the spices, then stir in the tomatoes and stock. Bring to a boil, add the salt, then lower the heat to maintain a simmer. Add the endive, pressing gently to submerge it in the rice. Cover and cook for 20 minutes. Stir only once, when halfway through the cooking time, being careful not break up the endive.

3. Uncover and gently stir the pot from the bot-

tom so as to keep the endive intact. Add the asparagus and peas, gently stirring to combine, and cook for 5 minutes. Taste and adjust the seasonings if necessary and test the endive to ensure that it's tender. Serve hot, allotting half an endive per serving and garnishing with the lemon wedges.

▶ LEFTOVERS: Stored in an airtight container, this dish will keep for 1 day in the refrigerator.

▶ PREPARATION AND COOKING TIME: 45 minutes

MUSHROOM STROGANOFF WITH TURNIPS

GROWING UP, BEEF stroganoff, one of my grandmother's specialties, was among my favorite wintertime dishes—and I often requested it for my birthday, which falls in February. Her recipe called for a hefty squirt of ketchup, a not insignificant amount of Wondra flour as a thickener, a tub of sour cream, and, of course, beef sirloin strips, and at the time I thought it was heaven on a fork. The first time I made it myself, I realized how much potential it had as a vegetarian dish. This version, with its medley of mushrooms, tender turnips, and rich, creamy sauce, rivals the original. It's best served over egg noodles or rice.

▶ SERVES 4

FOR THE MUSHROOM BROTH

1 teaspoon neutral oil (canola, grapeseed, peanut, or vegetable oil)

3 garlic cloves, smashed

1 shallot, or ½ white or yellow onion, coarsely chopped

3 black peppercorns

1 clove

1 tablespoon tomato paste

Stems from 1 pound (450 g) mushrooms (from the mushrooms in the stroganoff recipe)

1 small carrot, coarsely chopped

1 celery stalk, coarsely chopped

2 parsley sprigs, or ½ teaspoon dried parsley

3½ (840 ml) cups water

½ teaspoon salt

FOR THE STROGANOFF

2 tablespoons butter

1 tablespoon oil (canola, grapeseed, peanut, or vegetable oil)

1 onion, halved and sliced into thin half-moons

8 ounces (230 g) cremini mushrooms, stemmed and halved

8 ounces (230 g) shiitake mushrooms, stemmed and sliced

2 garlic cloves, minced

1 tablespoon tomato paste

1 teaspoon smoked paprika

3 tablespoons all-purpose flour

1 cup (240 ml) full-bodied red wine

1 recipe mushroom broth (recipe at left)

8 ounces (230 g) turnips, halved or quartered if baby turnips, and cut into ½-inch (1 cm) cubes if mature turnips

½ cup (120 ml) sour cream or crème fraîche

1 pound (450 g) egg noodles or 3 cups (350 g) cooked white rice (page 12)

Minced fresh parsley for garnish

1. To make the broth, heat the oil in a small saucepan over medium heat. Add the garlic, shallot, peppercorns, clove, and tomato paste and sauté until fragrant, about 1 minute. Stir in the mushroom stems, carrot, celery, and parsley. Cover and cook for 5 minutes. Pour in the water, bring to a boil, then stir in the salt. Lower the heat and simmer until the flavors come into focus, 30 to 40 minutes. Strain out the vegetables.

2. To make the stroganoff, heat 1 tablespoon of the oil and 1 tablespoon of the butter in a large, deep sauté pan over medium heat. When the foaming subsides, add the onion and cook until softened and beginning to brown, about 15 minutes. Add the mushrooms and cook,

stirring periodically, until they release their moisture and it cooks off, about 10 minutes. Remove the mushrooms and onion with a slotted spoon and set aside.

3. Put the remaining tablespoon of butter in the sauté pan, still over medium heat. After the foaming subsides, add the garlic, tomato paste, and paprika and sauté until fragrant, about 30 seconds. Sprinkle the flour over the mixture and cook, stirring constantly, until the mixture smells slightly nutty, 2 to 3 minutes. Gradually add the wine and 2 cups (480 ml) of the mushroom broth, whisking constantly until the mixture comes to a boil. (Reserve any remaining broth to thin the sauce later, if necessary.) Lower the heat to maintain a simmer. Stir in the reserved mushrooms and onion, as well as the turnips. Cook, uncovered, until the turnips are tender and the sauce has thickened, about 25 minutes. If the sauce seems too thin, transfer a ladleful or two of the sauce into a small bowl and whisk in 1 tablespoon flour until smooth. Stir this mixture back into the stroganoff and let simmer for 3 to 5 minutes more, until thickened. Stir in the sour cream.

4. Meanwhile, if preparing pasta, cook in a pot of salted water until al dente.

5. Before serving, stir the sour cream into the stroganoff mixture. Serve hot, over the freshly cooked pasta or rice, garnished with parsley.

▶ LEFTOVERS: Stored in an airtight container, this dish will keep for 1 day in the refrigerator.

▶ PREPARATION AND COOKING TIME:
1 hour and 30 minutes

STIR-FRIES

MY APPROACH to stir-frying is "Well, let's see what we've got." Stir-fries are always an easy meal option for me, but they're also a favorite way to take advantage of whatever vegetables are available and in season. And what a way to showcase those vegetables—there's so little disguising them! When combined with a scoop of your favorite rice, a stir-fry makes for a filling, nutritious meal that couldn't be easier to assemble.

Yet the stir-fry is such an obvious candidate for a vegetarian entrée that I half considered not mentioning it in this book. Who doesn't already have a favorite way of making stir-fries? Still, in the event that you don't—or if you're interested in branching out—I've outlined a few tips.

What I like best about a stir-fry is the textural contrasts of the vegetables, so the most important aspect of the method is making sure each vegetable is cooked correctly. This could mean adding the vegetables to the pan in the order of longest to shortest cooking times. Carrots, celery, and bell peppers can bring a welcome crunch, but if you prefer that they be somewhat tender, add them earlier. Asparagus and cabbage need at least 3 to 4 minutes of cooking time. A fail-safe option is to cook vegetables individually, transferring them to a bowl as you continue to cook other ingredients, and then throwing all of the cooked items from the bowl into the pan and heating at the finish.

A wok is designed so that a small portion of the ingredients have direct access to the heat in the bottom part of the pan, and other ingredients can be pushed up against the sides of the pan, where they'll stay warm but won't continue to cook as rapidly. A wok is the best way to prepare your stir-fry, but if you don't have one, then just keep this principle in mind as you cook your vegetables.

Stir-fries are traditionally made over high heat, which gives the vegetables color and flavor without collapsing their textures. It also makes for a relatively quick cooking time. So don't be afraid to crank up the heat, but do keep in mind that this makes it very important to cook with oil that has a high smoke point. Peanut oil is the best choice, with grapeseed or canola oil being good alternatives.

There are a couple of ways to incorporate the sauce into a stir-fry. (I've provided a sauce recipe on page 115 or you can use your own favorite recipe or a store-bought sauce.) One way is to put the sauce in the wok or sauté pan first and cook the vegetables in it. A second option is to use the sauce as a marinade and then transfer the vegetables and their marinade to the pan. A third option is to add the sauce at the end of the cooking and continue to cook until most of it reduces. Or you could use a combination of these methods. The more time the vegetables spend with the sauce, the more they will be infused with its flavor.

Here are a few of my favorite vegetables and other ingredients to include in stir-fries:

VEGETABLES FOR BULK

- Broccoli, cut into small florets
- Cauliflower, cut into small florets
- Carrots, julienned or cut into thin rounds
- Onions, sliced into rings ½ to ¾ inch (1–2 cm) thick
- Bell peppers, cut into thin strips
- Zucchini or yellow squash, julienned or thinly sliced
- Bok choy, cut into 1-inch (3 cm) strips
- Mushrooms, such as shiitake, cremini, or white button, halved or thinly sliced
- Asparagus, cut into 1-inch (3 cm) pieces

VEGETABLES (AND FRUITS!) FOR COLOR, TEXTURE, AND BURSTS OF FLAVOR

- Snow peas
- Mung bean sprouts
- Pineapple, cut into small chunks
- Mandarin oranges, separated into wedges
- Scallions, cut diagonally into 1-inch (3 cm) pieces
- Fresh or frozen peas
- Slivers of garlic
- Radishes, sliced thinly

FILLING PROTEIN TOPPINGS

- Panfried tofu
- Panfried seitan, chopped into bite-size pieces
- Panfried tempeh
- Scrambled or fried egg

NUTS AND GARNISHES FOR FINISHING

- Julienned ginger (see page 13)
- Roasted peanuts (see page 13)
- Toasted sesame seeds (see page 13)
- Roasted cashews (see page 13)
- Roasted walnuts (see page 13)
- Coarsely chopped fresh cilantro or parsley
- Wedges of lemon or lime

STIR-FRY SAUCE

▶ **MAKES ABOUT 1 CUP (240 ml)**

⅔ cup (160 ml) vegetable stock, preferably homemade
(page 15)

¼ cup (60 ml) soy sauce

1 tablespoon molasses

1 tablespoon toasted sesame oil

1 tablespoon rice vinegar

2 teaspoons packed brown sugar

1½ teaspoons cornstarch

1 teaspoon chili paste, such as sambal oelek

½ teaspoon salt

1 tablespoons neutral oil, preferably peanut oil

3 garlic cloves, minced

2 teaspoons grated fresh ginger (see page 13)

1. Whisk together the stock, soy sauce, molasses,
sesame oil, vinegar, sugar, chili paste, cornstarch, and salt, ensuring that the sugar and
cornstarch are dissolved.

2. Heat the neutral oil over medium-high heat
in a small saucepan. Add the garlic and ginger and sauté, stirring, until fragrant, about
1 minute. Pour in the soy sauce mixture and
boil until thickened and glossy, 1 to 2 minutes.
Adjust the seasonings if necessary, then transfer to a heat-safe container and cool. Store in
an airtight container until ready to use.

▶ **LEFTOVERS:** Stored in an airtight container,
this dish will keep for up to 2 weeks in the
refrigerator.

▶ **PREPARATION AND COOKING TIME:**
10 minutes

BRAISED FENNEL WITH TOMATOES, EGGPLANT, AND ISRAELI COUSCOUS

A FRIEND INVITED a group of us over for dinner one night and made a version of this dish in a gigantic, industrial-size frying pan, which she plopped down in the center of the table for us to serve ourselves from. Initially, I was taken aback by how much food it was. But then we scraped that enormous frying pan clean, digging in for seconds and thirds. This dish is addictive, hearty, and fragrant—fennel has one of the most distinctive aromas I know, though it mellows as it cooks. Israeli couscous, sometimes labeled "pearled couscous" or "pearl couscous" is about the size of peppercorns and plumps up into chewy little morsels.

▶ **SERVES 4**

1 medium globe eggplant

1 fennel bulb, stalks trimmed off, fronds reserved

2 tablespoons neutral oil (canola, grapeseed, peanut, or vegetable oil)

½ cup (120 ml) dry white wine

One 28-ounce (794 g) can whole tomatoes

1½ teaspoons salt

¼ teaspoon freshly ground black pepper

4 cups (1 l) water

1½ cups (240 g) Israeli couscous

⅓ cup (20 g) thinly sliced fresh basil for garnish

1. Preheat the oven to 400°F (200°C). Line a baking sheet with foil.

2. Place the eggplant on the baking sheet and roast for 30 to 40 minutes, until flattened and blistered. Let stand until cool enough to handle, then peel off the skin (it should come off in strips) and coarsely chop the flesh.

3. Meanwhile, cut the fennel in half from top to bottom and trim off any discolored parts. Put it on a cutting board flat side down and cut it into thin strips. Finely chop 1 heaping tablespoon of the fronds and reserve a few fronds for garnish. (The rest can be discarded or put to another use.)

4. Heat the oil in a deep sauté pan or Dutch oven over medium-high heat. Add the fennel and cook, stirring periodically, until it begins to color and then soften, 15 to 20 minutes. Turn the heat up to medium-high. Pour in the wine and cook until the liquid is reduced by half.

5. Add the tomatoes and their juices and bring to a boil. Stir in ½ teaspoon of the salt and the pepper, then lower the heat and simmer for 15 minutes, crushing the tomatoes with a potato masher or the back of a spoon from time to time. Stir in the cooked eggplant.

6. Meanwhile, bring the water to a boil over high heat. Add the remaining 1 teaspoon salt and then the couscous. Lower the heat to low, cover, and cook for 10 minutes, then remove from the heat and let stand for at least 5 minutes. The couscous should have absorbed all the water in the pan, but if not simply drain off the excess water.

7. Stir the cooked couscous into the eggplant mixture, then stir in the minced fennel fronds. Garnish with the basil and the reserved fennel fronds and serve.

▶ **LEFTOVERS:** Stored in an airtight container, this dish will keep for up to 2 days in the refrigerator.

▶ **PREPARATION AND COOKING TIME:** 1 hour and 30 minutes

Cassoulet with Tomato-Roasted Carrots and Chard

CASSOULET, A SLOW-COOKED dish that originated in southern France, traditionally features white beans and various cuts of meat. In this cleanly flavored vegetarian adaptation, the beans are cooked using a method described in Amanda Hesser's 2001 *New York Times* profile of Paola di Mauro, who lives in Italy and has imparted her knowledge to such powerhouse chefs and restaurateurs as Mario Batali and Lidia Bastianich. Rather than cooking the beans in double or triple their volume of water, they're just barely covered and brought to a very gentle simmer. Then a heatproof bowl of water is set on top of the pot, functioning as a lid. As the beans cook and soak up their cooking liquid, the warm water from the bowl is added in small increments. I like this method because it keeps the cook actively involved and therefore always results in perfectly cooked beans, which is important in such a simple dish. In place of the meat, I feature bright and tender tomato-roasted carrots, but you can substitute any roasted vegetable you please—beets, potatoes, turnips, squash, celery root, or a combination of vegetables. Just be sure to cook each vegetable in its own pan, as cooking times vary. One final note: The beans must be soaked in advance, so plan ahead.

▶ SERVES 4

FOR THE BEANS

1½ cups (300 g) cannellini beans, soaked for at least 4 hours or overnight

4 garlic cloves, smashed

5 black peppercorns

1 bay leaf

1 thyme sprig

½ teaspoon salt

1 tablespoon olive oil

1 bunch Swiss chard (about 12 ounces, 325 g), stemmed and cut into 1-inch (3 cm) strips

FOR THE CARROTS

2 tablespoons tomato paste

2 tablespoons olive oil

1 tablespoon packed brown sugar

¼ teaspoon salt

1 pound (450 g) carrots, cut diagonally into 2- to 3-inch (3–5 cm) lengths

1. To prepare the beans, drain off the soaking water and put the beans in a soup pot or Dutch oven. Add the garlic, peppercorns, bay leaf, and thyme. (If you'd like, tie these items up in a small square of cheesecloth to make a bouquet garni, which will make it easier to fish them out later.) Add enough water to barely cover the beans, about 2½ to 3½ cups (600–750 ml); they should be just submerged. Bring to a boil, then lower the heat to maintain a very gentle simmer. Place a wide heatproof mixing bowl on the pot as a lid and pour about 2 cups (475 ml) of water into the bowl. As the beans are cooking, the water will heat up. Every 15 minutes or so, check on the beans. If they're no longer completely submerged, pour

**CASSOULET WITH TOMATO-ROASTED
CARROTS AND CHARD**

in just enough water from the bowl to barely cover them. Continue cooking in this way for 45 minutes, then stir in the salt and continue to cook in the same way until the beans are creamy and tender, up to 45 more minutes.

2. Remove the garlic, peppercorns, bay leaf, and thyme. Stir in the olive oil, then taste the broth for salt and add more if necessary. Add the chard, gently pressing it under the broth and stirring until the greens are wilted and tender, about 10 minutes. Taste for salt again. Cover and remove from the heat.

3. Meanwhile, prepare the carrots. Preheat the oven to 425°F (220°C). Stir together the tomato paste, olive oil, sugar, and salt in a mixing bowl. Add the carrots and toss until evenly coated. Spread the carrots on a roasting pan and roast for 5 to 8 minutes, until they begin to caramelize and even burn at the edges. Turn the oven down to 300°F (150°C) and continue baking for 30 to 40 minutes, until completely tender.

4. To assemble the cassoulet, use a slotted spoon to divide the cooked beans and chard among 4 wide, shallow bowls. Taste the broth again and adjust the seasoning if necessary. Top with the carrots, then pour a ladleful of the bean broth around the edges of the bowl. Serve hot, passing a pepper mill at the table.

▶ LEFTOVERS: Stored separately in airtight containers, the beans and the carrots will keep for up to 2 days in the refrigerator.

▶ PREPARATION AND COOKING TIME: About 1 hour and 30 minutes

SUMMER SQUASH GRATINS

summer squash gratins

THIS IS A great dish for late spring and early summer, when small zucchini and yellow squash show up at the farmers' market and it's still cool enough in the evenings that using the oven is pleasant. People often look down on summer squash, largely because they have a reputation as a late summer glut vegetable. But when young and tender, they can be treated as something of a delicacy, as here, where they're coated with a light béchamel sauce and paired with walnuts and bitter greens, then baked under a delicate blanket of salty, crispy bread crumbs. And while I always recommend making your own bread crumbs (see page 17 for instructions), in this dish it's especially important. If you must use store-bought crumbs, opt for panko. I like to serve this with a crisp salad of romaine or red leaf lettuce, thin rounds of carrots, cucumbers, and radishes, and a scattering of cold, cooked French green lentils, dressed with my Basic Vinaigrette (page 135).

▶ SERVES 4

1 bunch chard, kale, or other braising greens (about 12 ounces, 325 g), tough stems removed

2 tablespoons butter

2 shallots, minced

3 garlic cloves, thinly sliced

4 teaspoons all-purpose flour

⅔ cup (160 ml) reduced-fat milk (1% or 2%)

⅔ cup (160 ml) vegetable stock (page 15)

Salt

¼ teaspoon freshly ground black pepper

Pinch of finely grated lemon zest

1 heaping tablespoon coarsely chopped fresh basil, dill, or parsley

⅔ cup (75 g) coarsely chopped roasted walnuts (see page 13)

1½ pounds (675 g) assorted summer squash, sliced into rounds ¼-inch (5 mm) thick

¾ cup (90 g) toasted bread crumbs, preferably homemade (page 17)

1 tablespoon olive oil

2 tablespoons grated Parmesan cheese

1. Preheat the oven to 350°F (180°C). Grease a medium gratin dish or baking dish, preferably one with a capacity of 1½ quarts (1.5 l), or 4 individual gratin dishes.

2. Blanch or boil the chard (see page 10). Using a tea towel or cheesecloth, squeeze out as much liquid as possible. Roughly chop it into bite-size pieces.

3. Melt the butter in a medium saucepan or Dutch oven over medium heat. Add the shallots and sauté until fragrant and slightly softened, 2 to 3 minutes. Add the garlic and sauté until fragrant, about 30 seconds. Sprinkle the flour over the shallots, stirring constantly to evenly distribute the flour, and cook, still stirring, until the mixture is a shade darker and smells nutty, 2 to 3 minutes. Gradually add the milk and stock, whisking constantly to break up any lumps. Bring to a boil, then lower the heat and simmer just until thickened, 3 to 5 minutes. Remove from the heat.

4. Stir in ½ teaspoon salt and the pepper, zest, and parsley. Taste and adjust the seasoning if necessary. Add the walnuts, chard, and squash

and stir gently until all of the vegetables are evenly coated with the sauce. Transfer the mixture to the prepared gratin dish or dishes.

5. Put the bread crumbs, olive oil, Parmesan, and a big pinch of salt in a small bowl and mix gently until well combined. Sprinkle the mixture evenly over the vegetables.

6. Bake for 15 to 20 minutes, until the edges are bubbling and the top is browned. If the top begins to brown too quickly, cover with aluminum foil, then remove the foil for the last 4 or 5 minutes of cooking time. Serve immediately.

▶ LEFTOVERS: This dish is best eaten freshly cooked, but wrapped tightly or stored in an airtight container, it will keep for 1 day in the refrigerator.

▶ PREPARATION AND COOKING TIME:
40 minutes

QUINOA AND CELERY ROOT GRATIN

HERE'S ONE OF those dishes where the magic is in the simplicity. Celery root and quinoa are deeply complementary, and they find perfect harmony with the small amount of cream that lightly binds the dish together. The quinoa and bread crumbs provide some crunch, while the celery root becomes fork-tender in the oven. In a dish like this, it's important to use homemade bread crumbs, ones that you could snack on. Celery root, also known as celeriac, has a knotty, hairy appearance that belies its clean taste and wonderful texture—snappy and fresh when raw, and tender and nuanced when cooked, as in this recipe. Just be careful as you're cleaning it. A vegetable peeler doesn't cut deeply enough to do the job efficiently, so I've provided instructions for peeling it with a knife. This kind of gratin is wonderful with a crusty loaf of bread and a simple arugula salad—tender baby leaves of arugula, a few shavings of fennel, and a shower of fresh Parmesan—dressed lightly with Lemon-Cumin Vinaigrette (page 136).

▶ SERVES 3 OR 4

1 cup (170 g) quinoa

2 cups (475 ml) water

2 tablespoons cold butter

2 leeks, white and pale green parts, halved lengthwise, sliced into thin half-moons, and cleaned (page 13)

¼ cup (30 g) toasted bread crumbs, preferably homemade (page 17)

1 teaspoon olive oil or melted butter

Salt

1 large celery root (about 1 pound, 450 g)

8 tablespoons (240 ml) heavy cream or half-and-half

Freshly ground black pepper

1. Preheat the oven to 375°F (190°C). Butter a 1½-quart gratin or soufflé dish.

2. Thoroughly rinse the quinoa in a fine-mesh sieve. Combine the quinoa and water in a small saucepan over high heat. Bring to a boil, then lower the heat, cover, and simmer for 15 minutes, until the water is absorbed and the tail-like germ of the quinoa is exposed. Drain off any excess water.

3. Meanwhile, melt 1½ tablespoons of the butter in a sauté pan over low heat. Add the leeks and sauté until tender, about 10 minutes.

4. Put the bread crumbs, oil, and a pinch of salt in a small bowl and mix gently until well combined.

5. To prepare the celery root, trim the ends so as to make flat surfaces. With a flat end on the cutting board, peel the celery root with a sharp, sturdy knife, cutting off the skin in strips from top to bottom. Trim off or carve out any hairy spots with a paring knife. Quarter the celery root lengthwise, then lay the quarters on the cutting board flat side down and cut crosswise into thin, ⅛-inch (3 mm) slices. (If you do this ahead of time, keep the prepared celery root in a bowl of cold water to prevent discoloration.)

6. To assemble the gratin, layer one-fourth of the quinoa over the bottom of the prepared gratin

QUINOA AND CELERY ROOT GRATIN

dish. Drizzle 2 tablespoons of the cream over the quinoa, then sprinkle with salt and pepper. Arrange one-third of the celery root over the quinoa. Repeat these layers two more times. Top with the remaining quinoa, drizzle with the remaining 2 tablespoons cream, then scatter the bread-crumb mixture evenly over the top. Cut the remaining 1 tablespoon of cold butter into small pieces and dot them over the surface.

7. Cover tightly with aluminum foil and bake for 30 minutes. Remove the foil and bake for 5 to 15 more minutes, until a thin knife inserted into the center meets no resistance from the celery root. Serve hot.

Variation

Substitute béchamel sauce (see page 126) made from 2 tablespoons butter, 2 tablespoons flour, and 2 cups (475 ml) milk for the cream, using ½ cup (120 ml) atop each layer of quinoa, and scatter ⅓ cup (85 g) of grated Gruyère cheese over each layer of celery root.

▶ LEFTOVERS: This dish is best eaten freshly cooked, but wrapped tightly or stored in an airtight container, it will keep for 1 day in the refrigerator.

▶ PREPARATION AND COOKING TIME: 1 hour and 15 minutes

Béchamel sauce

Béchamel IS one of the four "mother sauces" designated by nineteenth-century French chef Antonin Carême (the other three are *espagnole*, a dark stock-based sauce, *velouté*, a light stock-based sauce, and *allemande*, which is *velouté* with egg beaten into it).

For béchamel, you must first prepare a roux, which is made by melting butter, whisking flour into it, and continuing to whisk constantly as the roux cooks. A pale-colored roux is considered a white roux and a darker one is a blond roux, but a whole color spectrum can be applied to roux, where they're cooked to chestnuts and dark browns. For the recipes in this book, I recommend cooking the roux just until it smells nutty and turns a shade darker, which takes only 2 to 3 minutes over medium-low heat. Roux can serve as a base for many sauces or be used to thicken soups.

To transform the roux into béchamel sauce, you need to add milk or other liquid. Working in increments, pour warm or room-temperature milk into the roux while whisking constantly, which will ensure that the roux is fully incorporated into the milk. Bring to a very gentle boil, then lower the heat and simmer, stirring frequently, until thickened; this usually takes 8 to 10 minutes, but the timing can vary depending on the volume and how well your saucepan retains heat. In the recipes that follow, the sauce should have the consistency of glue and just coat the back of a spoon.

Béchamel sauce is used in gratins and baked pasta dishes—it appears, for example, in Whole Wheat Spaghetti with Creamed Kale and Chickpeas (page 71) and in many of the baked pasta dishes, as well as the gratins. In some ways it replicates an Alfredo sauce, especially if you stir in some cheese.

Vegan béchamel sauce is also very good. Simply replace the butter with canola, vegetable, or grapeseed oil and use nondairy milk, such as soy, almond, or oat milk. Similarly, in the manner of a *velouté*, vegetable stock can be substituted for some or all of the milk; this will lighten the stock in both richness and body, and will change the flavor slightly.

MUSHROOM MACARONI WITH GOAT CHEESE

THIS RICH AND tangy macaroni dish is inspired by the exponentially richer Wild Mushroom Mac and Cheese at ChipShop, a restaurant in Brooklyn I used to live near. While my version isn't exactly health food either, it's an appropriately hearty and heartwarming dish for winter holidays and special occasions. The tangy goat cheese is amplified by the red wine and the hint of rosemary but grounded by the mushrooms. This dish can easily be assembled ahead of time and it also freezes well, making for excellent leftovers. Feel free to mix and match the mushrooms and the cheese; for example, using cubed portobellos and a sharp, aged Cheddar. (If you try the Cheddar, I recommend nixing the rosemary.)

▶ SERVES 6

4 tablespoons butter

2 shallots, minced

8 ounces (230 g) cremini or white button mushrooms, thinly sliced

6 ounces (170 g) shiitake mushrooms, stemmed and thinly sliced

½ cup (120 ml) full-bodied red wine

2 cups (230 g) elbow macaroni

2 tablespoons all-purpose flour

2 cups (475 ml) reduced-fat milk (1% or 2%)

6 ounces (170 g) creamy goat cheese

1 teaspoon minced fresh rosemary

1 teaspoon salt

¼ teaspoon freshly ground black pepper

⅔ cup (80 g) toasted bread crumbs, preferably homemade (page 17)

1 teaspoon olive oil or melted butter

2 ounces (60 g) Parmesan cheese, grated (½ cup)

1. Preheat the oven to 375°F (190°C). Grease a 3-quart casserole dish or 9 × 13-inch (23 × 33 cm) baking dish.

2. Melt 2 tablespoons of the butter in a large, deep sauté pan or Dutch oven over medium heat. When the foaming subsides, add the shallots and sauté until just beginning to soften, about 3 minutes. Add the mushrooms and sauté until they release their liquid, about 5 minutes. Turn the heat up to high. Pour in the wine to deglaze the pan, scraping up any browned bits with a wooden spoon or spatula. Continue cooking until the liquid is reduced by half. Remove from the heat.

3. Meanwhile, bring a large pot of salted water to a boil. Add the macaroni and cook until just barely al dente. Drain and rinse under cold running water to halt the cooking.

4. Melt the remaining 2 tablespoons butter in a medium saucepan over medium-low heat. Sprinkle the flour over the butter, whisking constantly to evenly distribute the flour, and continue to cook, still whisking constantly, until the mixture is a shade darker and smells nutty, 2 to 3 minutes. Gradually add the milk, whisking constantly to break up any lumps. Bring to a boil, then lower the heat and simmer until the sauce thickens and has the consistency of glue, 8 to 10 minutes total. Remove from the heat and stir in the goat cheese, rosemary, ¾ teaspoon of the salt, and the pepper. Combine the mushrooms and sauce, then gently stir in the macaroni.

5. Put the bread crumbs, olive oil, and remaining ¼ teaspoon salt in a small bowl and mix gently until well combined.

MUSHROOM MACARONI
WITH GOAT CHEESE

6. Pour the macaroni mixture into the prepared casserole dish. Scatter the bread-crumb mixture evenly over the top and bake for 35 to 40 minutes, until bubbling at the edges and a knife inserted in the center comes out hot to the touch. Serve hot.

▶ LEFTOVERS: Stored in an airtight container, this dish will keep for up to 3 days in the refrigerator and 1 month in the freezer.

▶ PREPARATION AND COOKING TIME: 1 hour and 15 minutes

Baked Shells with Tomatoes and Gouda

THIS RECIPE IS inspired, in part, by Macaroni with Tomato Sauce and Goat Cheese, a recipe in Martha Rose Schulman's wonderful Recipes for Health column in the *New York Times* several years ago. I like béchamel as a base and thickening agent, and then mildly assertive Gouda as my cheese. Normally, I'm not a huge fan of smoked Gouda, but in this recipe it can be a nice alternative to its standard (unsmoked) counterpart. The tomato manages to tame it so that its smoky dimension harmonizes with the tomato rather than overwhelms it.

▶ SERVES 6

1 pound (450 g) conchiglie or shell pasta

3 tablespoons olive oil

2 tablespoons all-purpose flour

1 cup (240 ml) reduced-fat milk (1% or 2%)

1 recipe Twenty-Minute Tomato Sauce (page 24), or 2½ cups (500 ml) of simple tomato sauce

8 ounces (230 g) Gouda cheese, grated (about 2 cups)

¼ teaspoon freshly ground black pepper

½ cup (60 g) toasted bread crumbs, preferably homemade (page 17)

¾ teaspoon salt

1 tablespoon minced fresh parsley

1. Preheat the oven to 375°F (190°C). Grease a 3-quart casserole dish or 9 × 13-inch (23 × 33 cm) baking dish.

2. Bring a large pot of salted water to a boil. Add the pasta and cook until almost al dente. Drain and rinse under cold running water to halt the cooking.

3. Meanwhile, heat 2 tablespoons of the oil in a medium saucepan or Dutch oven over medium heat. Sprinkle the flour over the oil, whisking constantly to evenly distribute the flour, and continue to cook, still whisking constantly until the mixture is a shade darker and smells nutty, 2 to 3 minutes. Gradually add the milk, whisking constantly to break up any lumps, and then whisk in the tomato sauce in increments. Bring to a boil, then lower the heat and simmer until the sauce thickens slightly, 2 to 3 minutes. Remove from the heat. Stir in the cheese and the pepper.

4. Put the bread crumbs, salt, parsley, and remaining 1 tablespoon of oil in a small bowl and mix gently until well combined.

5. Combine the pasta and sauce and stir gently until evenly incorporated. Pour the mixture into the prepared dish, spreading it in an even layer with the back of a spoon or a spatula. Scatter the bread crumb mixture evenly over the top and bake for 30 to 35 minutes, until browned on top and bubbling on the edges. Let rest for 5 or 10 minutes to set up slightly before serving.

▶ LEFTOVERS: Stored in an airtight container, this dish will keep for up to 3 days in the refrigerator and 1 month in the freezer.

▶ PREPARATION AND COOKING TIME: 1 hour

Kale and Swiss Baked Penne

WHEN I FIRST tried out this recipe, I had doubts. I thought the kale would be too unusual, and that even if it turned out to be a fine dish, it would be a bit of an oddball: not quite mac 'n' cheese, and not quite anything else. Not the case! No one turns down second helpings. While you can certainly use standard, grocery store Swiss cheese in this recipe, it's worth seeking out something a little more nuanced, like Emmentaler. And feel free to substitute chard or any other hearty braising green for the kale.

▶ **SERVES 6**

1 bunch kale (about 12 ounces, 325 g), tough stems removed

1 pound (450 g) penne

2 tablespoons butter

2 shallots, minced

3 garlic cloves, minced

2 tablespoons all-purpose flour

2 cups (475 ml) reduced-fat milk (1% or 2%)

8 ounces (230 g) Swiss cheese, grated (2 cups)

Salt

¼ teaspoon freshly ground black pepper

½ cup (60 g) toasted bread crumbs, preferably homemade (page 17)

2 ounces (60 g) Parmesan cheese, grated (½ cup)

1 tablespoon olive oil or melted butter

1. Preheat the oven to 375°F (190°C). Grease a 3-quart casserole dish or 9 × 13-inch (23 × 33 cm) baking dish.

2. Blanch the kale (see page 10) in a large pot of salted water until tender, removing it from its cooking water with tongs or a slotted spoon so as to reserve the cooking water. Finely chop the kale.

3. Return the pot of water to a boil. Add the penne and cook until barely al dente. Drain and rinse under cold running water to stop the cooking.

4. Meanwhile, melt the butter in a medium saucepan or Dutch oven over medium heat. Add the shallots and sauté until fragrant and just beginning to soften, about 2 minutes. Add the garlic and sauté until fragrant, about 1 minute. Sprinkle the flour over the shallots, whisking constantly to evenly distribute the flour, and cook, still whisking constantly, until the mixture is a shade darker and smells nutty, 2 to 3 minutes. Gradually add the milk, whisking constantly to break up any lumps. Bring to a boil, then lower the heat and simmer until the sauce thickens, 8 to 10 minutes. Remove from the heat. Stir in the kale, Swiss cheese, ¾ teaspoon of salt, and the pepper. Taste and adjust the seasonings if necessary.

5. Put the bread crumbs, Parmesan, oil, and a big pinch of salt in a small bowl and mix gently until well combined.

6. Combine the pasta and sauce and stir gently until evenly incorporated. Pour the mixture into the prepared baking dish, spreading it in an even layer with the back of a spoon or a spatula. Scatter the bread crumb mixture evenly over the top and bake for 30 to 35 minutes, until browned on top and bubbling on the edges. Let rest for 5 or 10 minutes to set up slightly before serving.

▶ **LEFTOVERS:** Stored in an airtight container, this dish will keep for up to 3 days in the refrigerator and 1 month in the freezer.

▶ **PREPARATION AND COOKING TIME:**
1 hour and 30 minutes

**BUTTERNUT SQUASH, BLACK BEAN,
AND SPINACH LASAGNA**

BUTTERNUT SQUASH, BLACK BEAN, AND SPINACH LASAGNA

THIS RICH, INDULGENT lasagna features one of my favorite trios: squash, spinach, and black beans. It's a dish for a crowd, but it freezes well, so you can tuck a couple of portions away for nights when you want to treat yourself to something special. Admittedly, it's difficult to give lasagna a healthy bent. I tried several versions that weren't so rich, but in the end I concluded that lasagna simply must have an oozing, creamy factor to be worth the effort. Here, that creaminess takes the form of a béchamel sauce and mozzarella cheese. It can be made up to a day in advance and kept in the refrigerator, unbaked and covered tightly with plastic wrap.

▶ **SERVES 8**

1 medium butternut squash (about 2 pounds, 1 kg)

1 tablespoon olive oil

8 ounces (230 g) lasagna noodles (9 to 12 noodles)

1 pound (450 g) fresh or 10 ounces (280 g) frozen spinach

3 tablespoons butter

3 tablespoons all-purpose flour

3 cups (750 ml) reduced-fat milk (1% or 2%)

¾ teaspoon salt

¼ teaspoon cayenne pepper

1 pound (450 g) fresh mozzarella cheese, thinly sliced or grated

2 cups cooked black beans, or one 15-ounce (425 g) can, drained and rinsed

1½ ounces (45 g) Parmesan cheese, grated (⅓ cup)

1. Preheat the oven to 400°F (200°C).

2. Trim the ends of the squash and cut the squash in half at the point where the narrow neck transitions into the bulbous bottom. With the flat surface on the cutting board, carefully cut the skin off in thin strips from top to bottom. Cut each piece of squash in half lengthwise, scoop out the seeds, and then cut crosswise into ¼-inch (5 mm) slices. Arrange on a baking sheet and using your hands, toss with the olive oil. Roast, stirring and flipping periodically, for 20 to 30 minutes, until tender and slightly caramelized. Let stand until cool enough to handle.

3. Turn the oven down to 375°F (190°C). Lightly grease a 9 × 13-inch (23 × 33 cm) baking dish.

4. Bring a large pot of salted water to a boil. Add the lasagna noodles and cook until soft and pliable but not limp. Drain and rinse under cold running water, then separate the noodles or spread them out on a baking sheet or cutting board so they don't stick together.

5. If using fresh spinach, blanch or steam it until tender (see page 10). If using frozen spinach, cook it in the microwave, cooking at 2 minute intervals on medium heat, stirring at each interval with a fork. Continue to cook until thawed, then drain and, once cool enough to handle, squeeze out as much liquid as possible. Finely chop the spinach.

6. Melt the butter in a medium saucepan over medium-low heat. When the foaming subsides, sprinkle the flour over the butter, whisking constantly to evenly distribute the flour, and continue to cook, still whisking constantly, until this mixture is a shade darker

and smells nutty, 1 to 2 minutes. Gradually add the milk, whisking constantly to break up any lumps. Bring to a boil, then lower the heat and simmer until the mixture thickens, 6 to 8 minutes. Remove from the heat and stir in the spinach, salt, and cayenne.

7. To assemble the lasagna, spread about ½ cup (120 ml) of the spinach sauce on the bottom of the prepared baking dish. Arrange 3 cooked lasagna noodles over the sauce, followed by about 1 cup (240 ml) of spinach sauce, half of the butternut squash, half of the mozzarella, and 1 cup (210 g) of the beans, distributing each component evenly. Place 3 more lasagna noodles on top of the beans, followed by another 1 cup (240 ml) of the spinach sauce, then layer on the remaining squash, cheese, and beans. Top with a final layer of noodles. Spread any remaining spinach sauce on top, then sprinkle the Parmesan cheese evenly over the top. Cover with foil and bake for 30 minutes. Remove the foil and continue baking for another 10 to 15 minutes, until bubbling at the edges and browned on top. Let rest for at least 15 minutes to set up slightly before serving.

▶ LEFTOVERS: Wrapped tightly or stored in an airtight container, this dish will keep for up to 3 days in the refrigerator and 1 month in the freezer.

▶ PREPARATION AND COOKING TIME: 1 hour and 45 minutes

five salad Dressings

Few meals seem complete without some greens, which on my table usually come in the form of a simply dressed salad: a pile of fresh greens with a topping or two, such as cucumber, radishes, and maybe a crumble of cheese, tossed with a shimmer of salad dressing. I've never understood buying bottled salad dressing; it's so easy to make it at home. In vinaigrettes, the traditional proportion of vinegar to oil is three parts oil to one part vinegar, but I greatly prefer using only two parts oil, or even just one part. The result is a dressing that's a thick emulsion and also contains less fat.

Basic vinaigrette

I MAKE THIS salad dressing so often I've had dreams about it. And I have the proportions down pat, so I make it in my serving bowl, then throw in the greens and other salad ingredients and toss everything together, sparing me a few dirty dishes. It's nice over a medley of greens, say red leaf lettuce and endive, or watercress and Bibb lettuce—topped with shavings of Parmesan or bits of creamy goat cheese.

▶ **MAKES ABOUT ½ CUP (120 ml)**

1 small garlic clove, optional
Kosher salt or other coarse salt
3 tablespoons balsamic or sherry vinegar
1 tablespoon Dijon mustard
Pinch of dried thyme
¼ to ⅓ (60–80 ml) cup olive oil
Freshly ground black pepper

If using the garlic, place it on a cutting board and smash it with the flat side of a knife. Sprinkle ¼ teaspoon of salt on the garlic, then mince and smash it until it turns into a paste. Place the paste in a mixing bowl (or a serving bowl) and whisk in the vinegar, mustard, and thyme. Slowly add the olive oil, whisking constantly, until the desired consistency is reached. Season with salt and pepper to taste.

Lemon-Cumin Vinaigrette

MY FRIEND BRIAN introduced me to his version of this wonderful dressing. I'd always found lemon vinaigrettes to be too bracing—they made my mouth ache. Here, the earthiness of cumin helps balance the lemon juice. This dressing is excellent served over romaine tossed with cucumber, radishes, and, if in season, wedges of tomato.

▶ **MAKES ABOUT ½ CUP (120 ml)**

1 small garlic clove

¼ teaspoon kosher salt or other coarse salt

1 small shallot, minced

Juice of 1 lemon (2 to 3 tablespoons)

1 tablespoon white vinegar

½ teaspoon ground cumin

2 teaspoons Dijon mustard

¼ to ⅓ cup (60–80 ml) olive oil

Freshly ground black pepper

Sugar

Place the garlic on a cutting board and smash it with the flat side of a knife. Sprinkle the salt over it, then mince and smash it until it turns into a paste. Transfer to a small bowl with the shallot, lemon juice, vinegar, and salt and let sit for 10 minutes. Whisk in the cumin and mustard, then slowly add the olive oil, whisking constantly, until the desired consistency is reached. Season with pepper and sugar to taste, then adjust the seasonings if necessary.

Carrot-Ginger Dressing

THIS BRIGHT DRESSING is so thick that it could almost be called carrot-ginger hummus—it's practically a dip. Serve over a crisp lettuce, like iceberg, Bibb, or romaine, garnished with a shower of scallions and toasted sesame seeds.

▶ **MAKES ABOUT 1 CUP (240 ml)**

1 medium carrot, coarsely chopped

1-inch (3 cm) piece of fresh ginger (one small knob), peeled and cut into small chunks (see page 13)

1 scallion, white part only, coarsely chopped

1 tablespoon neutral oil (canola, grapeseed, peanut, or vegetable oil)

1 small garlic clove, minced

2 teaspoons rice wine vinegar

½ teaspoon toasted sesame oil

2 teaspoons soy sauce

Pinch of brown sugar

¼ teaspoon salt

Squeeze of lemon juice

Combine all the ingredients in a blender or food processor and pulse until smooth. Thin the dressing with water, 1 tablespoon at a time, if desired. Taste and adjust the seasoning if necessary.

TAHINI-SCALLION DRESSING

THIS ROBUST SALAD dressing is especially nice over a salad of baby spinach and summer squash that's been cut into thin strips, brushed with olive oil, and grilled or roasted. The hot squash wilts the spinach a bit, and the dressing coats everything with a nutty, tart sheen.

▶ **MAKES ABOUT ¾ CUP (180 ml)**

Juice of ½ lemon

2 teaspoons soy sauce

2 tablespoons tahini

1 garlic clove, minced

1 teaspoon grated fresh ginger (see page 13)

¼ teaspoon salt

¼ cup (60 ml) grapeseed or canola oil

1 bunch scallions, white part and 1 inch (3 cm) of the dark green part, thinly sliced

Whisk together the lemon juice, soy sauce, tahini, garlic, ginger, and salt. Add the oil in a steady stream while whisking constantly, then stir in the scallions. Taste and adjust seasoning with more lemon juice, soy sauce, or salt if necessary.

GREEN GODDESS DRESSING

I'VE ALWAYS SMILED at the name *green goddess*, and what's not to love about a salad dressing that's chock-full of greens? Most green goddess recipes are based on mayonnaise, but I much prefer the richness and creaminess that crème fraîche or sour cream contribute in my variation. Serve over a wedge of iceberg lettuce, wedges of roasted beets, and, at the peak of summer, tomato slices.

▶ **MAKES ABOUT 1¼ CUPS (300 ml)**

10 plump green olives, such as Manzanilla, pitted

½ bunch watercress, tough stems removed

¼ cup (8 g) fresh flat-leaf parsley leaves

1 tablespoon fresh lemon juice

2 tablespoons crème fraîche or sour cream

1 tablespoon capers, rinsed

2 teaspoons sherry vinegar

1 garlic clove, minced

¼ teaspoon salt

¼ teaspoon freshly ground black pepper

¼ to ⅓ cup (60–80 ml) grapeseed or canola oil

Put the olives, watercress, parsley, lemon juice, vinegar, crème fraîche, capers, garlic, salt, sugar, and pepper in a blender or food processor and pulse until combined. With the motor running, pour in the oil in a thin, steady stream, until the desired consistency is reached. Taste and adjust the seasoning with lemon juice, sugar, salt, or pepper if necessary.

VEGETARIAN KITCHEN ESSENTIALS

5

GRAIN and VEGETABLE CAKES, HANDHELD ENTRÉES, and SIMPLE PROTEINS

MY ENTHUSIASM FOR handheld entrées was one force behind my first book, *Veggie Burgers Every Which Way*. There is something hugely appealing about an entrée that's compact and dense with flavor and can be sandwiched between two pieces of bread. That exactly defines what veggie burgers are—more accurately than any comparison to their meaty counterparts.

I was shocked to learn that sandwiches are one of the most frequent entrées to grace the American dinner plate, but after some consideration it made sense. After all, what's not to like in a sandwich? What better communicates nourishment and ease? This chapter covers more than sandwiches, but that ease and nourishment characterize all of the offerings here. There are savory cakes made from vegetables and grains, some special recipes for sandwiches, and a few related offerings, like tostadas and burritos.

And while one way to think about these recipes focuses on their transportability, I'm not a big fan of eating in motion—in the car, walking to the bus station, or even standing up. But I do believe that handheld entrées are perfect meals for dining in solitude. My Favorite Grilled Cheese Sandwich (page 153) is a restorative private dinner, best enjoyed after an exhausting catering job (at least this is how I enjoy it). A frittata sandwich (see page 151 for one specific recipe) is a surprisingly rewarding meal that can be slapped together from leftovers. The ideas here will get your creative juices flowing, so that you'll soon have your own repertoire of handheld entrées, and hopefully a special "veg out" entrée of your own.

GLUTEN-FREE ZUCCHINI LATKES

I FIRST MADE these zucchini latkes when I was spending the weekend at my friend Ilsa's farm in western Massachusetts, using vegetables that were left over from the morning's farmers' market. I was cooking for someone with a gluten intolerance, so I used rice flour to bind the mixture, and to my surprise it resulted in the best latkes I'd ever made. Latkes make a terrific snack or side dish, with sour cream and applesauce for dipping, but I especially like to use them as a base for cooked vegetables, like greens or stewed tomatoes. See page 146 for a few topping ideas. You can serve these with bread and salad, but I find that latkes go especially well with unfussy cooked vegetables, like steamed or roasted turnips dressed with salt and olive oil, or roasted carrots.

▶ **MAKES 8 LATKES; SERVES 4**

3 medium Yukon Gold or other waxy potatoes (about 12 ounces, 325 g)

1 medium zucchini

½ teaspoon salt

1 egg, beaten

3 tablespoons coarsely chopped fresh herbs, such as basil, parsley, or chives

3 to 5 tablespoons rice flour

3 tablespoons neutral oil (canola, grapeseed, peanut, or vegetable oil)

1. Preheat the oven to 400°F (200°C).
2. Prick the potatoes all over with a fork. Arrange them on a baking sheet and roast for 25 to 35 minutes, until just tender; a skewer inserted in the center should meet just a bit of resistance. When they're cool enough to handle, grate the potatoes using the large holes of a box grater, discarding the large pieces of potato skin that remain.
3. Meanwhile, grate the zucchini using the large holes of a box grater. Toss with the salt and place in a cheesecloth-lined colander to drain for at least 15 minutes. Gather the zucchini up in the cheesecloth and squeeze out as much excess liquid as possible.
4. Combine the grated potato and zucchini in a bowl. Fold in the egg and herbs. Sprinkle 3 tablespoons of the rice flour over the mixture and fold it in gently, until the mixture just comes together, adding additional rice flour if necessary.
5. Heat the oil in a sauté pan over medium-high heat. Scoop up a ¼-cup portion of the mixture and put it in the sauté pan, pressing it gently to flatten it into a 4-inch (10 cm) round. Continue adding latkes to the pan in this way, making sure they don't touch and working in batches as need be. Cook, flipping once, until browned on each side and firmed to the touch, 8 to 10 minutes total. To keep cooked latkes warm while you continue frying the rest, place them on a parchment-lined baking sheet and keep in a 250°F (120°C) oven. Serve hot.

▶ **LEFTOVERS:** Wrapped tightly or stored in an airtight container, latkes will keep for 1 day in the refrigerator and up to 1 month in the freezer.

▶ **PREPARATION AND COOKING TIME:** 45 minutes

BAKED QUINOA AND CARROT CAKES

Baked Quinoa and Carrot Cakes

QUINOA IS AN excellent grain to work into your diet. For one thing, it's a complete protein, containing all of the essential amino acids. It's also filling and inexpensive, though its grassy notes can be an acquired taste. If at first you're put off by this, I recommend using it in seasoned dishes, such as this one, where it won't dominate the flavor of the dish. These cakes, which are zingy and have a faint crunch, make a very colorful plate when paired with cold, roasted beets that have been gently tossed in a spoonful of thick, Greek-style yogurt.

▶ MAKES 10 CAKES; SERVES 4 TO 5

1 cup (170 g) quinoa

2 cups (475 ml) water

2 tablespoons olive oil

2 shallots, minced

8 ounces (230 g) carrots, peeled and grated

1 tablespoon sherry vinegar

2 tablespoons minced fresh dill

2 eggs, beaten

½ teaspoon salt

¼ teaspoon freshly ground black pepper

1. Preheat the oven to 375°F (190°C). Line a baking sheet with parchment paper.
2. Thoroughly rinse the quinoa in a fine-mesh sieve. Combine the quinoa and water in a small saucepan over high heat. Bring to a boil, then lower the heat, cover, and simmer for 10 to 15 minutes, until the water is absorbed and the tail-like germ of the quinoa is exposed.

3. Meanwhile, heat the oil in a sauté pan over medium heat. Add the shallots and sauté until just tender, 3 to 4 minutes. Add the carrots and sauté until softened but still a bit crunchy, 8 to 10 minutes. Pour in the vinegar to deglaze the pan, scraping up any browned bits with a wooden spoon or spatula. Set aside to cool slightly.
4. Combine the quinoa, carrots, and dill in a bowl, then stir in the eggs, salt, and pepper. Shape into 10 patties, about 3 inches (8 cm) in diameter and 1 inch (3 cm) in thickness and arrange them on the lined baking sheet. Bake for 10 to 15 minutes, until crisp on the exterior and firm to the touch. Serve hot.

▶ LEFTOVERS: Wrapped tightly or stored in an airtight container, these cakes will keep for up to 2 days in the refrigerator and 1 month in the freezer.

▶ PREPARATION AND COOKING TIME: 40 minutes

SAVORY CORN AND YOGURT CAKES

A LITTLE BIT flapjack, a little bit veggie burger, these corn cakes are substantial without being heavy and sweet without being cloying, with a gentle tang from the yogurt and an addictive, crispy crust. You can't go wrong pairing these cakes with tomatoes. Twenty-Minute Tomato Sauce (page 24) or your favorite simple tomato sauce makes a perfect topping. Salsa is another obvious choice. I also love to top them with tart little heirloom cherry tomatoes that have been marinated in a bit of olive oil for 20 or 30 minutes.

▶ **MAKES 6 CAKES; SERVES 3**

½ cup (70 g) stone-ground cornmeal or polenta

¼ cup (30 g) all-purpose flour

½ teaspoon baking powder

½ teaspoon sugar

½ teaspoon salt

¼ teaspoon freshly ground black pepper

2 eggs

½ cup (120 g) plain, unsweetened yogurt

1½ cups (180 g) fresh corn kernels (from about 3 ears) or frozen corn kernels, thawed and drained

4 scallions, white and pale green parts, thinly sliced

2 tablespoons olive oil, or more as needed

1. Put the cornmeal, flour, baking powder, sugar, salt, and pepper in a mixing bowl and whisk to combine.
2. Put the eggs, yogurt, and two thirds of the corn in a food processor and pulse until coarsely pureed, about 10 to 12 pulses. Pour the mixture into the cornmeal mixture and gently fold it in until combined. Fold in the scallions and the remaining corn.
3. Heat the oil in a sauté pan over medium heat. Scoop up a scant ¼-cup (60 ml) portion of the mixture and put it in the sauté pan, pressing it gently to flatten into a 4-inch (10 cm) round and cooking in batches to avoid crowding. (If there are too many cakes in the pan, they will be difficult to flip.) Cook until golden brown on the bottom, 2 to 4 minutes. Carefully flip and cook until the second side is golden brown and the cakes are firm in the center, another 2 to 4 minutes, adding more oil to the pan as needed. To keep cooked cakes warm while you continue frying the rest, place them on a parchment-lined baking sheet and keep in a 250°F (120°C) oven. Serve hot.

▶ **LEFTOVERS:** Wrapped tightly or stored in an airtight container, these cakes will keep for up to 2 days in the refrigerator and 1 month in the freezer.

▶ **PREPARATION AND COOKING TIME:** 25 minutes

Panko-Crusted Risotto Cakes

RISOTTO CAKES MAKE excellent use of leftover risotto—much tastier than it would be if simply reheated. Feel free to use whatever type of risotto you please. This recipe calls for shaping the risotto into larger cakes so that they can be served as an entrée, but mini cakes make an excellent appetizer. I recommend topping these with the Twenty-Minute Tomato Sauce (page 24), but you can substitute any tomato sauce you please, or eat them unadorned—which is tempting. If you use another type of risotto, choose whatever savory sauce seems complementary.

▶ MAKES 6 CAKES; SERVES 3

2 cups (475 ml) Basic Vegetable Risotto (or any variation; see page 63), chilled

½ cup (60 g) all-purpose flour

1 egg, beaten

1 cup (120 g) panko

3 tablespoons neutral oil (canola, grapeseed, peanut, or vegetable oil)

1½ cups (360 ml) warm Twenty-Minute Tomato Sauce (page 24) or other simple tomato sauce

1. Shape the risotto into 6 patties using about ⅓ cup of risotto per patty.
2. Place the flour and the panko on separate plates, and place the beaten egg in a small mixing bowl. Dredge a risotto patty in the flour until evenly coated, then dip it in the egg, turning as needed to coat evenly, and then dredge it through the panko, once again coating it completely. Repeat with the remaining risotto patties.
3. Heat the oil in a sauté pan over medium heat. Add the patties and sauté until golden brown and crisp on both sides, carefully flipping halfway through, about 10 minutes total.
4. If desired, puree the tomato sauce using an immersion blender, food processor, or regular blender.
5. Serve hot, topped with the tomato sauce.

▶ LEFTOVERS: Wrapped tightly or stored in an airtight container, these cakes will keep for 1 day in the refrigerator and up to 1 month in the freezer.

▶ PREPARATION AND COOKING TIME:
25 minutes

TOPPINGS FOR
Grain and Vegetable Cakes

GRAIN AND vegetable cakes are excellent as hearty snacks or side dishes, but to qualify as filling entrées, they usually need something additional to dress them up. They can certainly be turned into sandwiches or veggie burgers, but another approach is to treat them as a base for flavorful vegetables. Here are several of my favorite options. All of these toppings make an amount sufficient for three to four servings of cakes.

BRAISED COLLARD GREENS: Remove the stems from 1 bunch of collard greens and chop the leaves into 1-inch (3 cm) pieces. Heat 1 tablespoon of butter or olive oil in a sauté pan over medium heat. When hot, add 1 small minced onion and sauté until softened, 6 to 8 minutes. Add a minced seeded jalapeño and sauté until fragrant, 2 to 3 minutes. Deglaze the pan with 2 tablespoons cider vinegar. Add the collard greens and ¼ cup water (if the leaves have just been cleaned and have water still clinging to them, omit the additional water, but add more if needed). Cook until the leaves are uniformly dark green, 12 to 15 minutes, tossing periodically and adding more water as the liquid in the pan dries up. Season with salt and freshly ground black pepper, then spoon over the hot cakes and serve.

TOMATO SAUCE AND POACHED EGGS: Warm 1½ cups (360 ml) of simple tomato sauce (such as Twenty-Minute Tomato Sauce, page 24). If desired, puree the sauce with an immersion blender, food processor, or regular blender. Poach 4 eggs (see page 172). Divide the sauce over each serving of cakes, then top with a poached egg. Garnish with a drizzle of olive oil, a few grinds of black pepper, and a dusting of Parmesan cheese if desired.

ROASTED EGGPLANT AND TOMATOES: Preheat the oven to 450°F (230°C). Arrange 1 globe eggplant or 2 small Japanese eggplants on one side of a foil-lined baking sheet and 1 pint (340 g) of cherry tomatoes on the other side. Prick the eggplants all over with a sharp knife. Roast for 20 minutes, then remove the tomatoes. Return the eggplant to the oven and bake for 20 more minutes, until it's flattened and tender. When cool enough to handle, trim the ends, peel off the skin, and coarsely chop the flesh. Toss with the tomatoes, a big pinch of salt, and 1 to 2 tablespoons olive oil, to taste. Divide the mixture over the cakes and garnish with minced fresh basil or oregano if desired.

MARINATED CHARD WITH GOAT CHEESE: Cut 1 bunch of chard into 1-inch (3 cm) strips and sauté in 1 tablespoon olive oil. When cool enough to handle, squeeze out any excess moisture, then toss with 1 tablespoon olive oil, salt to taste, a pinch of lemon zest, and a pinch of red pepper flakes. Arrange on top of the cakes, followed by 1 tablespoon crumbled creamy goat cheese per serving.

ZUCCHINI-ALMOND VEGGIE BURGERS

I DEVELOPED THIS veggie burger after *Veggie Burgers Every Which Way* was published. It was inspired by two things: The first was an overflowing bag of zucchini I picked up from my CSA one week. The second was a revelatory discovery of what a delicious flavor combination zucchini and almonds make, with almonds complementing the delicate flavor of the zucchini and rounding it into something mature. This burger is moist, succulent, and nicely textured. The recipe has plenty of room for improvisation; play with the herbs, substitute a parboiled potato for part of the zucchini, or consider using walnuts or pecans in place of the almonds. I like to serve these with pickled red onions and slices of juicy summer tomato on classic hamburger buns.

▶ SERVES 4

4 small zucchini, yellow squash, or a combination (about 1 pound, 450 g)

½ teaspoon salt

¼ cup (25 g) roasted almonds (see page 13), finely chopped

3 tablespoon minced fresh basil

1 tablespoon all-purpose flour

1 egg, beaten

¼ teaspoon freshly ground black pepper

¼ cup (30 g) toasted bread crumbs, preferably homemade (page 17), or more as needed

1 tablespoon neutral oil (canola, grapeseed, peanut, or vegetable oil)

1. Preheat the oven to 350°F (180°C).
2. Grate the zucchini using the large holes of a box grater. Toss with the salt and place in a cheesecloth-lined colander to drain for at least 15 minutes. Gather the zucchini up in the cheesecloth and squeeze out as much excess liquid as possible.
3. Combine the zucchini with the almonds, basil, flour, egg, and pepper in a bowl. Add the bread crumbs and stir gently until the mixture just comes together, adding more bread crumbs if necessary. The mixture will be quite wet. Shape into 4 patties.
4. Heat the oil in an oven-safe sauté pan over medium heat. Put the burgers in the pan and cook until golden brown on the bottom, 2 to 4 minutes. Carefully flip and cook until the second side is golden brown, another 2 to 4 minutes. Transfer the pan to the oven and bake for 12 to 15 minutes, until the burgers are firm.

▶ LEFTOVERS: Wrapped tightly or stored in an airtight container, these burgers will keep for up to 2 days in the refrigerator and 1 month in the freezer.

▶ PREPARATION AND COOKING TIME: 40 minutes

vegetarian banh mi ✺

BANH MI, KNOWN sometimes simply as "Vietnamese sandwiches," are a culinary product of the French colonization of Vietnam that have recently become trendy in the States. Traditional *banh mi,* which include pâté and usually some version of pork, have long been appreciated as inexpensive, handheld takeout food. In this vegetarian version, the tofu marinade produces enticing aromas and also hardens slightly in the oven to create something akin to spicy-savory tofu candy. The challenge in making these is to find Vietnamese baguettes, which are about 10 inches (25 cm) long and have a brittle crust and an interior so pillowy soft and light that they're practically weightless. If you can't find them, look for baguettes that are very light—nothing too chewy or tough. This isn't necessarily a complicated recipe, but between the sheer number of steps and the help you might need to find the baguettes, it's a good candidate for cooking with friends!

▶ SERVES 4

One 14-ounce (380 g) block extra-firm tofu
2 tablespoons chili paste, such as sambal oelek
3 tablespoons soy sauce
¼ cup (60 g) packed brown sugar
2 garlic cloves, minced
2 teaspoons grated fresh ginger (see page 13)
¼ cup (60 ml) plus 2 teaspoons rice vinegar
1 carrot
1 daikon radish, or 8 standard radishes

1 teaspoon salt
1 tablespoon granulated sugar
¼ cup (60 ml) mayonnaise
1 teaspoon sriracha sauce
4 Vietnamese baguettes (see headnote)
1 cup (20 g) loosely packed cilantro sprigs

1. Drain the tofu and put it on the cutting board, broad side facing up. Cut it into 4 pieces lengthwise, then turn each piece onto its skinniest side and cut lengthwise into three thin rectangles, about 2½ inches (6 cm) by 1¼ inches (3 cm), and slightly less than ½ inch (1 cm) thick. Line a baking sheet with a tea towel or double layer of paper towels and arrange the tofu in a single layer. Top with another layer of towels, and then cover with something flat and wide enough to cover all the tofu, like a baking sheet or Pyrex baking dish. Place something heavy, such as a few cans or a heavy pan, on top. The goal is to squeeze out as much moisture as possible. Let sit for 20 to 30 minutes.

2. Put the chili paste, soy sauce, brown sugar, garlic, and ginger in a small bowl. Add the 2 teaspoons vinegar and stir until thoroughly combined. Spread half of the mixture on the bottom of a 9 × 13-inch (23 × 33 cm) baking pan. Arrange the pressed tofu on top of the mixture, then spread the remainder of the mixture over the tofu, being sure to distribute it evenly. Let sit for at least 20 minutes and up to 2 hours.

3. Meanwhile, peel the carrot and cut it into long, very thin strands, ideally the thickness of matchsticks. (If you have a mandoline, use it to julienne the carrot.) Do the same with the daikon; if using standard radishes, slice

them into paper-thin rounds. Place the carrot and radish in separate bowls. Whisk together the ¼ cup (60 ml) rice vinegar, salt, and sugar until dissolved. Drizzle the mixture over the carrot and radish, dividing it evenly, and toss to combine. Allow to stand for at least 20 minutes and up to 1 hour.

4. Preheat the oven to 400°F (200°C).

5. Bake the tofu, still in the same pan and with its marinade, for 30 to 40 minutes, carefully flipping it every 15 minutes, until it has toughened a bit and the exterior seems candy-coated and feels slightly crisp.

6. Stir together the mayonnaise and the sriracha sauce. When the tofu has 5 more minutes to cook, place the baguettes in the oven to warm them up.

7. To assemble the sandwiches, cut the baguettes in half lengthwise. Spread the mayonnaise mixture on both cut faces, using 1 tablespoon per baguette. Layer 3 rectangles of tofu on the bottom half, then divide the carrots, radishes, and cilantro among the sandwiches on top of the tofu. Top with the other half of the baguette and serve warm.

▶ LEFTOVERS: The assembled sandwiches are best eaten freshly prepared, but stored separately in airtight containers, the baked tofu, carrot, and radish will keep for up to 2 days in the refrigerator.

▶ PREPARATION AND COOKING TIME: 1 hour and 30 minutes

FRITTATA SANDWICH WITH PICKLED RED ONION

FRITTATAS, UNLIKE OTHER basic egg preparations like scrambled, fried, or poached eggs or omelets, keep very well in the fridge overnight. I'm always wrapping up portions for bag lunches, but they can also be repurposed as delicious sandwiches, which in some ways make them a serious improvement on a classic egg salad sandwich. Anytime eggs are involved, I think textural contrast is key, so I'm partial to using a crusty baguette or ciabatta and crisp romaine lettuce for such sandwiches. Otherwise, you can make the sandwich as plain or fussy as you choose. I especially enjoy adding roasted red peppers (page 19) and onion marmalade (page 23). And while I've included the recipe for a small frittata below, feel free to substitute your favorite recipe or your leftovers.

▶ SERVES 4

½ cup (120 ml) water

¼ cup (60 ml) red wine vinegar

1 tablespoon kosher salt

1 teaspoon sugar

6 eggs

1 small red onion, sliced into thin rings

1 tablespoon reduced-fat milk (1% or 2%)

⅓ cup (25 g) grated Parmesan cheese

¼ teaspoon salt

A few grinds of black pepper

2 tablespoons butter or olive oil

1 standard baguette, or 4 ciabatta rolls, halved lengthwise

FOR THE SANDWICH TOPPINGS

Roasted red bell pepper (page 19), cut into ½-inch (1 cm) strips

Fresh mozzarella cheese, thinly sliced

Avocado slices

Romaine lettuce leaves

Tomato slices

1. Preheat the oven to 400°F (200°C).
2. Whisk together the water, vinegar, kosher salt, and sugar until dissolved. Add the onions and let stand for at least 30 minutes.
3. Whisk together the eggs, milk, Parmesan, salt, and pepper.
4. Melt the butter in an oven-safe 10-inch (25 cm) nonstick sauté pan over medium heat, swirling to ensure that the entire inside surface of the pan is coated. When hot, pour in the eggs, using a rubber spatula to scrape every last bit from the bowl. Let the eggs cook undisturbed for 1 or 2 minutes, until beginning to set around the edges. Run the spatula around the perimeter of the mixture, then tuck the spatula underneath one edge of the mixture to lift it up and, at the same time, tilt the pan toward the spatula so some of the uncooked egg can run underneath. Let the mixture cook undisturbed for 1 more minute, then repeat. Continue in this way until the frittata is mostly set on top.
5. Transfer the pan to the oven and bake for 8 to 10 minutes, until just set and dry in the center. Remove from the pan and allow to cool slightly.
6. Slice the bread in half lengthwise and toast until just crispy. Cut the cooked frittata into wedges and arrange on the bottom halves of

the bread. Drain the onion and arrange the rings atop the frittata. Add other toppings as desired, then cover with the top half of the bread and serve right away.

▶ LEFTOVERS: The assembled sandwiches are best eaten within a few hours, but stored separately in the refrigerator, the frittata will keep for 2 days and the onion will keep for 1 week. Wrap the frittata tightly and store the onion in an airtight container.

▶ PREPARATION AND COOKING TIME:
40 minutes

MY FAVORITE GRILLED CHEESE SANDWICH

MAKING A GREAT grilled cheese sandwich begins with using great ingredients. When there are so few, you can't take any risks, and I feel it is especially important to begin with good bread. My favorite kind is an Italian-style loaf that has a crisp, sesame-seed covered crust and a tender, moist interior and that toasts beautifully. This sandwich is easiest to pull together when you have roasted tomatoes on hand (which, once you start incorporating them into your meals, you surely will). And what a treat after a long day's work—to sink into a cushioned chair with a delicious grilled cheese sandwich in your hand and a napkin draped over your lap. The tomatoes offer bursts of sweetness; the olives, counterbalancing salt; the sriracha sauce, a whisper of heat; and the Fontina, which is an Italian cow's milk cheese, a blanket of earthy, creamy nuttiness that carries the sandwich to sublimity.

▶ **SERVES 1**

2 slices rustic bread, 1 inch (3 cm) thick

1 teaspoon sriracha sauce

Two or three ¼-inch (5 mm) thick slices of Fontina cheese (enough to cover the bread)

6 to 8 kalamata olives, smashed with the flat side of a knife and pitted if necessary

5 roasted cherry tomatoes (page 21), coarsely chopped

Cold butter for frying

1. Spread the facing surfaces of the two slices of bread with the sriracha sauce. Arrange the cheese, olives, and tomatoes atop one slice of bread. Top with the other piece of bread and dot the upper surface with flecks of cold butter.

2. Heat a sauté pan over medium-low heat. Place the sandwich in it, buttered side down, and cook until golden brown and crisp on the first side, 3 to 5 minutes, applying pressure with a spatula or covering the pan for a while if necessary to encourage the cheese to melt. Dot the top of the uncooked side with butter, then flip the sandwich. Cook until the second side is golden brown and crisp and the cheese is beginning to ooze out, 3 to 5 minutes. Serve hot.

▶ **LEFTOVERS:** Grilled cheese sandwiches are best eaten freshly cooked.

▶ **PREPARATION AND COOKING TIME:** 15 minutes

MY FAVORITE GRILLED CHEESE SANDWICH

SQUASH, SPINACH, AND BLACK BEAN BURRITOS

CONTRARY TO WHAT U.S. chain restaurants may have led you to believe, burritos don't have to be the size and weight of a brick. It's refreshing to be served a reasonable burrito, especially one that's bursting with fresh vegetables and nuanced flavor, as in this recipe. To simulate the effect of steaming the tortillas to make them soft and malleable before filling them, as they do at burrito shops, wrap them, in a stack, tightly in foil and place in a warm oven for 10 minutes.

▶ **SERVES 6**

1 medium butternut squash (about 2 pounds, 1 kg)

3 tablespoons neutral oil (canola, grapeseed, peanut, or vegetable oil)

Salt

Freshly ground black pepper

6 flour tortillas

1 bunch spinach (about 14 ounces, 380 g), tough stems removed and roughly chopped

2 cups cooked black beans, or one 15-ounce (425 g) can, drained and rinsed

2 ounces (60 g) crumbled queso fresco or cotija cheese (½ cup)

¼ cup (5 g) coarsely chopped fresh cilantro

½ cup pickled jalapeño peppers, drained (about one 7-ounce can, 205 g)

4 ounces (115 g) mozzarella cheese, grated (1 cup)

1. Preheat the oven to 400°F (200°C).
2. Trim the ends of the squash and cut the squash in half at the point where the narrow neck transitions into the bulbous bottom. With the flat surface on the cutting board, carefully cut the skin off in thin strips from top to bottom. Cut each piece of squash in half lengthwise, scoop out the seeds, and then cut into ¾-inch (2 cm) cubes. Arrange on a baking sheet. Using your hands, toss with 1 tablespoon of the oil, sprinkle with salt and pepper, then roast, stirring and flipping periodically, for 20 to 30 minutes, until tender and slightly caramelized. Remove from the oven and set aside.
3. Turn the oven down to 275°F (140°C). Stack the tortillas and wrap them tightly in foil. Place them in the oven to warm for up to 20 minutes before assembling the burritos.
4. Heat the remaining 2 tablespoons of oil. Add the spinach and sauté, tossing frequently with tongs, until collapsed and tender, 2 to 3 minutes. Compress the spinach against the side of the pan with a spatula and pour out any liquid that collects.
5. Put the squash, spinach, black beans, queso fresco, cilantro, and jalapeños in a mixing bowl and mix gently until well combined.
6. Divide the mozzarella among the tortillas, using about 3 tablespoons of cheese per tortilla, then divide the squash mixture evenly among the tortillas. Roll into burritos, tucking in one or both ends if desired. Serve hot. To keep warm, wrap the burritos individually in foil and keep them in a 275°F oven until ready to serve.

▶ **LEFTOVERS:** The assembled burritos are best eaten freshly cooked, but stored in an airtight container, the squash filling will keep for up to 2 days in the refrigerator.

▶ **PREPARATION AND COOKING TIME:**
40 minutes

CHIPOTLE BLACK BEAN TOSTADAS WITH AVOCADO AND MANGO

TOSTADAS ARE SUCH a simple meal—but, oh, what a yummy one. In this version, corn tortillas are topped with homemade refried black beans and baked, then topped with cheese and a simple salad made from iceberg lettuce, avocado, mango, and radishes. There's lots of room for improvisation. You can substitute refried beans made using your favorite recipe or, for an even easier dish, use canned refried beans. Also feel free to take whatever liberties you please with the salad. That said, the contrasts here—sweet mango, bitter radishes, crunchy lettuce, and creamy, cooling avocado tossed in cumin-spiked lime juice—make for an entrée that's as flavorful and fresh as it is filling.

▶ **SERVES 4**

2 tablespoons olive oil, plus more for brushing

1 onion, diced

2½ teaspoons ground cumin

4 cups cooked black beans, or two 15-ounce (425 g) cans, drained and rinsed

2 chipotle peppers in adobo sauce, seeded and finely diced, or ¼ teaspoon cayenne pepper

Salt

8 corn tortillas

Juice of 1 lime

½ head iceberg lettuce, cut into thin strips

1 mango, cut into thin wedges

1 avocado, cut into thin wedges

6 radishes, cut into thin rounds

6 ounces (170 g) Monterey Jack cheese, grated (1½ cups)

1. Preheat the oven to 400°F (200°C).
2. Heat the oil in a deep sauté pan over medium heat. Add the onion and 2 teaspoons of the cumin and sauté until the onion is softened, 5 to 7 minutes. Add the beans, chipotles, and ½ teaspoon salt and cook until heated through. Using a potato masher, mash the beans until the desired consistency is reached. If they seem too thick, stir in a bit of water, 1 tablespoon at a time.
3. Brush both sides of the tortillas with oil and arrange them on 2 baking sheets. Divide the refried beans on top of them, spreading them so that most of each tortilla is covered. Bake for 8 to 10 minutes, until the tortillas are crisp.
4. Meanwhile, put the lime juice, remaining ½ teaspoon of cumin, and a big pinch of salt in a large mixing bowl and whisk to combine. Add the lettuce, mango, avocado, and radishes and gently toss until evenly coated.
5. After removing the tostadas from the oven, immediately scatter the cheese over the beans, using about 3 tablespoons cheese per tostada, followed by the salad. The tostadas are best served on the hot side of warm, while the cheese is still melted, 2 tostadas per person.

▶ **LEFTOVERS:** The assembled tostadas are best eaten freshly cooked, but stored in an airtight container, the refried beans will keep for up to 3 days in the refrigerator.

▶ **PREPARATION AND COOKING TIME:** 30 minutes

five TOFU MARINADES

BY NO means is a chunk of tofu my favorite thing to eat, and this is evidenced by the recipes in this book, where tofu doesn't make an appearance very often. But I can't argue with the fact that it is an easy, filling protein to put in the center of the plate.

You always hear how tofu is such an excellent protein because it's a blank slate, absorbing the flavor of whatever it's cooked with. This, unfortunately, is not my experience. I find that tofu does indeed have a flavor, and even if it's mild, it isn't especially pleasant. And while it's true that marinades and sauces can turn tofu into something scrumptious, unless you're careful that flavor will only penetrate the exterior of the tofu, leaving the interior tasting as unappealing as a few layers of wet cardboard.

One trick that will help is to press tofu before cooking to extract as much moisture as possible; this allows the tofu to absorb more of the marinade. You can further amp up the flavor quotient by creating as much surface area as possible. Rather than cutting tofu into large, fat slabs, try thin triangles or rectangles, as in the recipe for Vegetarian Banh Mi (page 149). If you're adverse to cooking with tofu, as I've often been, you'll be astounded by what a difference these two steps will make.

As to marinades, the possibilities are endless. Here are a few that I particularly like. Each makes enough for about 1 pound (450 g) of tofu.

sesame-pineapple marinade

¾ cup (180 ml) pineapple juice

¼ cup (60 ml) soy sauce

2 tablespoons toasted sesame oil

1 tablespoon packed brown sugar

2 tablespoons neutral oil (canola, grapeseed, peanut, or vegetable oil)

Whisk together the juice, soy sauce, sesame oil, and sugar. Add the neutral oil in a steady stream, whisking constantly until thoroughly incorporated. If making ahead of time, store the marinade in the refrigerator in an airtight container for up to 3 days. Rewhisk just before use.

peanut-cilantro marinade

⅓ cup (140 g) creamy, unsalted natural peanut butter

1 bunch cilantro, coarsely chopped

1 bunch scallions, coarsely chopped

2 tablespoons neutral oil (canola, grapeseed, peanut, or vegetable oil)

2 tablespoons fresh lime juice

1 tablespoon soy sauce

¼ teaspoon salt

Combine all the ingredients in a food processor and process until smooth. If the marinade is too thick, add hot water, 1 tablespoon at a time, to achieve the desired consistency. If making ahead of time, store the marinade in the refrigerator in an airtight container for up to 3 days. Rewhisk just before use.

VEGETARIAN KITCHEN ESSENTIALS

Balsamic and Soy Sauce Marinade

¼ cup (60 ml) balsamic vinegar

¼ cup (60 ml) soy sauce

3 tablespoons Dijon mustard

½ teaspoon freshly ground black pepper

⅓ cup (80 ml) neutral oil (canola, grapeseed, peanut, or vegetable oil)

Whisk together the vinegar, soy sauce, mustard, and pepper. Add the oil in a steady stream, whisking constantly until thoroughly incorporated. If making ahead of time, store the marinade in the refrigerator in an airtight container for up to 3 days. Rewhisk just before use.

Honey-Mustard Marinade

¼ cup (60 ml) Dijon mustard

2 tablespoons honey

2 tablespoons packed brown sugar

1 teaspoon kosher salt

¼ teaspoon cayenne pepper

½ cup (120 ml) neutral oil (canola, grapeseed, peanut, or vegetable oil)

Whisk together the mustard, honey, sugar, salt, and cayenne. Add the oil in a steady stream, whisking constantly until thoroughly incorporated. If making ahead of time, store the marinade in the refrigerator in an airtight container for up to 3 days. Rewhisk just before use.

Spicy Orange-Ginger Marinade

⅓ cup (80 ml) fresh orange juice (about 1 orange)

2 tablespoons rice vinegar

1 tablespoon grated fresh ginger (see page 13)

1 serrano chile, coarsely chopped

1 teaspoon kosher salt

2 garlic cloves, minced

3 tablespoons neutral oil (canola, grapeseed, peanut, or vegetable oil)

Whisk together the orange juice, vinegar, ginger, serrano, and salt until combined. Add the oil in a steady stream, whisking constantly until thoroughly incorporated. If making ahead of time, store the marinade in the refrigerator in an airtight container for up to 3 days. Rewhisk just before use.

seitan and pineapple skewers

SEITAN CAN TASTE alarmingly meatlike, and for that reason I like it best when it has lots of brightly flavored vegetable company. These skewers, inspired by something similar at the Mexican restaurant Alma in Brooklyn, get it exactly right. The pineapple is the winning factor here; it's juicy and candy-sweet, with its flavor balanced by the savory marinade, seitan, and vegetables. It's perfectly fine to substitute tofu or tempeh, or even additional vegetables, for the seitan if you like. This makes a perfect meal when paired with a scoop of freshly cooked white or brown rice, drizzled with any leftover marinade.

▶ SERVES 4

¾ cup (180 ml) pineapple juice

2 tablespoons soy sauce

2 tablespoons olive oil

1 tablespoon packed brown sugar

1 garlic clove, minced

1 teaspoon grated fresh ginger (see page 13)

½ teaspoon salt

¼ teaspoon freshly ground black pepper

1 pound (450 g) seitan, cut into 1-inch (3 cm) cubes

1 pineapple, cut into 1-inch (3 cm) cubes

2 bell peppers (any color or a combination), cut into 1-inch (3 cm) squares

1 red onion, cut into 1-inch (3 cm) cubes

1. Soak 8 wooden skewers in hot water for at least 20 minutes.
2. Put the pineapple juice, soy sauce, olive oil, sugar, garlic, ginger, salt, and pepper in a small bowl and whisk until thoroughly combined.
3. Thread the seitan, pineapple, bell peppers, and onion on the skewers, alternating on the skewers and beginning and ending with the seitan if possible.
4. Place the skewers in a shallow baking dish or resealable plastic bag. Pour the marinade over them and let stand for at least 30 minutes and up to 2 hours, turning periodically.
5. Heat a grill pan or sauté pan over medium heat. Alternatively, prepare a medium-hot grill and allow it to preheat for at least 20 minutes. Cook or grill the skewers, turning periodically, until the seitan has firmed slightly and has browned, and the pineapple and vegetables have developed some char marks, 4 to 5 minutes per side. Serve hot, 2 skewers per person.

▶ LEFTOVERS: Wrapped tightly or stored in an airtight container, the cooked skewers will keep for up to 2 days in the refrigerator.

▶ PREPARATION AND COOKING TIME: 40 minutes

LETTUCE CUPS WITH SMOKED TOFU AND CRISPY CHOW MEIN NOODLES ✵

LETTUCE WRAPS HAVE always struck me as an ideal vessel for food. I love the idea that they provide a crisp exterior and a hint of flavor with no bulk or flavor-concealing density, I even like to eat veggie burgers wrapped in lettuce. In this recipe for lettuce cups, the filling is richly textured and features a savory assortment of meaty mushrooms, chewy smoked tofu, and crispy chow mein noodles. It makes for a dramatic, somewhat interactive dish to serve at the table, with everyone filling their own lettuce cups. It's a fun meal to eat with friends.

▶ **SERVES 4**

8 ounces (230 g) chow mein "stir-fry" noodles

2 tablespoons soy sauce

2 teaspoons rice vinegar

1 teaspoon chili paste, such as sambal oelek

1 head iceberg lettuce

1 teaspoon toasted sesame oil

3 tablespoons neutral oil (canola, grapeseed, peanut, or vegetable oil)

2 shallots, minced

1 pound (450 g) cremini or white button mushrooms, coarsely chopped

3 garlic cloves, minced

2 teaspoons grated fresh ginger (see page 13)

8 ounces (230 g) smoked or baked tofu, cut into small cubes

½ cup (20 g) very thinly sliced fresh basil or coarsely chopped fresh cilantro

¼ cup (30 g) coarsely chopped roasted walnuts (see page 13)

1. Bring a large pot of unsalted water to a boil. Add the noodles and cook until just tender. Drain and rinse under cold running water. Shake vigorously to remove as much excess water as possible.

2. Put the soy sauce, vinegar, and chili paste in a small bowl and stir to combine.

3. Cut the lettuce in half lengthwise. Cut out the stem and separate the lettuce leaves into 8 individual cups (reserve remaining leaves and the core for another use). Put them in a large bowl of ice water to make them crisp.

4. Heat the sesame oil and 1 tablespoon of the neutral oil in a sauté pan over medium heat. Add the shallots and sauté until just softened, 2 to 3 minutes. Add the mushrooms and sauté until they release their liquid and it cooks off, 6 to 8 minutes. Add the garlic and ginger and sauté until fragrant, about 1 minute. Pour in the soy sauce mixture and cook, stirring occasionally, for 1 minute, then remove from the heat. Stir in the tofu, basil, and walnuts.

5. Transfer the mushroom mixture to a serving dish and wipe out the sauté pan, then heat the remaining 2 tablespoons of neutral oil in a sauté pan over medium-high heat. Divide the cooked noodles into 8 small piles and place as many in the sauté pan as will fit without crowding. Fry the noodles until browned and crisp on each side, 2 to 3 minutes per side.

6. Arrange the noodle cakes, filling, and lettuce cups separately at the table. To serve, place one noodle cake in a lettuce cup, then top with the mushroom-tofu filling.

▶ **LEFTOVERS:** The assembled lettuce cups are best eaten freshly prepared, but stored in an airtight container, the filling will keep for up to 2 days.

▶ **PREPARATION AND COOKING TIME:**
45 minutes

FIVE EASY DESSERTS

I always wish I had more time to make desserts. So when I have people over to eat, I like to take it as an opportunity to make something sweet. While it can be fun to go all out and make a spectacular cake from *The Cake Bible*, it's equally nice for dessert to be a less bombastic affair. Here are a few of my favorite recipes for desserts that aren't terribly involved, all of them easy enough to throw together without too much advance planning.

CHOCOLATE TRUFFLES

THE INFORMALITY OF finger foods for dessert can be a relief for the cook as well as for guests. These truffles can be made days ahead of time; in fact, they'll keep in the freezer for up to a month. Dust them with ground nuts, cocoa powder, superfine sugar, or whatever you please. It's worthwhile to use a good-quality chocolate. With so few ingredients, it will make a noticeable difference.

▶ **MAKES ABOUT 30 TRUFFLES**

12 ounces (325 g) bittersweet chocolate, chopped into small pieces

⅔ cup (160 ml) heavy cream

1 tablespoon brandy, cognac, or fruity liqueur

Pinch of salt

½ cup (50 g) cocoa powder, superfine sugar, confectioners' sugar, or finely ground nuts for coating

1. Place the chocolate in a heatproof mixing bowl. Scald the cream, heating it in a small saucepan over medium-high heat until it just begins to bubble at the edges and an active steam cloud lingers over the surface. Pour the hot cream over the chocolate and add the brandy and salt. Stir with a rubber spatula a few times, then let sit for 5 minutes. Whisk the mixture until completely smooth. If there are still lumps of unmelted chocolate, place the bowl over a pot of simmering water and whisk constantly until smooth. Spread the chocolate into a 9 × 13-inch (23 × 33 cm) baking dish and refrigerate until just set, about 30 minutes.

2. Using a melon baller or 1-teaspoon measuring spoon, scoop up a mound of chocolate and, working quickly with your hands, shape it into a lumpy truffle. Set aside and continue until all of the chocolate has been shaped. Refrigerate, in a single layer, until the truffles are firm, about 30 minutes. The shaped truffles can be stored in an airtight container in the refrigerator for up to 1 week, and in the freezer for up to 1 month.

3. To serve, bring the truffles to room temperature. Put the cocoa or other coating in a small container with a lid. Add the truffles to the container in batches of 4 or 5 and gently shake until they're fully coated.

RIESLING POACHED PEARS

THIS SIMPLE, CLEAN fruit dessert could hardly be less labor-intensive. Have the poaching liquid ready to go, and when your guests start to help you clear the dinner plates, put it over the heat.

▶ **SERVES 4**

3 cups (750 ml) water

2 cups (475 ml) Riesling

¼ cup (60 ml) honey, or 3 tablespoons agave syrup

¼ cup (50 g) sugar

1 cinnamon stick

3 cloves

Zest of 1 orange, removed in thick strips with a vegetable peeler

4 pears

Ground cinnamon for dusting

4 mint sprigs for garnish

1. Combine the water, the wine, honey, sugar, cinnamon stick, cloves, and orange zest in a medium saucepan. Bring to a boil, then lower the heat, cover, and simmer.

2. Meanwhile, peel the pears using a vegetable peeler and once the poaching liquid is simmering, add the whole peeled pears. Cook for 20 to 30 minutes, until the pears are completely tender.

3. Use a slotted spoon to transfer the pears from the saucepan to serving dishes. Transfer a few ladlefuls of the poaching liquid to a smaller saucepan, bring to a boil, and continue to boil until reduced by half and syrupy.

4. Serve the pears while still warm, drizzled with the reduced poaching liquid, dusted with cinnamon, and garnished with a sprig of mint.

AFFOGATO

YEARS AGO I bought a little stovetop espresso maker that looks something like a percolator. As someone who only enjoys the occasional espresso (and wouldn't have the countertop space for an electric espresso maker anyway), I love putting it to use for this simple but always impressive dessert. Use decaf espresso beans if you or any of your guests are concerned about sleep.

▶ SERVES 4

1 pint (475 ml) vanilla ice cream

½ cup (120 ml, 4 shots, 1 ounce each) hot espresso

Roasted hazelnuts, cashews, pecans, or almonds (see page 13), coarsely chopped, for garnish

Dark chocolate shavings for garnish

Divide the ice cream among 4 serving dishes. Pour 2 tablespoons of espresso over each dish. Garnish with the nuts and chocolate shavings and serve immediately.

BAKED CREPES

CREPES CAN BE a fun interactive dessert, something for everyone to put together while digesting dinner. Prepare an array of fillings and let your guests customize their desserts. The crepes can be made up to a day ahead of time.

▶ MAKES 8 CREPES

1 recipe Basic Crepes (page 224), made with all-purpose or whole wheat flour, and with 2 teaspoons of sugar added to the batter

Fillings, such as cinnamon-sugar with flecks of butter, honey and mascarpone cheese, chunks of chocolate, thinly sliced fresh fruit, jam, or chocolate hazelnut butter

Confectioners' sugar for dusting

1. Preheat the oven to 400°F (200°C).
2. Arrange the fillings of your choice on the crepes, then fold the crepes into quarters. Arrange them on a baking sheet and dust generously with confectioners' sugar. Bake in the top third of the oven for 8 to 12 minutes, until the sugar has caramelized, the fillings are heated through and the crepes are crisp. Serve immediately, dusted with additional confectioners' sugar if desired.

NECTARINE CRISP

FEW DESSERTS ARE as satisfying as a fruit crisp. This one would work for any fruit—apples, peaches, rhubarb, plums, or a combination—but nectarines are a special treat when they're in season. The topping is nutty and textured, and it comes together very quickly with the aid of a food processor. You can assemble the dessert up to two hours ahead of time and then keep it in the refrigerator until ready to bake. This crisp is best served very warm, with a spoonful of fresh, gently whipped cream.

► **SERVES 6**

FOR THE FILLING

3 pounds (1.5 kg) nectarines or other fruit, sliced ½-inch (1 cm) thick (about 2 quarts total)

1 tablespoon packed brown sugar

1 tablespoon all-purpose flour

1 teaspoon ground cinnamon

Pinch of salt

FOR THE TOPPING

⅔ cup (90 g) all-purpose flour

⅔ cup (140 g) packed brown sugar

½ cup (70 g) roasted unsalted almonds

½ cup (50 g) rolled oats

Pinch of salt

6 tablespoons cold unsalted butter, cut into small pieces

1. Preheat the oven to 375°F (190°C). Butter an 8-inch (20 cm) square baking dish.

2. TO MAKE THE FILLING, toss the fruit with the sugar, flour, cinnamon, and salt. Spread into the prepared baking dish.

3. TO MAKE THE TOPPING, combine the flour, sugar, almonds, oats and salt in a food processor. Pulse until most of the almonds are finely chopped, 20 to 30 seconds. Add the cold butter and pulse until it's cut into small pieces about the size of peas, 25 pulses or so. Pour the topping over the fruit, spreading it evenly with your hands and gently pressing it into the fruit if needed.

4. Bake for 30 to 40 minutes, until the fruit is tender and collapsed and the juices are bubbling around the edges. Let stand for at least 15 minutes before serving.

6

EGGS EVERY WHICH way

THERE ARE SO many ways of cooking eggs; don't let a single cooking method become a badge of your identity. I used to take my eggs the way my mother did, which was scrambled and dry as Styrofoam, with no trace of runniness. But as my culinary curiosity evolved, dry, scrambled eggs became boring. So I started experimenting, first by making omelets and frittatas. Then one day I wanted to turn spaghetti with pesto into a more substantial meal, so I topped it with a poached egg. (I'd been offered such meals at dinner parties, but had always asked that my egg be practically hard-boiled.) It was a revelation.

Since then, I've discovered a multitude of delicious ways to prepare and enjoy eggs—a good thing, as they are hearty and filling and therefore have an important role to play in creating satisfying vegetarian entrées. They are also a simple, invaluable way to add a boost of protein, as well as a host of other vitamins and nutrients, including vitamins A, B_2, and D and iron, to the vegetarian plate. In this section, I'll take you through a variety cooking methods, from simple scrambled eggs to soufflés.

Whatever cooking method you use, start with the best-quality eggs available, from chickens raised in the most humane manner. Consider looking for such eggs at farmers' markets, where they are often cheaper, not to mention fresher. In addition, the vendors can vouch firsthand for how their chickens are raised. This is reassuring in light of the fact that farm-fresh eggs produced by humanely raised chickens may not taste or look different from those of their factory-farmed counterparts. You may have heard that you can identify the humanely produced eggs by their more vibrant orange yolks, but yolk color actually has more to do with feed than farming practices, though feed and farming practices are sometimes related. Just remember, even if you can't tell the difference, the chickens certainly can!

AND A NOTE ABOUT EGG SAFETY: Numerous *Salmonella* outbreaks in recent years have made egg safety (as well as the safety of many other types of foods) a reasonable concern. If you are concerned or if you are pregnant, it's important to cook your eggs until they're fully set. This means that for fried or poached eggs, for example, there should be no runny yolk.

SCRAMBLED EGGS WITH VARIATIONS

THOUGH SCRAMBLED EGGS are considered more of a breakfast food than an entrée, I still eat them for dinner quite often. Chefs and other foodies tend to exalt the merits of custardy, slow-cooked scrambled eggs, but I don't like my scrambled eggs to be overwhelmingly custardy, so I cook them over a slightly higher heat for a significantly shorter cooking time. The key is frequent stirring, which encourages the eggs to break into curds. Butter or oil is necessary for greasing the pan, and each has its merits. Butter lends its characteristic richness, while olive oil gives the eggs slightly fruity notes. If you're not a pro at scrambling eggs, I recommend that you start with the basic recipe below so you can devote your attention to the cooking process and how it affects the outcome, and then start exploring variations, including the options I've listed below the recipe.

▶ SERVES 1

2 eggs
1 teaspoon reduced-fat milk (1% or 2%)
Big pinch of salt
A few grinds of black pepper
1 tablespoon butter or olive oil

1. Crack the eggs into a mixing bowl and add the milk, salt, and pepper. Beat with a fork just until the yolks and whites are combined.

2. Heat a sauté pan over medium heat or, if you prefer custardy scrambled eggs, over low or medium-low heat. Add the butter and swirl to ensure that the entire inside surface of the pan is coated. When hot, pour in the eggs, using a rubber spatula to scrape every last bit from the mixing bowl. Cook, stirring leisurely with a rubber spatula, until cooked to the desired doneness. This will take anywhere from 2 to 8 minutes, depending on the temperature and how you prefer your eggs. When cooked to your liking, remove immediately, as the eggs will continue to cook in the pan even after it's removed from the heat.

▶ LEFTOVERS: Scrambled eggs are best eaten freshly cooked.

▶ PREPARATION AND COOKING TIME: 5 to 10 minutes, not including time to prepare accompaniments for variations

variations

SCRAMBLED EGGS WITH PESTO: Fold in 1 tablespoon pesto (preferably homemade; see pages 25 and 26) during the last 30 seconds to 1 minute of cooking time. Optional: Stir in 2 tablespoons creamy goat cheese along with the pesto.

SCRAMBLED EGGS WITH CHEESE: Grated hard cheeses can be mixed in with the beaten eggs, whereas soft cheeses like mascarpone or a creamy goat cheese should be folded in during the last 30 seconds or 1 minute of cooking time. I usually use about 1 to 2 tablespoons cheese per serving. Much more than that will overwhelm the eggs.

SCRAMBLED EGGS WITH SPINACH AND OLIVE TAPENADE: When beating the eggs in the mixing bowl, add 2 tablespoons of grated Parmesan cheese. After the butter has melted, add ¼ cup (60 g) blanched or steamed and coarsely chopped spinach (see page 10) and cook just until heated through. Pour in the eggs and cook as described on page 169, folding in 2 teaspoons Olive Tapenade (page 27) during the last 30 seconds to 1 minute of cooking time.

FRIED AND POACHED EGGS WITH VARIATIONS

HARDLY ANYTHING IS easier than frying an egg, yet a fried or poached egg can turn almost any dish into an entrée, whether on pasta, a sandwich, crepes, or a bowl of stew, to name a few. Several recipes in this book call for using eggs this way. Generally, you can swap a poached egg for a fried egg, or vice versa. Poached eggs have the merit of not being cooked in fat, whereas fried eggs have an irresistible crispy crust, due to that fat they're cooked in.

FRIED EGGS

FRIED EGGS NEED a generous amount of grease to prevent them from sticking to the pan; it also helps make those delicious, crispy edges, packed with flavor. Here's a trick that will increase the crispy factor and help cook the top surface more quickly: Tilt the pan so that the butter or oil pools at one end, then tilt the other way to distribute it over the top of the eggs.

▶ SERVES 1

3 tablespoons butter or olive oil
2 eggs
Salt
Freshly ground black pepper

Heat the butter in a 10-inch (25 cm) sauté pan over medium heat. When hot, crack the eggs into the pan, being careful not to break the yolks. Cook for 1 or 2 minutes, periodically swirling the pan to redistribute the oil and tilting it so that the butter or oil pools at one side

of the pan, and then can be redistributed over the tops of the eggs with a spoon or by tilting the pan in the opposite direction. Continue cooking the eggs for 2 to 4 minutes, until the whites are set and the yolks are cooked to the desired doneness. Sprinkle with salt and pepper and serve.

▶ LEFTOVERS: Fried eggs should only be eaten freshly cooked.

▶ PREPARATION AND COOKING TIME:
5 minutes

POACHED EGGS

ADDING A SMALL amount of vinegar to the poaching liquid helps keep the egg whites from splaying into threads when they hit the water. You can use any type of vinegar you like, and if its flavor will complement the finished dish, you can increase the amount slightly. Recipes vary greatly from one cookbook to the next in terms of how much vinegar is specified—some recipes call for as much as 2 tablespoons, which lends a strong vinegar flavor. I prefer a smaller amount, which gives just a whisper of flavor to the finished dish.

▶ **SERVES 1**

2 teaspoons vinegar, or more as desired
2 eggs, at room temperature

Put at least 3 inches (8 cm) of water in a small saucepan over high heat. Bring to a boil, add the vinegar, then lower the heat to maintain a very gentle simmer. Crack one egg into a small bowl, being careful not to break the yolk. Lower the bowl into the simmering water and gently transfer the egg into the saucepan, then do the same with the second egg. (If poaching more eggs, don't try to cook more than 2 at a time.) Cook until the whites are set and the yolks are cooked to the desired doneness, about 2½ minutes for a yolk that's runny, 4 minutes for partially set, and 5 minutes for hard. To check doneness, lift the egg up from the water using a slotted spoon and gently touch the yolk with your finger. When each egg is cooked, remove it with the slotted spoon and gently blot the surface dry with a tea towel or paper towel. If cooked in batches, poached eggs can be stored in room-temperature water and then quickly reheated in simmering water for 30 seconds.

▶ **LEFTOVERS:** Poached eggs should only be eaten freshly cooked.

▶ **PREPARATION AND COOKING TIME:** 10 minutes

VARIATIONS

POACHED OR FRIED EGGS ON TOAST WITH GREENS
▶ **SERVES 2**

Sauté 1 bunch (about 12 ounces, 325 g) of chard or spinach (see page 10). After the greens are squeezed dry, stir in 1 tablespoon olive oil, a squeeze of lemon juice, a pinch of red pepper flakes, and salt to taste. Meanwhile toast 4 slices of bread and poach or fry 4 eggs. Divide the greens evenly over each piece of toast, then top each with an egg. Drizzle with a bit of olive oil and sprinkle with salt, freshly ground black pepper, and a dusting of Parmesan cheese if desired. Serve two per person.

POACHED OR FRIED EGGS ON FRISÉE SALAD
▶ **SERVES 4**

Clean 1 bunch of frisée and dry thoroughly. Toss with 1 minced shallot, 1 thinly sliced pickling cucumber, peeled if desired, 1 cup roasted cherry tomatoes (page 21), and ⅓ cup (30 g) roasted, roughly chopped or slivered almonds.

Dress with Basic Vinaigrette (page 135), tasting along the way for balance. Fry or poach 4 eggs. Divide the salad among 4 serving plates or bowls and top each with 1 fried or poached egg. Sprinkle with salt and freshly ground black pepper.

POACHED EGGS OVER STEWED LENTILS
▶ SERVES 2

Pick through 1 cup (200 g) French green lentils. Put them in a small saucepan with 2 cups water. Bring to a boil, then lower the heat, cover, and simmer until the lentils are tender, 25 to 35 minutes. Drain off any excess water, then stir in 1 cup (170 g) roasted cherry tomatoes (page 21), 2 tablespoons coarsely chopped fresh parsley, 1 tablespoon olive oil, 1 tablespoon balsamic vinegar, ½ teaspoon salt, and ¼ teaspoon freshly ground black pepper. Toast 4 thick slices of bread and poach 4 eggs. Spoon the lentils over the bread, distributing them evenly, then top each slice of bread with 1 poached egg. Drizzle with a bit of olive oil and sprinkle with salt and freshly ground black pepper. Serve two toasts per person.

Baked Eggs with Variations

BAKING IS MY favorite way of cooking eggs. To use this method, you'll need ramekins or oblong gratin dishes. I prefer the latter, as they can accommodate two eggs, whereas smaller ramekins may only fit 1 egg after you've added the accompaniments. Speaking of which, there are endless variations for what you might add to the eggs: cooked greens (see page 10), roasted bell peppers (page 19), roasted cherry tomatoes (page 21), pesto (pages 25 and 26), caramelized onions (page 22), Olive Tapenade (page 27) or Onion Marmalade (page 23), fresh tomatoes, any kind of cheese . . . the list goes on. Simply distribute the accompaniments among the individual baking dishes, then crack the eggs over them. Here, I've provided three specific recipes to get you started. Once you're familiar with the method, try experimenting with your own combinations.

Baked Eggs with Caramelized Onions

▶ SERVES 2

Butter or oil for greasing

¼ cup caramelized onions (page 22)

1 ounce (30 g) Gruyère or Parmesan cheese, grated (¼ cup) 4 eggs

2 tablespoons cream

Salt and freshly ground black pepper

Olive oil for garnish

Minced fresh parsley for garnish

1. Preheat the oven to 375°F (190°C).
2. Grease 2 ramekins or gratin dishes with softened butter or oil. Divide the caramelized onions and cheese evenly between the dishes, then crack 2 eggs into each dish, being careful not to break the yolks. Drizzle the cream on top. Sprinkle with salt and pepper.
3. Bake for 15 to 20 minutes, until the whites are set and the yolks are cooked to the desired doneness (you can gently press the surface of the egg with a thin spatula or butter knife to determine how cooked it is). Garnish with the parsley, drizzle with a bit of olive oil, and serve hot.

▶ LEFTOVERS: Baked eggs should only be eaten freshly cooked.

▶ PREPARATION AND COOKING TIME: 30 minutes, not including time to prepare the onions

**BAKED EGGS WITH TOMATO SAUCE,
OLIVES, AND PARMESAN**

BaKED EGGS WITH ARUGULA, ROASTED TOMATOES, AND GARLIC

▶ SERVES 2

1 tablespoon olive oil

2 cups baby arugula or coarsely chopped arugula

Butter or oil for greasing

⅓ cup (70 g) roasted cherry tomatoes (page 21)

Pulp or flesh from 1 head roasted garlic, skins discarded (page 20), peeled

4 eggs

3 tablespoons fresh ricotta cheese, optional

Salt and freshly ground black pepper

1. Preheat the oven to 375°F (190°C).
2. Heat the oil in a sauté pan over medium-low heat. Add the arugula and sauté until fully wilted, 2 to 4 minutes.
3. Grease 2 ramekins or gratin dishes with softened butter or oil. Divide the arugula, cherry tomatoes, and roasted garlic between the ramekins. Crack 2 eggs into each dish, being careful not to break the yolks. If using the ricotta, dollop it over the eggs.
4. Bake for 15 to 20 minutes, until the whites are set and the yolks are cooked to the desired doneness (you can gently press the surface of the egg with a think spatula or butter knife to determine how cooked it is). Sprinkle with salt and pepper and serve hot.

▶ LEFTOVERS: Baked eggs should only be eaten freshly cooked.

▶ PREPARATION AND COOKING TIME: 30 minutes

BaKED EGGS WITH TOMATO SAUCE, OLIVES, AND PARMESAN

▶ SERVES 2

Butter or oil for greasing

1 cup (240 ml) Twenty-Minute Tomato Sauce (page 24) or other simple tomato sauce

4 eggs

8 kalamata, niçoise, or dry-cured olives, pitted

Shaved Parmesan cheese for garnish, made with a vegetable peeler

Very thinly sliced fresh basil for garnish

Freshly ground black pepper

1. Preheat the oven to 375°F (190°C).
2. Grease 2 ramekins or gratin dishes with softened butter or oil. Divide the tomato sauce between the dishes. For each dish, make two slight indentations in the sauce, then crack an egg into each indentation, being careful not to break the yolks. Scatter the olives on top.
3. Bake for 15 to 20 minutes, until the whites are set and the yolks are cooked to the desired doneness (you can gently press the surface of the egg with a thin spatula or butter knife to determine how cooked it is). Garnish with the Parmesan shavings and basil. Sprinkle with pepper and serve hot.

▶ LEFTOVERS: Baked eggs should only be eaten freshly cooked.

▶ PREPARATION AND COOKING TIME: 30 minutes

omelets and Frittatas with variations

PRACTICALLY ANYTHING CAN go into an omelet or a frittata, as long as it can be contained by the eggs. The difference between the two is that in omelets the eggs are cooked, then fillings are folded or rolled inside, whereas in frittatas the filling is mixed into the uncooked eggs, which are then cooked flat in the pan and finished off in the oven. In either case, the vegetables don't get much cooking once they're added to the eggs; it's more that they're heated through. For that reason, many vegetables must be cooked before being added to these dishes.

Basic omelet

OMELETS CAN BE intimidating. I've made my share of them that have ripped apart, either while I was trying to fold them in half or as I was attempting to coax them out of the frying pan and onto the plate. Leaving the omelet in the pan, covered, for a few minutes after cooking is a huge help, as it encourages the omelet to fully set. If you don't have a lid that's large enough, use an inverted heatproof mixing bowl or a piece of aluminum foil.

▶ **SERVES 2**

4 eggs

1 tablespoon reduced-fat milk (1% or 2%)

¼ teaspoon salt

A few grinds of black pepper

2 tablespoons butter or olive oil

Fillings of your choice (see variations)

1. In a mixing bowl, whisk together the eggs, milk, salt, and pepper.
2. Heat the butter in a 10-inch (25 cm) nonstick sauté pan over medium heat, swirling to ensure that the entire inside surface of the pan is coated. When hot, pour in the eggs, using a rubber spatula to scrape every last bit from the mixing bowl. Let the eggs cook undisturbed for 1 or 2 minutes, until beginning to set around the edges. Run the spatula around the perimeter of each egg, then tuck the spatula underneath one edge of the egg to lift it up and, at the same time, tilt the pan toward the spatula so some of the uncooked egg can run underneath. Let the eggs cook undisturbed for 1 more minute, then repeat the spatula maneuver to transfer more of the uncooked egg to the bottom of the pan. Continue doing this until the eggs are mostly set on top. Arrange fillings over the entire surface.
3. Remove from the heat, cover the pan, and let sit for 3 minutes. Run the spatula around the perimeter of the omelet to loosen the edges, then lift half of it up and fold it over the fillings, using a flat spatula to assist if necessary. Transfer to a plate and serve immediately.

▶ **LEFTOVERS:** Omelets are best eaten freshly cooked.

▶ **PREPARATION AND COOKING TIME:** 20 minutes, not including time to prepare fillings

BASIC OMELET

Variations

OMELET WITH COLLARD GREENS AND SHARP CHEDDAR: Remove the stems and stalks of 1 bunch of collard greens, then chop into 1-inch (3 cm) pieces and sauté (see page 10). Press out the excess liquid with a spatula. Once the eggs are mostly set on top, spread the cooked greens over the entire surface, followed by ¾ cup grated sharp Cheddar cheese (3 ounces, 85 g). Proceed with finishing and folding as described in the recipe.

OMELET WITH ONION MARMALADE AND GOAT CHEESE: Once the eggs are mostly set on top, spread ⅓ cup (120 g) Onion Marmalade (page 23) and ½ cup creamy goat cheese (2 ounces, 60 g) over the top. Proceed with finishing and folding as described in the recipe.

OMELET WITH CORN, ROASTED TOMATOES, AND FETA: Heat 1 tablespoon oil in a sauté pan. Add 4 thinly sliced scallions (white and pale green parts only) and 1 cup (120 g) fresh or frozen corn kernels. Cook until the scallions are softened, 3 to 5 minutes. Set aside until cooled slightly, then stir in 1 cup (170 g) roasted cherry tomatoes (page 21) and ½ cup crumbled feta cheese (2 ounces, 60 g). Once the eggs are mostly set on top, spread the corn mixture over the entire surface. Proceed with finishing and folding as described in the recipe.

Basic Frittata

THE FINAL STAGE of cooking frittatas can be done either on the stovetop or in the oven. I have terrible luck flipping them out of the pan when cooked completely on the stovetop, so the method below calls for finishing in the oven. An oven-safe sauté pan (ideally a nonstick one) is best for this method. When combining the eggs with any sautéed fillings, don't just pour the eggs over the fillings in the sauté pan. Rather, once the fillings have finished cooking, stir them into the eggs and then return the mixture to the sauté pan used to cook the fillings (I don't wipe it out first—this way I don't need to add more oil to the pan). This makes the frittata is easier to slip out of the pan. If you don't have an oven-safe sauté pan, you can pour the mixture into a greased square or small rectangular baking dish and cook the frittata entirely in the oven.

▶ **SERVES 4**

Fillings of your choice (see variations)
8 eggs
2 tablespoons reduced-fat milk (1% or 2%)
½ teaspoon salt
A few grinds of black pepper
3 tablespoons butter or olive oil

1. Preheat the oven to 375°F (190°C).
2. Cook your frittata fillings, following the instructions on page 181 or improvising your own filling.

3. Whisk together the eggs, milk, salt, and pepper. Allow the frittata fillings to cool slightly, then fold them into the eggs.
4. Melt the butter in an oven-safe 10-inch (25 cm) nonstick sauté pan over medium heat, swirling to ensure that the entire inside surface of the pan is coated. (If you used a sauté pan to prepare the filling, it's fine to reuse it to finish cooking the frittata; subtract the butter or oil used in preparing the fillings from the 3 tablespoons called for at left.) When hot, pour in the egg mixture, using a rubber spatula to scrape every last bit from the bowl. Let the eggs cook undisturbed for 1 or 2 minutes, until beginning to set around the edges. As when cooking an omelet, run the spatula around the perimeter of the mixture, then tuck the spatula underneath one edge of the mixture to lift it up and, at the same time, tilt the pan toward the spatula so some of the uncooked egg can run underneath. Let the mixture cook undisturbed for 1 more minute, then repeat. Continue in this way until the frittata is mostly set on top.
5. Transfer the pan to the oven and bake for 5 to 10 minutes, until just set and dry in the center. Serve hot, warm, or chilled.

▶ **LEFTOVERS:** Wrapped tightly, frittatas will keep for 1 day in the refrigerator.

▶ **PREPARATION AND COOKING TIME:**
25 minutes, not including time to prepare the fillings

Variations

FRITTATA WITH PARMESAN, SHALLOTS, AND PARSLEY: Whisk ½ cup grated Parmesan cheese (2 ounces, 60 g) with the eggs in step 3. Add 2 minced shallots to the melting butter in step 4 and sauté until just translucent, 3 to 5 minutes. Add 3 tablespoons fresh parsley and stir until fragrant, about 30 seconds. Pour in the eggs and proceed with the recipe. (Because the volume of shallots and parsley is so minimal, in this case it's fine to add the eggs directly to the pan after sautéing the filling.)

FRITTATA WITH ASPARAGUS, SHALLOTS, AND PARMESAN: Heat 1 tablespoon butter and 2 tablespoons water in a sauté pan. Add ¾ cup (115 g) chopped asparagus and 2 minced shallots. Cover and cook until the asparagus is just tender, about 3 minutes. Drain off the liquid, and let cool slightly. Stir the asparagus and shallots into the beaten eggs in step 3, along with ½ cup grated Parmesan cheese (2 ounces, 60 g). Proceed with the recipe.

FRITTATA WITH POTATOES AND RICOTTA: Heat 2 tablespoons oil in a sauté pan over medium-high heat. Add 5 very thinly sliced small waxy potatoes (about 8 ounces, 230 g), such as red bliss or Yukon gold. Cook, gently tossing every few minutes, until browned at the edges and almost cooked through, 4 to 6 minutes. Using a slotted spoon, transfer the potatoes to a bowl. Lower the heat to medium and sauté 1 chopped white or yellow onion until just softened, 6 to 8 minutes. Transfer to the bowl with the potatoes and let cool slightly. Gently stir the potatoes and onion into the beaten eggs in step 3 and proceed with the recipe. Before transferring the pan to the oven, dot the surface with ⅓ cup (75 g) fresh ricotta cheese. Garnish with minced fresh chives just before serving if desired.

KALE QUICHE WITH FONTINA

Basic Quiche with Variations

QUICHE IS ONE of those things, like cheese soufflé, that one instinctively knows not to eat too often. But when you want quiche, nothing else will really suffice. Standard quiches, inspired in part by Julia Child's recipe, call for ½ cup heavy cream per egg in the custard, a proportion that's far too rich for me. I've found that using mostly milk and a smaller amount of heavy cream results in quiche that is rich but not exceedingly so, and slightly less custardy when fully cooked due to the larger proportion of egg. Almost anything can go into a quiche. Just be sure to cook vegetables before adding them, and to completely submerge the fillings in the custard (if they're above the surface, they're likely to burn). Some of my favorite vegetable fillings are included after the Basic Quiche recipe, but others I enjoy are: asparagus, roasted or fried potatoes, roasted bell peppers, sautéed mushrooms, an assortment of whatever I have on hand, or even just cheese. And for the cheese, it's best to use something that melts nicely.

BASIC QUICHE

▶ SERVES 5 OR 6

1 to 2 cups (240–475 ml) vegetable fillings of your choice (see above)

3 eggs

¾ cup (180 ml) milk (whole or 2%)

½ cup (120 ml) heavy cream

½ teaspoon salt

¼ teaspoon freshly ground black pepper

2 ounces (60 g) cheese of your choice, grated (½ cup)

1 prebaked 10-inch (25 cm) tart shell, preferably homemade (page 214)

1. Preheat the oven to 375°F (190°C), then prepare your desired fillings.
2. Whisk together the eggs, milk, cream, salt, and pepper, then stir in the prepared fillings.
3. Sprinkle the cheese over the bottom of the tart shell. Carefully pour the custard into the shell.
4. Bake for 30 to 40 minutes, until set in the center. Let rest for at least 20 minutes before serving.

▶ LEFTOVERS: Stored in an airtight container, quiche will keep for up to 2 days in the refrigerator.

▶ PREPARATION AND COOKING TIME: 45 minutes, not including time to prepare the crust or fillings

Kale Quiche with Fontina

▶ SERVES 5 OR 6

1 bunch kale (about 12 ounces, 325 g)

1 tablespoon butter

3 shallots

1 garlic clove, minced

3 tablespoons minced fresh parsley

3 eggs

¾ cup (180 ml) milk (whole or 2%)

½ cup (120 ml) heavy cream

½ teaspoon salt

¼ teaspoon freshly ground black pepper

6 ounces (170 g) Fontina cheese, grated (1½ cups)

1 prebaked 10-inch (25 cm) tart shell, preferably homemade (page 214)

1. Preheat the oven to 375°F (190°C).
2. Blanch or steam the kale (see page 10) and chop it very finely.
3. Melt the butter in a sauté pan and sauté the shallots until tender, 3 to 5 minutes. Add the garlic, followed by the kale and the parsley, and sauté for 2 to 3 minutes, until the garlic and parsley are fragrant. Remove from the heat and allow to cool slightly.
4. Whisk together the eggs, milk, cream, salt, and pepper. Stir in the kale mixture and 1 cup (120 g) of the grated cheese.
5. Sprinkle remaining ½ cup (50 g) of cheese over the bottom of the tart shell. Carefully pour the custard into the shell.
6. Bake for 30 to 40 minutes, until set in the center. Let rest for at least 20 minutes before serving.

▶ LEFTOVERS: Stored in an airtight container, quiche will keep for up to 2 days in the refrigerator.

▶ PREPARATION AND COOKING TIME: 1 hour

Caramelized Onion Quiche

▶ SERVES 5 OR 6

2 white or yellow onions

3 tablespoons butter

½ cup (120 ml) dry white wine

3 eggs

¾ cup (180 ml) milk (whole or 2%)

½ cup (120 ml) heavy cream

1 tablespoon chopped fresh thyme, or 1 teaspoon dried

½ teaspoon salt

¼ teaspoon freshly ground black pepper

2 ounces (60 g) Gruyere or Parmesan cheese, grated (½ cup)

1 prebaked 10-inch (25 cm) tart shell, preferably homemade (page 214)

1. Preheat the oven to 375°F (190°C).
2. Caramelize the onions in the butter, using the method described on page 22. Once the onions are tender, collapsed, and richly golden brown, deglaze with the wine and cook until the liquid is reduced by half. Allow to cool.
3. Whisk together the eggs, milk, cream, thyme, salt, and pepper. Stir in the onions, including any liquid that remains in the pan the onions were cooked in.
4. Sprinkle the cheese over the bottom of the tart shell. Carefully pour the custard into the shell.
5. Bake for 30 to 40 minutes, until set in the center. Let rest for at least 20 minutes before serving.

▶ LEFTOVERS: Stored in an airtight container, quiche will keep for up to 2 days in the refrigerator.

▶ PREPARATION AND COOKING TIME: Up to 2 hours and 30 minutes

BROCCOLI QUICHE WITH CHEDDAR

► **SERVES 5 OR 6**

2 cups (200 g) small broccoli florets

3 eggs

¾ cup (180 ml) milk (whole or 2%)

½ cup (120 ml) heavy cream

½ teaspoon salt

¼ teaspoon cayenne pepper

6 ounces (170 g) sharp Cheddar cheese,
   grated (1½ cups)

1 prebaked 10-inch tart (25 cm) shell, preferably
   homemade (page 214)

1. Preheat the oven to 375°F (190°C).

2. Steam the broccoli florets until tender, 6 to 9
   minutes. Allow to cool slightly.

3. Whisk together the eggs, milk, cream, salt, cayenne, and 1 cup (120 g) of the grated cheese.

4. Sprinkle the remaining ½ cup (50 g) of the
   cheese over the bottom of the tart shell.
   Arrange broccoli over the cheese in an even
   layer. Carefully pour the custard into the shell.

5. Bake for 30 to 40 minutes, until set in the center.
   Let rest for at least 20 minutes before serving.

► **LEFTOVERS:** Stored in an airtight container,
quiche will keep for up to 2 days in the
refrigerator.

► **PREPARATION AND COOKING TIME:** 1 hour

CLASSIC CHEESE SOUFFLÉ

Classic cheese soufflé with variations

ONE DAY IN the dead of winter I was working the lunch shift as a server at a restaurant in Manhattan. A serious blizzard had come through, and aside from my miserable commute from Brooklyn, I had so few tables during my shift that I'd have made more money scrounging underneath the sofa cushions. I was slipping into a grumpy mood but assuaged it by deciding to make cheese soufflé for dinner. On my way home, trudging through the snow, I picked up the ingredients. As soon as I got home, I pried off my snow boots, preheated the oven, and got cooking. It turned out to be the best remedy ever. As evidenced by the ingredients, this dish qualifies more as comfort food than health food, but on some days that's just what's called for. There are endless variations, and I've described a few after the recipe to get you started. If you don't have ramekins or a soufflé dish, you can bake individual soufflés in oven-safe coffee cups; shallow, wide cups work better than tall, skinny ones.

▶ SERVES 3 OR 4

Grated Parmesan cheese for dusting

4 eggs

2 tablespoons butter

1 leek, white and pale green parts, halved lengthwise, sliced into thin half-moons, and cleaned (see page 13), or 2 shallots, minced

1 garlic clove, minced

2 tablespoons all-purpose flour

1 cup (240 ml) milk (whole or 2%)

¾ teaspoon salt

¼ teaspoon freshly ground black pepper

3 ounces (85 g) creamy goat cheese, blue cheese, or Gruyère cheese, crumbled or grated (¾ cup)

1. Preheat the oven to 400°F (200°C). Generously butter four 10-ounce (300 ml) round ramekins or a 1½-quart soufflé dish, and then dust with Parmesan cheese.

2. Separate the eggs, placing the yolks in a small bowl and the whites in a very clean, dry mixing bowl.

3. Melt the butter in a small saucepan over medium-low heat. Add the leek and sauté until tender, about 10 minutes. Stir in the garlic and sauté until fragrant, about 1 minute. Sprinkle the flour over the mixture and cook, whisking constantly, until the mixture has darkened just a shade and smells nutty, 2 to 3 minutes. Pour in the milk in increments, whisking constantly to break up any lumps, then continue cooking and stirring, until thickened and has the consistency of glue, 3 to 5 minutes. Remove from the heat. Whisk in the egg yolks, salt, and pepper, then stir in the cheese.

4. Using an electric mixer on medium to medium-high speed or a good, strong arm, whisk the egg whites until they form soft peaks (see box on page 191). This will take about 2 minutes with a mixer and up to 5 minutes by hand. The whites will quadruple in volume and should just hold their shape on the tip of the whisk. In four batches, fold the whites into the yolk mixture, being careful not to overmix and deflate the whites. Carefully pour the mixture into the prepared baking dish. If making individual soufflés, divide the mixture among

the 4 prepared dishes and place them on a baking sheet.

5. Bake for 20 to 30 minutes for individual soufflés or 30 to 40 minutes for one large soufflé. The top should be browned and set in the center. The soufflé will jiggle a bit but shouldn't appear liquid underneath the surface. Dust the top with Parmesan and serve immediately.

▶ **LEFTOVERS:** Soufflé is best eaten freshly cooked.

▶ **PREPARATION AND COOKING TIME:** 1 hour

variations

CHARD AND CHEESE SOUFFLÉ: Blanch or steam 1 bunch of chard (see page 10) and finely chop it. When you add the cheese to the yolk mixture in step 3, stir in the chard and continue with the recipe. A crumbled, creamy goat cheese is my favorite for this soufflé.

BLACK OLIVE, PARMESAN, AND HERB SOUFFLÉ: Substitute ½ white or yellow onion, minced, for the leek. Omit the garlic. Use Parmesan for the cheese in step 3, and when you stir it in, also add 2 tablespoons Olive Tapenade (page 27, made with black olives), 2 tablespoons minced fresh parsley, and 2 tablespoons minced fresh chives. Proceed with the recipe.

MUSHROOM AND GRUYÈRE SOUFFLÉ: Heat 1 tablespoon oil or butter in a sauté pan over medium heat. Add 8 ounces (230 g) of coarsely chopped cremini mushrooms and sauté until the mushrooms have released their liquid and it cooks off, 6 to 8 minutes. Use Gruyère for the cheese in step 3, and when you stir it in, also add the mushrooms. Proceed with the recipe.

SPINACH, CORN, AND POLENTA SOUFFLÉ

THIS SOUFFLÉ IS more textured and bulkier than the Classic Cheese Soufflé (page 186), and for that reason it's not a temperamental soufflé that sets the clock ticking as soon as it comes out of the oven. I first discovered the idea of using polenta as a base when my editor, Matthew Lore, loaned me Jeanne Lemlin's classic (and, sadly, out of print) cookbook *Vegetarian Pleasures*. Subsequently I learned about corn soufflé as a Christmas dish on Southern tables, and that connection brought me to see it as a hybrid of soufflé and spoon bread. Whatever its genesis, it's a winning vegetarian entrée, and when baked in individual soufflé dishes, it looks as elegant as it tastes. Rogue Creamery in Oregon makes a delicious blue cheese that is actually smoked, called "Smokey Blue," which is especially good in this soufflé, but in lieu of that use your favorite salty blue.

▶ **SERVES 4**

4 eggs

5 ounces (140 g) frozen spinach, or 8 ounces (230 g) fresh

1 cup (240 ml) milk (whole or 2%)

½ cup (120 ml) water or vegetable stock (page 15)

½ cup (70 g) coarse-grind cornmeal or polenta

2 tablespoons butter

¾ cup (90 g) fresh corn kernels (from about 1½ ears) or frozen corn kernels, thawed and drained

4 ounces (115 g) blue cheese, crumbled

½ teaspoon salt

¼ teaspoon freshly ground black pepper

1. Preheat the oven to 375°F (190°C). Generously butter four 10-ounce (300 ml) round ramekins or a 1½-quart soufflé dish.

2. Separate the eggs, placing the yolks in a small bowl and the whites in a very clean, dry mixing bowl.

3. If using fresh spinach, blanch or steam it until tender (see page 10), then finely chop it. If using frozen spinach, defrost it in the microwave, cooking at 2-minute intervals on medium heat, stirring at each interval with a fork, and continuing to cook until thawed. Then drain it and, once cool enough to handle, squeeze out as much liquid as possible. If using whole frozen spinach, finely chop it.

4. Combine the milk and water in a medium saucepan over high heat. Bring to a boil, then turn the heat down to maintain a simmer. Add the polenta in a steady stream, whisking constantly to break up any lumps. Continue simmering and stirring until the polenta has the consistency of oatmeal or porridge (thick, but not so stiff that it appears congealed), 8 to 10 minutes. Remove from the heat and whisk in the butter and egg yolks, then stir in the spinach, corn, cheese, salt, and pepper.

5. Using an electric mixer on medium to medium-high speed or a good, strong arm, whisk the egg whites until they form soft peaks (see sidebar). This will take about 2 minutes with a mixer and up to 5 minutes by hand. The whites will quadruple in volume and should just hold their shape on the tip of a whisk. In four batches, fold the whites into the yolk mixture, being careful not to overmix and deflate the whites. Carefully pour the mixture into the prepared baking dish. If

making individual soufflés, divide the mixture among the prepared dishes and place them on a baking sheet.

6. Bake for 25 to 30 minutes for individual soufflés or 30 to 40 minutes for one large soufflé. The top should be browned, set in the center, and firm to the touch. Serve hot or warm.

▶ **LEFTOVERS:** Wrapped tightly, this soufflé will keep for 1 day in the refrigerator.

▶ **PREPARATION AND COOKING TIME:** 1 hour

AND A NOTE ABOUT EGG SAFETY: Numerous Salmonella outbreaks in recent years have made egg safety (as well as the safety of many other types of foods) a reasonable concern. If you are concerned or if you are pregnant, it's important to cook your eggs until they're fully set. This means that for fried or poached eggs, for example, there should be no runny yolk.

A NOTE ON WHISKING EGG WHITES

WHEN WHISKING egg whites, always wipe the bowl with a clean towel before placing the egg whites in it. Any kind of debris, and especially residual fats or oils—even a slight trace—will hinder the whites from forming peaks. For the same reason, if a yolk breaks while you're separating the egg, it's far preferable to have a bit of whites with the yolks than even a small spot of yolk in the whites.

Recipes for baked goods often recommend adding a bit of cream of tartar to the whites. This gives them a glossy appearance and helps stabilize them, which is important in something like a macaroon, where the stability of the egg whites is crucial. For soufflés and other egg dishes, however, I don't find it necessary to add cream of tartar since the whites don't sit for very long before getting folded into the custard.

sHaKsHuKa

SHAKSHUKA, A POPULAR Israeli dish, is a simple stovetop version of baked eggs. There are limitless variations, especially in terms of spice profiles. The tomato base typically has a spicy kick, with many recipes calling for hot peppers. If you like spicy food, try adding a small chile pepper with a high heat index when you add the onion in the recipe below. While in Paris several years ago, I picked up a jar of *ras el hanout*, a North African spice blend that, like curry powder and garam masala, can vary widely in composition. It's terrific in this kind of tomato sauce. If you can get your hands on some, add a heaping ½ teaspoon with the onion and use only ¾ teaspoon of paprika. Shakshuka makes nice leftovers, as well. Sometimes I like to make a full recipe of the sauce, transfer half of it to a smaller saucepan to cook just two eggs, and save the rest for lunch the next day. I pack the sauce up in a reusable container and eat it cold, with a chopped-up hard-boiled egg mixed in.

▶ SERVES 2

1 tablespoon neutral oil (canola, grapeseed, peanut, or vegetable oil)

1 medium red or yellow onion, diced

1½ teaspoons smoked paprika

Pinch of cayenne pepper

One 28-ounce (794 g) can crushed or diced tomatoes

½ teaspoon packed brown sugar

½ teaspoon salt

4 eggs

Minced fresh parsley for garnish

1. Heat the oil in a sauté pan over medium-high heat. Add the onion, 1 teaspoon of the paprika, and the cayenne and sauté until the onion just begins to soften but still has a bit of crunch, 6 to 8 minutes. Add the tomatoes, sugar, and salt. Lower the heat to maintain a simmer and cook, stirring periodically, until the sauce has reduced slightly and the tomatoes are soft, about 20 minutes. Stir in the remaining ½ teaspoon paprika and taste for salt.

2. Crack an egg into a ¼-cup (60 ml) ladle or measuring cup. Press the bottom of the ladle into the sauce to create a well, then quickly rotate the ladle to slip the egg into the well. (This helps prevent the egg from spreading too much on top of the sauce.) Proceed in the same way with the remaining eggs.

3. Lower the heat, cover, and simmer for 5 to 8 minutes, until the whites are set and the yolks are cooked to the desired doneness (you can gently press the surface of an egg with a thick spatula or butter knife to determine how cooked it is). Garnish with the parsley and serve hot.

VARIATION

To make shakshuka with tofu, substitute tofu for the eggs. Slice 7 ounces (205 g) of tofu (half of a 14-ounce block) into thin rectangles. Line a baking sheet with paper towels and transfer the tofu to the pan in a single layer. Top with more paper towels and a second baking sheet, then place some weight (such as cans or a heavy pot) on top. Let sit for 15 minutes to squeeze out some of the moisture. Cut the tofu slices into any smaller shape you please, stir them into the sauce at the end of step 1, and cook until heated through.

▶ LEFTOVERS: Made with eggs, shakshuka should only be eaten freshly cooked.

▶ PREPARATION AND COOKING TIME:
35 minutes

COOKING FOR ONE

COOKING FOR one should be treated as a special little indulgence, even if you do it all the time. If you cook for yourself often, you probably rely on one or two standbys. Mine is a big salad that I eat out of a mixing bowl. I make it by tossing a bunch of lettuce with other stuff that happens to be in my fridge and topping it with a poached egg. I probably wouldn't ever serve it to someone else, but the ritual of sitting down to eat it every so often—with a stack of reading material, a Rickie Lee Jones album, or the most recent iteration of *The Real Housewives*—is something I take enough pleasure in that I never dread having to eat alone. But there are other ways to cook for one and here are some tips on doing so:

- **USING LEFTOVERS:** Follow recipes as written, rather than scaling them back for smaller quantities, and pack away the leftovers in individual containers. This works well for refrigerated items that will keep for at least a couple of days, like hearty bean salads or pasta dishes. Soups and some baked dishes reheat well, but their recipes may yield more than you can eat in a couple of days. For these and other entrées with higher yields, look for dishes that freeze well.

- **COOKING INDIVIDUAL PORTIONS:** Sometimes the temptation inherent in facing a four-person portion in the privacy of the kitchen (and the comfort of sweatpants) creates an irresistible opportunity to overeat. When cooking for myself, I often use my set of small baking dishes to create built-in portion control. One is a miniature rectangular baking pan that's perfect for an individual piece of lasagna. I also have mini tart shells and individual gratin and soufflé dishes. It can be tricky to scale recipes down to individual portions, but with some tweaking and practice, it's not impossible. Though not a vegetarian cookbook, Jane Doerfer's book *Going Solo in the Kitchen* has wonderful recipes and guidelines on this subject.

- **MAKING A ROUNDED MEAL:** Something I've learned from several excellent cooks is that serving yourself a complete meal enhances the experience of eating alone. Accompaniments need not be complex. A salad is easy enough to throw together for one person, and the same is true of roasted carrots or steamed asparagus. And don't hesitate to treat yourself to dessert—either one of the easy recipes included in this book (see pages 163–166), or a prepared treat from a bakery or grocery store.

■ **SHOPPING AND PLANNING SMART:** It can be tricky to find time to shop properly, let alone make a habit of eating home-cooked food on those nights when you get home from work late and exhausted. A little planning will go a long way toward turning this around. In advance of your workweek, consider what the upcoming week will entail and how much time you'll have to cook. It may be a good idea to spend part of the weekend stocking your freezer and refrigerator with prepared dishes or their components. Soups and baked pastas keep extremely well in the freezer. The main-dish salads in this book keep for a day or two, and also make for excellent lunches. One last tip: If you shop on the weekend, when purchasing perishables consider how much you'll reasonably be able to use during the week so you don't have food going to waste because you've run out of time to cook it.

VEGETARIAN KITCHEN ESSENTIALS

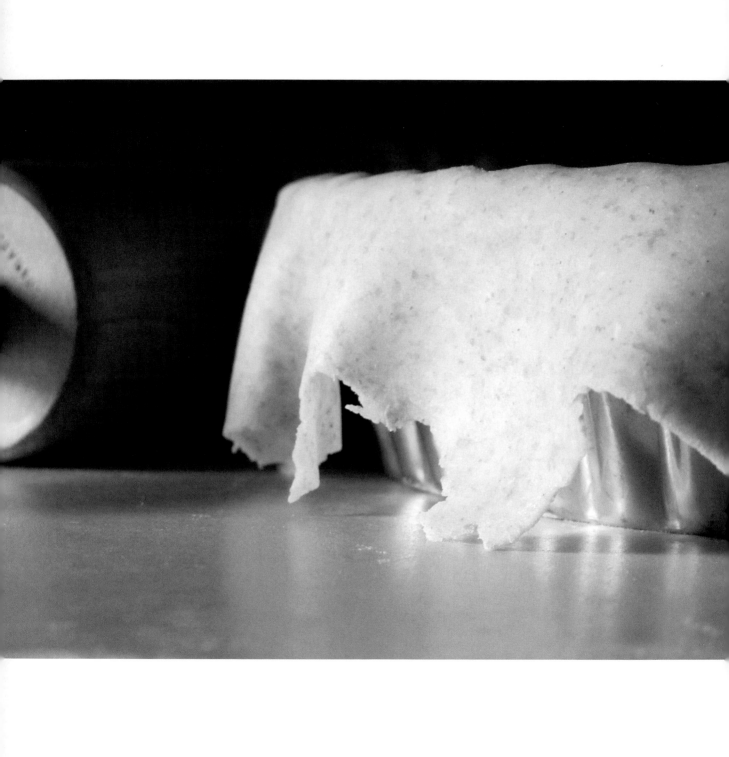

7

PIZZAS, TARTS, GALETTES, AND CREPES

THIS CHAPTER PROVIDES recipes for some of my favorite types of vegetarian entrées. Pizza, tarts, galettes, and crepes are essentially ways of serving vegetables in a vessel fashioned from dough or batter. They can be elegant centerpieces for festive meals, and since many of these dishes don't need to be served hot, you can prepare them in advance and have them sitting on the counter or dinner table to deliciously foreshadow the meal ahead. These entrées can also be made in individual portions, allowing you to experiment with fillings or cater to specific appetites.

I've had wonderful parties where pizzas and crepes acted as interactive entrées. Homemade pizza is especially fun for kids; not only do they enjoy playing with dough, they can also help arrange toppings. I especially enjoy crepe parties with friends. I cook the crepes in advance, along with a smorgasbord of fillings, and then spread everything out on the table. Everyone assembles crepes to order and places them on baking sheets for a brief heating in the oven. These memorable, relatively easy gatherings break the mold of the standard dinner party, where guests are expected to show up, mingle, sit down to eat, and then head home.

Typical recipes for doughs and batters tend to rely on all-purpose flour. These recipes in this chapter, however, aim to capitalize on a few alternative flours by incorporating small doses of whole wheat, spelt, or buckwheat flour. I used to resist this kind of thing. With alternative flours being somewhat expensive, I was discouraged by recipes that called for such small amounts. Once in a while I'd buy a new flour for a recipe, but it would sit around because I didn't know what else to do with it. Eventually, my outlook changed and I began to approach alternative flours with a more adventurous attitude, thinking that as long as I had it on hand, I might as well use it. Now these flours find their way into nearly every baked good I make: cookies, biscuits, breads, waffles, pancakes, flatbreads, you name it. A good place to start is by substituting an alternative flour for one-fourth to one-third of the all-purpose flour in a recipe. Using more than that can compromise the texture and usually requires making adjustments to other ingredients, amounts, or cooking times or temperatures. If this subject interests you, be sure to check out Kim Boyce's excellent book on baking with alternative flours, *Good to the Grain*.

Vegan adaptations for these doughs and batters are relatively easy. In crepes, Ener-G egg replacer can be substituted for the eggs, and any kind of nondairy milk, such as rice, oat, soy, or almond milk, or even water or vegetable stock, can be substituted for the milk. In tart and galette doughs, nondairy margarine (such as Earth Balance) can be substituted for the butter with good results.

Pizza

FOR a long time I believed it wasn't worth the trouble to attempt homemade pizza. Good results seemed impossible without a proper pizza oven, which can reach the high temperatures needed to create the characteristic crusty-chewy crust. My early efforts yielded crusts more like loaf bread: thick, spongy, and overly yeasty. The recipe for pizza dough in this chapter, however, got me very excited about homemade pizza's potential. It features a shortcut sourdough-style starter made with commercial yeast, in which a small amount of flour is mixed with yeast and water and left to ferment. From there, the recipe is traditional as far as home bread making goes. Here are a few helpful guidelines:

■ Get comfortable working with wet dough. This will improve almost all of your bread making, as too much flour makes any bread dense and dry. When kneading, use additional flour as sparingly as possible. I recommend that you knead with one hand and hold a dough scraper in the other, using the scraper to get underneath and flip the dough, as wetter doughs are more inclined to stick to the work surface.

■ Pizza needs to cook in a very hot oven, ideally on a pizza stone, a heavy ceramic or earthenware platter that comes in round, square, and rectangular shapes. My oven only goes up to 500°F, but if yours can go higher, turn it up all the way and give it the time it needs to preheat. If you have a pizza stone, put it in the oven prior to preheating so it will be as hot as possible when the pizza is placed on top of it.

■ Transferring an uncooked pizza onto the hot stone can be tricky. A pizza peel makes the job very easy, but few people own one. If you don't have one, put the pizza on a rimless baking sheet or inverted rimmed baking sheet that's been dusted with semolina or all-purpose flour and bake it on this surface for about 5 minutes, after which the pizza will be sturdy enough to quickly slide onto the stone for the remainder of its time in the oven.

■ If you don't have a pizza stone, you can keep cooking the pizza on the baking sheet, or you can transfer it to the floor of your oven. Just be sure to wipe it down before preheating.

■ One of the nicest things about pizza, in my opinion, is the beauty of its imperfections: the charred splotches on the crust, the cheese that makes a stringy mess when you remove a slice, the rustic, informal scattering of toppings. Free yourself from any notion that your crust must be perfectly round or uniform in thickness. I don't even recommend using a rolling pin to shape the pizza; I like to either stretch it out over my clenched fists or pat it out into a rough circle with my hands. But if you're a person who leads a more orderly life, then by all means use a rolling pin.

Basic Whole Wheat Pizza Dough

THIS RECIPE IS endlessly adaptable. In this chapter it's used in recipes for baked, grilled, and panfried pizzas, as well as calzones, but it's also great for flatbreads, focaccia, or soft bread sticks. Feel free to substitute another whole-grain flour for the whole wheat; spelt and rye both make for flavorful variations.

▶ MAKES ONE 14-INCH (35 cm) PIZZA, WHICH WILL SERVE 4

1 packet active dry yeast (2¼ teaspoons, 21 g)

⅓ cup (80 ml) warm water, 105° to 115°F

¾ cup (90 g) whole wheat flour

⅔ cup (160 ml) room-temperature water

¾ teaspoon kosher salt

1 tablespoon olive oil, plus more for coating

1 cup (120 g) all-purpose flour, plus more if needed

1. In a mixing bowl or the bowl of a stand mixer, dissolve the yeast in the warm water. Stir in ¼ cup (30 g) of the whole wheat flour until it forms a tacky paste. Let stand for 20 to 25 minutes, until the surface is dimpled with air bubbles.

2. Add the ⅔ cup (160 ml) room-temperature water, along with the salt, olive oil, ⅔ cup (80 g) of the all-purpose flour, and the remaining ½ cup (60 g) of the whole wheat flour.

3. **If using a stand mixer,** mix with the paddle attachment on medium-low speed until the ingredients are combined, about 2 minutes, and switch to the dough hook. Knead at medium speed adding more of the all-purpose flour as needed, until the dough is smooth but still somewhat sticky, 5 to 8 minutes. Resist adding more flour than needed. It should pull off the sides of the bowl but stick to the bottom in a somewhat viscous mass.

   If making the dough by hand, stir with a wooden spoon or spatula, adding more of the all-purpose flour as needed until the dough just holds its shape and can be turned out onto a kneading surface. The dough should be sticky, so I recommend kneading with one hand and using a dough scraper in the other to assist with flipping the dough; if you add too much flour the crust will be dense and not chewy. Knead until the dough is smooth but still somewhat sticky, 8 to 10 minutes.

4. (*Note:* To save the dough for use later, skip this step and see the box at right.) Rub a bit of olive oil over the dough, cover with a tea towel or plastic wrap, and let rest in a warm place until doubled in size, 45 minutes to 1 hour.

FREEZING PIZZA DOUGH

IF YOU'RE dividing pizza dough into smaller portions, you may want to refrigerate or freeze some of the dough. To do this, divide the dough into portions prior to the first rise and place the portions in individual airtight containers.

* The dough won't rise in the freezer, so if freezing, use a container that is as close to the size of the dough as possible. The night before you want to cook the pizza, rub a bit of oil on the dough, transfer it to a bowl, cover with plastic wrap, and refrigerate overnight. About 1 hour before shaping the dough, move it to the countertop and let rest at room temperature until doubled in size, then proceed with shaping as directed in the recipe.

* Dough stored in the refrigerator will continue to rise slowly, so it should be placed in a container that is at least double the size of the dough. It can be refrigerated for up to 2 days. About 1 hour before shaping the dough, move it to the countertop and let rest at room temperature until doubled in size, then proceed with shaping as directed in the recipe.

BAKED PIZZA

AS PREVIOUSLY NOTED, it's tricky for a home oven to mimic a proper pizza oven, which is typically large, sometimes domed, and always capable of very high heats. But crank your oven dial up as high as it will go and be sure to use a pizza stone, and you'll have homemade pizza that certainly rivals any pizza you can order in.

▶ SERVES 4

1 recipe Basic Whole Wheat Pizza Dough (page 200)
Cornmeal, semolina, or all-purpose flour for dusting
Toppings of your choice (see pages 208–212)

1. Oil a baking sheet. Turn the dough out onto a clean surface that's been lightly dusted with flour. Gently shape the dough into a 6-inch (15 cm) round. Place it on the oiled baking sheet and let rest until doubled in size, 30 to 45 minutes. Meanwhile, place a pizza stone in the oven and preheat the oven to 500°F (260°C) or as high as it will go. While you're waiting for the dough to rise, prepare your pizza toppings.

2. Dust another baking sheet with cornmeal, semolina, or all-purpose flour. To shape the dough, pat it into a 14-inch (35 cm) round on the baking sheet. Alternatively, stretch the dough by hand, by draping it over your clenched fists and moving your fists in opposite directions; rotate the dough 90 degrees and stretch it in the other direction until you have a round that's roughly 14 inches (35 cm) in diameter. Place the round on the cornmeal-dusted baking sheet. Don't worry if it isn't perfectly round or perfectly even in thickness.

3. Place your toppings on the pizza and brush the edges of the crust with olive oil.

4. Bake the pizza, still on the dusted baking sheet, for 5 minutes, just until the bottom is firm. Using gloved hands and a large spatula, carefully transfer the pizza to the pizza stone. Bake for 5 to 7 more minutes, until the edges of the crust are golden and the bottom of the pizza is deeply browned.

▶ LEFTOVERS: Pizza is best eaten freshly cooked, but wrapped tightly, it will keep for up to 2 days in the refrigerator.

▶ PREPARATION AND COOKING TIME: About 3 hours

GRILLED PIZZA

GRILLED PIZZA IS a delicacy for me, since I don't often have access to a grill where I live in New York. When stretched as directed below, this crust is especially good on the grill. The thin patches of crust char into flavorful, crispy bites, and the thicker parts become plump and tender without being overly bready.

▶ MAKES TWO 10-INCH (25 cm) PIZZAS; SERVES 4

1 recipe Basic Whole Wheat Pizza Dough (page 200)
Cornmeal, semolina, or all-purpose flour for dusting
Toppings of your choice (see pages 208–212)

1. Oil a baking sheet. Turn the dough out onto a clean surface, lightly dusting the surface with flour if the dough is too loose or sticky to manage. Divide it into 2 equal portions and gently shape them into rounds. Set the rounds on the oiled baking sheet with at least 4 inches (10 cm) between them and let rest until doubled in size, 30 to 45 minutes.

2. Meanwhile, prepare a very hot grill at least 30 minutes before grilling the pizzas so that you have very hot embers. While you're waiting for the dough to rise, also prepare your pizza toppings.

3. Dust 2 baking sheets with cornmeal, semolina, or all-purpose flour. Shape each piece of dough by draping it over your clenched fists and moving your fists in opposite directions, rotating the dough so that it stretches somewhat evenly, until you have a round that's about 10 inches (25 cm) in diameter. Place the stretched dough directly on the hot grill.

4. Leaving the lid open, grill for 2 to 3 minutes, until the bottom is browned and charred. Using a large spatula, flip the crust onto a cornmeal-dusted baking sheet. Shape the second crust in the same fashion as the first one, and place it on the grill. While it cooks, arrange your toppings on the cooked side of the first crust. With grilled pizzas, it's best to go light on the toppings.

5. After removing the partially cooked second crust from the grill and transferring it to a cornmeal-dusted baking sheet, close the lid and allow the grill to heat up again. As it heats up, arrange your toppings on the second pizza.

6. Quickly place the first topped pizza on the grill and close the lid. Cook for 3 to 4 minutes, until the bottom is browned and charred, the toppings are heated through, and the cheese melted. Quickly remove the first pizza, place the second pizza on the grill, and cook in the same way. Serve immediately.

▶ LEFTOVERS: Pizza is best eaten freshly cooked, but wrapped tightly, it will keep for up to 2 days in the refrigerator.

▶ PREPARATION AND COOKING TIME:
About 3 hours

PANFRIED PIZZA ✺

THIS IS A great method for making smaller portions of pizza. I love to make it this way for friends, letting them shape and dress their pizzas (and even cook them, especially if you have an extra sauté pan) as they please. If cooking for just one or two, you can freeze portions of the dough as described in the box on page 203, making it easier to prepare homemade pizza whenever you wish. And if you forgo the toppings, except perhaps a drizzle of olive oil and a dusting of flaky salt and fresh herbs, cooking the basic pizza dough in this way makes a great flatbread.

▶ **MAKES FOUR 8- TO 9-INCH (20–23 cm) PIZZAS; SERVES 4**

1 recipe Basic Whole Wheat Pizza Dough (page 200)
Cornmeal, semolina, or all-purpose flour for dusting
Toppings of your choice (see pages 208–212)

1. Oil a baking sheet. Turn the dough out onto a clean surface, that's been lightly dusted with flour. Divide the dough into 4 equal portions and gently shape them into rounds. Set the rounds on the oiled baking sheet with at least 4 inches between them and let rest until doubled in size, 30 to 45 minutes. While you're waiting for the dough to rise, prepare your pizza toppings.

2. Heat a 10-inch (25 cm) skillet over medium heat. Lightly grease the skillet with only a thin film of olive oil; I find it's best to use a brush or to wipe the pan with a paper towel that's been moistened with olive oil. While you cook the individual pizzas, keep the remaining portions of dough covered with a tea towel to prevent them from drying out.

3. To shape the dough, pat each portion into an 8- to 9-inch (20–23 cm) round on the baking sheet. Alternatively, stretch the dough by hand, by draping it over your clenched fists and moving your fists in opposite directions, rotating the dough so that it stretches somewhat evenly. If panfrying multiple pizzas, preheat the oven to 300°F (150°C).

4. Lay the stretched dough directly in the preheated sauté pan and cook until the bottom begins to brown and even char in places, 4 to 6 minutes. Placing the uncooked side down, transfer the dough to a plate or baking sheet that's been dusted with cornmeal, semolina, or all-purpose flour, then cook the next round. Proceed with the remaining dough. Avoid stacking the partially cooked crusts on top of each other, as they will stick together.

5. Once all of the crusts are cooked on one side, arrange your toppings on the cooked side of the first crust and place it back in the pan, uncooked side down. Cook until the bottom is browned and even slightly charred, the toppings are heated through, and the cheese is melted. Repeat with the other crusts. To keep the pizzas warm as you continue cooking, transfer them to the preheated oven.

▶ **LEFTOVERS:** Pizza is best eaten freshly cooked, but wrapped tightly, it will keep for up to 2 days in the refrigerator.

▶ **PREPARATION AND COOKING TIME:** About 3 hours

Calzones ✦

CALZONES, OR PIZZA POCKETS, are more of a
knife-and-fork affair than standard pizza,
served with tomato sauce on the side.
Of course, Twenty-Minute Tomato Sauce
(page 24) makes a good accompaniment.
Rather than filling calzones with
individual toppings, I like to cook a
mixed filling, such as in the recipe for
Three-Pepper Calzones (page 212). Like
Panfried Pizza (page 206), calzones are
fun to make with friends.

▶ **MAKES 4 LARGE CALZONES; SERVES 4**

1 recipe Basic Whole Wheat Pizza Dough (page 200)
Cornmeal, semolina, or all-purpose flour for dusting
Fillings of your choice (see pages 208–212)
1 egg, beaten, optional

1. Oil a baking sheet. Turn the dough out onto
   a clean surface that's been lightly dusted with
   flour. Divide the dough into 4 equal portions
   and gently shape them into rounds. Set the
   rounds on the oiled baking sheet with at least
   4 inches between them and let rest until doubled in size, 30 to 45 minutes.

2. Meanwhile, place a pizza stone in the oven
   and preheat the oven to 500°F (260°C) or as
   high as it will go. While you're waiting for the
   dough to rise, prepare your pizza toppings.

3. Dust a rimless baking sheet or an inverted
   rimmed baking sheet with flour. To shape the
   dough, pat each portion into a 7-inch (18 cm)
   round on the baking sheet. Lay each circle on
   the baking sheet and top with your fillings,
   just off center.

4. Fold the dough over the toppings and press to
   seal the edges together. Using the tines of a
   fork, press down all along the perimeter of the
   joined edge to ensure that it's sealed. Proceed
   in the same manner with the remaining portions of dough, assembling them on a dusted
   work surface, such as a cutting board, if there
   isn't adequate space on the baking sheet.

5. If desired, make an egg wash by whisking the
   egg with 1 tablespoon water. Brush the calzones with egg wash, if desired, then use a
   sharp paring knife to make a few slits across
   the tops of each calzone, which will allow
   steam to release as they cook. Place the baking sheet in the oven and bake until firmed
   slightly, about 8 minutes. Transfer the calzones to the pizza stone and continue cooking until browned and crisp, another 12 to 17
   minutes.

▶ **LEFTOVERS:** Calzones are best eaten freshly
cooked, but wrapped tightly, they will keep for
up to 2 days in the refrigerator.

▶ **PREPARATION AND COOKING TIME:**
About 3 hours

TOPPINGS FOR PIZZAS AND FILLINGS FOR CALZONES

HERE ARE SEVERAL different topping ideas for pizzas—some classic combinations as well as a few new ideas. To turn pizza into a hearty vegetarian dish, it's important to choose toppings that will add a nutritional punch, such as kale, lentils, or combinations of fresh vegetables, but that won't weigh down the pizza. My favorite approach is to find a way to fashion leftover vegetables, or even leftovers like sauces or salads, into toppings, so in that vein I encourage you to improvise. The farmers' market is also a source of inspiration, and my pizzas often showcase whatever vegetables are in season.

CLASSIC MARGARITA PIZZA

MARGARITA PIZZA GETS away with being so simple because every ingredient counts. The quality of the crust, sauce, cheese, and basil will result in a perfect pizza in which everything shines but nothing overwhelms.

▶ **MAKES ENOUGH FOR 1 BAKED PIZZA, 2 GRILLED PIZZAS, 4 PANFRIED PIZZAS, OR 4 CALZONES**

2 garlic cloves, minced

2 tablespoons olive oil

4 ounces (115 ml) fresh mozzarella cheese, thinly sliced

1 cup (240 ml) Twenty-Minute Tomato Sauce (page 24) or other simple tomato sauce

½ cup (20 g) loosely packed fresh basil leaves, coarsely torn

Freshly ground black pepper or red pepper flakes

1. Combine the garlic and olive oil in a small bowl. Infuse for at least 20 minutes as you prepare to cook the pizza.

2. Spread the sauce over the crust, then arrange the cheese on top. Cook according to your preferred crust method. Just before serving, scatter the basil leaves over the pizza, drizzle with the garlic oil, and sprinkle with pepper or pepper flakes to taste. (If making calzones, drizzle the oil over the fillings before sealing the calzones.)

Kale Pesto Pizza

THIS IS A good pizza for skeptics of dark greens like kale—everyone I serve this pizza to is surprised when I report that kale is the dominating ingredient.

▶ MAKES ENOUGH FOR 1 BAKED PIZZA, 2 GRILLED PIZZAS, 4 PANFRIED PIZZAS, OR 4 CALZONES

2 garlic cloves, minced
2 tablespoons olive oil
1 recipe Kale-Almond Pesto (page 26)
1 cup (225 g) fresh ricotta cheese
2 cups (280 g) cherry tomatoes, halved
½ medium red onion, very thinly sliced
Salt
Freshly ground black pepper

1. Combine the garlic and olive oil in a small bowl. Infuse for at least 20 minutes as you prepare to cook the pizza.

2. Spread the pesto over the crust, dividing it evenly among the crusts if making calzones or multiple smaller pizzas. Arrange dollops of the ricotta evenly over the pesto, followed by the tomatoes and onion. Cook according to your preferred crust method. Just before serving, drizzle with the garlic oil and season with the salt and pepper. (If making calzones, drizzle the oil over the fillings and add seasoning before sealing the calzones.)

Lentil, Roasted Garlic, Caramelized Onion, and Feta Pizza

THIS COMBINATION OF toppings is inspired by a favorite pasta dish, and the idea of making something like hummus from lentils. Make sure to fully caramelize your onions so that they are as sweet and rich as possible.

▶ MAKES ENOUGH FOR 1 BAKED PIZZA OR 4 PANFRIED PIZZAS (NOT RECOMMENDED FOR GRILLED PIZZA OR CALZONES)

¾ cup (120 g) green lentils
1½ cups water, or more as needed
2 tablespoons butter or olive oil
1 large white onion, sliced into thin rings
¼ teaspoon salt
¼ teaspoon freshly ground black pepper
¼ cup (5 g) fresh flat-leaf parsley
2 tablespoons olive oil, or more as needed
Pulp or flesh from 2 heads roasted garlic, skins discarded (page 20)
6 ounces (170 g) feta cheese, crumbled

1. Combine the lentils and water in a small saucepan. Bring to a boil, then lower the heat, cover, and simmer for 25 minutes, until tender, adding more water if necessary.

2. Melt the butter or heat the oil in a heavy-bottomed sauté pan and, using the method on page 22, caramelize the onion. Let stand until cool enough to handle.

3. Put the lentils, salt, pepper, parsley, and olive oil in a food processor and process until coarsely ground and spreadable, adding additional oil if the mixture seems too thick.

4. Spread the lentil puree over the crust, followed by the caramelized onions. Dot with the roasted garlic and feta cheese. Cook according to your preferred crust method.

"BREAKFAST" PIZZA

"BREAKFAST" PIZZA ISN'T named as such to discourage you from eating it at dinner—though I have eaten a few versions at restaurants for brunch—but rather to contextualize its combination of flavors and ingredients. It literally is breakfast on a pizza.

▶ MAKES ENOUGH FOR 1 BAKED PIZZA (NOT RECOMMENDED FOR GRILLED PIZZA, PANFRIED PIZZA, OR CALZONES)

1 large russet potato (about 12 ounces, 325 g)

2 tablespoons butter

1 tablespoon neutral oil (canola, grapeseed, peanut, or vegetable oil)

1 red, yellow, or orange bell pepper, diced

4 scallions, white and pale green parts, thinly sliced

Salt

Freshly ground black pepper

4 ounces (115 g) fresh mozzarella, thinly sliced

2 ounces (60 g) Parmesan cheese, grated (½ cup)

4 eggs

2 tablespoons minced fresh parsley

1. Preheat the oven to 400°F (200°C). Prick the potato all over with a fork and wrap it in aluminum foil. Bake for 1 hour, until completely tender. Alternatively, microwave for 10 minutes on high power, until completely tender. Let stand until cool enough to handle. (The potato can be prepared a day or two in advance.)

2. Grate the potato using the large holes of a box grater, discarding the large pieces of potato skin that remain. Blot the grated potato dry with a paper towel.

3. Melt the butter and oil in a sauté pan over medium heat. When the foaming subsides, add the bell pepper and sauté until softened, 5 to 7 minutes. Add the scallions and sauté until just fragrant, about 1 minute. Stir in the potato, press it into the pan, and cook, without stirring, for 5 minutes. Break up the potato with a spatula, flip so that the uncooked part is face-down on the pan, and continue cooking for another 5 minutes, until uniformly browned. Remove from the heat and season with salt and pepper.

4. To assemble the pizzas, arrange the mozzarella on the crust, then scatter the Parmesan over it. Arrange the potato on top, then crack the eggs directly onto the pizza. Bake until the whites are set and the yolks are cooked to the desired doneness, 8 to 12 minutes. Garnish with the parsley and additional pepper.

ZUCCHINI PIZZA WITH TOMATOES AND RICOTTA

THIS PIZZA IS bursting with the simple flavors of summer. I prefer using Mint-Walnut Pesto (page 26), but any variety will do. I especially recommend this pizza for cooking on the grill.

▶ **MAKES ENOUGH FOR 1 BAKED PIZZA, 2 GRILLED PIZZAS, OR 4 PANFRIED PIZZAS (NOT RECOMMENDED FOR CALZONES)**

2 small zucchini, cut into ⅛-inch (5 mm) rounds
Salt
1 cup (225 g) fresh ricotta cheese

1 ounce (30 g) Parmesan cheese, grated (¼ cup)
1 cup (140 g) cherry tomatoes, halved
1 cup (240 ml) Mint-Walnut Pesto (page 26; a double batch)
Big pinch of salt
Freshly ground black pepper

1. Lay out the zucchini rounds on a double layer of paper towels or a tea towel. Sprinkle with salt and let stand for 15 minutes. Blot off the moisture.
2. Spread the ricotta over the crust, then sprinkle with the Parmesan. Arrange the zucchini and tomatoes over the cheese, then dollop the pesto on top.
3. Cook according to your preferred crust method.

POTATO AND ROSEMARY PIZZA

ANOTHER SIMPLE PIZZA, this one becomes more refined by using fresh, young potatoes from the farmers' market. There's no way to describe them except "potato-ey"—I'm an Idaho native, but when I started shopping frequently at farmers' markets, the delicate flavor of a potato was a revelation.

► **MAKES ENOUGH FOR 1 BAKED PIZZA OR 2 GRILLED PIZZAS (NOT RECOMMENDED FOR PANFRIED PIZZA, OR CALZONES)**

2 garlic cloves, minced

2 tablespoons olive oil

1 pound (450 g) small Yukon Gold or red bliss potatoes

6 ounces (170 g) Gruyère cheese, grated (1½ cups)

1 tablespoon coarsely chopped fresh rosemary

Freshly ground black pepper

1. Combine the garlic and 1 tablespoon of the olive oil in a small bowl. Infuse for at least 20 minutes as you prepare to cook the pizza.

2. Cut the potatoes into rounds, slicing them as thinly as possible and using a mandoline if you have one.

3. Scatter the cheese over the crust and arrange the potatoes on top. Sprinkle the rosemary over the potatoes, then drizzle the remaining 1 tablespoon of olive oil over the potatoes.

4. Cook according to your preferred crust method. Just before serving, drizzle with the garlic oil.

THREE-PEPPER CALZONES

THIS IS MY go-to filling for calzones—the peppers are bulky, textured, and hugely flavorful, and all the more delicious when the mozzarella cheese oozes out once you take your first bite.

► **MAKES ENOUGH FILLING FOR 4 CALZONES**

2 tablespoons neutral oil (canola, grapeseed, peanut, or vegetable oil)

1 large onion, sliced into thin rounds

1 tablespoon coarsely chopped fresh oregano, or 1 teaspoon dried oregano

2 garlic cloves, minced

2 jalapeños, minced (seeded for a milder heat level)

1 green bell pepper, cut into ¼-inch (5 mm) strips

1 red, yellow, or orange bell pepper, cut into ¼-inch (5 mm) strips

¼ teaspoon salt

8 ounces (230 g) fresh mozzarella cheese, thinly sliced

1. Heat the oil in a wide sauté pan over medium-high heat. Add the onion and cook, stirring only periodically so as to encourage the onion to develop char marks, until just softened, 4 to 6 minutes. Add the oregano and garlic, stir briefly, then add all of the peppers. Cook, again stirring only periodically, until the peppers have softened on their exterior but still retain a bit of crunch, 10 to 12 minutes. Add the salt and taste for seasonings, then allow to cool.

2. Divide the cheese over the calzone crusts, distributing it slightly off center, then top with the pepper mixture. Proceed with the calzone recipe on page 207.

Tarts and Galettes

IF YOU'VE made piecrust, you'll be a pro with tart and galette crusts, because the principles here are the same. It's important to use restraint in breaking up the butter as you cut it into the dough; you want small morsels of butter to remain in the dough. Using ice-cold water helps prevent it from melting as you finish mixing the dough, and as the dough chills in the refrigerator, the butter will firm back up. Then, when you roll out the dough, the cold butter pieces will be flattened into long, thin disks that melt and leave hollows in the crust during baking. Those hollows are what makes the crust flaky.

If you use a food processor, making these crusts will be a breeze. But the dough can also be made by hand without too much fuss. In that case, it's worth owning a pastry blender, a very inexpensive tool that's much easier to use to cut in the butter than two knives or a fork, as some recipes suggest.

Just as with piecrusts, it's often important to prebake tart shells. You'll need pie weights or something similar for this step. Pie weights, which look like marbles with a dull finish, aren't expensive, but they do violate one of my kitchen rules, which is to never buy anything that only has one use (for example, an olive pitter, lemon zester, or egg separator). I first heard about using pennies as pie weights on an episode of *America's Test Kitchen* and haven't looked back. You only need enough pennies to cover the base of the tart, so about a dollar's worth will do. One caveat: Although a layer of parchment paper or foil prevents them from being in direct contact with the food, it's a good idea to give them a quick wash first.

As far as fillings go, there are limitless options. I think the best fillings for tarts are those with a custardlike element, which will set during baking. For many recipes, fillings are arranged inside the tart, then the custard is poured over them. With galettes, on the other hand, the filling must be able to hold its own on top of the crust, as it's only slightly contained by the edges of the crust, which are folded over the perimeter of the filling.

Basic Tart Shell

THIS IS AN all-purpose shell for tarts, quiches, and even desserts. (If using this recipe for a sweet tart, add 1 teaspoon of sugar when you add the flour.) As with pizza crust, making this provides a fun opportunity to experiment with alternate flours. The first step, making the dough and then refrigerating it, can be done up to a day in advance.

▶ MAKES ONE 9-INCH (23 cm) TART SHELL

1 cup (120 g) all-purpose flour, plus more for dusting

⅓ cup (40 g) whole wheat pastry flour or whole wheat, rye, or spelt flour

½ teaspoon salt

7 tablespoons (100 g) cold unsalted butter, cut into ¼-inch cubes

3 to 6 tablespoons ice water

1. **If using a food processor,** put the flours and salt in the food processor and pulse until combined. Add the butter all at once and pulse 30 to 35 times, until the butter is cut down to lumpy morsels about the size of peas. Add 3 tablespoons of the water and pulse a few times. Watching for the mixture to come together, add additional water, 1 tablespoon at a time. When the mixture is uniformly moistened and a handful holds together without crumbling, stop processing. Spread a piece of plastic wrap on a work surface and pour the mixture into the middle of it. Lift the wrap by its corners and, working from outside the wrap, gently compact the dough into a squat disk about 4 inches (10 cm) in diameter. Wrap it tightly and refrigerate for at least 30 minutes and up to 24 hours.

   If making the dough by hand, put the flours and salt in bowl and whisk to combine. Working quickly with a pastry blender, cut the butter into the flour until it's broken into lumpy morsels about the size of peas. Sprinkle 3 tablespoons of the water over the mixture and incorporate it using a spatula or your hands. Add more water, 1 tablespoon at a time, until the mixture just begins to gather into a mass. Using your hands, shape the mixture into a disk about 4 inches (10 cm) in diameter. Wrap it tightly with plastic wrap and refrigerate for at least 30 minutes and up to 24 hours.

2. Lightly dust a rolling pin and a work surface with flour and place the chilled dough in the center. Roll the disk into a circle about 13 inches (33 cm) in diameter and

about ⅛ inch (3 mm) thick, rolling outward from the center of the dough and rotating the dough 90 degrees after each roll. If the dough sticks to the work surface, use a dough scraper to lift it up and toss a bit of flour underneath. Don't fret if the dough begins to tear at the edges.

3. Preheat the oven to 400°F (200°C).

4. Drape the rolled-out dough over a rolling pin and carefully transfer it to a 10-inch (25 cm) tart pan. Gently tuck the dough into the pan without stretching it, then trim any excess. (You can do this by running the rolling pin across the rim of the tart pan.) Press the dough into the edges with your fingertips. Cover with plastic wrap and refrigerate for at least 20 minutes. (Note: At this point, the tart shell can be wrapped tightly and frozen for up to 1 month. Thaw it overnight in the refrigerator before proceeding with the recipe.)

5. Prick the base of the shell all over with the tines of a fork. Place a piece of parchment paper over it, then fill with pie weights, dried beans, or pennies. Bake for 15 minutes. Remove the parchment paper and weights and bake for 5 to 7 minutes, until the bottom of the shell begins to brown. At this point, the tart can be filled and baked.

CauLIFLOWER-LeeK TarT

THIS RICH, EASY tart uses much less
dairy than similar tarts and quiches
do, thanks in large part to the humble
cauliflower's natural richness. And the
cauliflower really shines here, with
the backdrop of Gruyère cheese and
leek and the final touch of scallions
elevating and transforming the
vegetable from a standby for crudité
platters to something refined. This type
of cauliflower dish will also be exactly
what you're craving when the vegetable
is in season—in early fall, as a cold
front starts to blow through.

▶ **SERVES 4**

1 tablespoon butter

1 leek, white part only, quartered lengthwise, thinly
    sliced, and cleaned (see page 13)

Pinch of sugar

¼ cup (60 ml) dry white wine

3 cups cauliflower florets (about 12 ounces)

2 eggs

⅓ cup (80 ml) cream or half-and-half

2 teaspoons Dijon mustard

½ teaspoon salt

¼ teaspoon ground white pepper

2 teaspoons all-purpose flour

2 scallions, white and green parts, thinly sliced

4 ounces (115 g) Gruyère cheese, grated (1 cup)

1 prebaked 10-inch (25 cm) tart shell, preferably
    homemade (page 214)

1. Preheat the oven to 325°F (160°C).
2. Heat the butter in a deep sauté pan or saucepan over medium-low heat. Add the leek and sugar, cover, and cook for 5 minutes to steam and soften. Uncover and cook until tender, 10 more minutes, lowering the heat if the leeks begin to burn. Stir in the wine and cauliflower. Cover and cook until the cauliflower is completely tender, about 10 minutes.
3. Transfer the cauliflower mixture, along with any liquid from the pan, to a food processor and process until smooth. Whisk the eggs, cream, mustard, salt, pepper, and flour together. Add the mixture to the food processor and pulse until combined. Add the scallions and half of the cheese and pulse a few times, just until distributed. Alternatively, puree the cauliflower with an immersion blender, then whisk in the custard mixture, followed by the scallions and half of the cheese.
4. Sprinkle the remaining cheese over the base of the prebaked tart shell. Pour in the cauliflower mixture and spread it evenly with a spatula. Bake for 25 to 35 minutes, until set in the center. Allow to cool for about 10 minutes before slicing and serving.

▶ **LEFTOVERS:** Wrapped tightly, this tart will keep for up to 2 days in the refrigerator.

▶ **PREPARATION AND COOKING TIME:** 1 hour

TOMATO AND RICOTTA TART WITH BASIL

ONLY MAKE THIS simple tart in the summer, when succulent, perfectly ripe tomatoes are at their absolute peak. Inferior ones will disappoint. The cheese custard can be taken in a number of different directions. Sometimes I make this tart with a lesser amount of pungent, creamy blue cheese (about ⅔ cup) to excellent effect. And if you're pressed for time, this tart is a good candidate for replacing the shell with frozen puff pastry. Allow the pastry to thaw in the refrigerator, then roll it out to a thickness of slightly less than ¼ inch (about 5 mm) and line the pan with it. It's not necessary to prebake the puff pastry. This adaptation works especially well for individual tart molds.

▶ SERVES 4

1 pound (450 g) ripe tomatoes, sliced ¼ inch (5 mm) thick

1 teaspoon kosher salt

2 eggs

1 cup (225 g) fresh ricotta cheese

½ cup (120 ml) reduced-fat milk (1% or 2%)

A few grinds of black pepper

¼ cup (60 ml) pesto, preferably homemade (such as Basil-Almond or Mint-Walnut, see pages 25 and 26)

1 prebaked 10-inch (25 cm) tart shell, preferably homemade (page 214), or 1 sheet frozen puff pastry, thawed

8 to 10 perfect fresh basil leaves for garnish

1. Preheat the oven to 375°F (190°C).
2. Arrange the tomato slices in a single layer in a colander or on a cooling rack placed over a baking sheet. Sprinkle with ¼ teaspoon of the salt and let sit for at least 10 minutes to drain.
3. Whisk the eggs, ricotta, milk, pepper, and the remaining ¾ teaspoon salt together.
4. Pour the ricotta mixture into the tart shell, then arrange the tomatoes on top, overlapping if necessary. Dollop the pesto over the tomatoes. Bake for 15 to 20 minutes, just until the filling is set. Scatter the basil leaves over the top and serve right away.

▶ LEFTOVERS: Wrapped tightly, this tart will keep for up to 2 days in the refrigerator.

▶ PREPARATION AND COOKING TIME: 45 minutes

GALETTE DOUGH

I WAS LATE to incorporate galettes into my repertoire, but I've been making up for lost time. With a galette you don't have to press the dough into a tart shell, and you also don't have that second chilling period, which shortens the prep time, making for a significantly more manageable weeknight meal. Fillings for galettes also don't need to set up as do those for custard-style tarts; in this book I have recipes that utilize braised red cabbage and roasted Brussels sprouts, and in neither case are the fillings bound together with eggs.

▶ **MAKES CRUST FOR ONE 9 TO 10-INCH (23–25 cm) GALETTE**

¾ cup (90 g) all-purpose flour, plus more for dusting

¼ cup (30 g) whole wheat pastry flour or whole wheat, rye, or spelt flour

½ teaspoon salt

6 tablespoons (85 g) cold unsalted butter, cut into ¼-inch cubes

2 to 4 tablespoons ice water

1. **If using a food processor,** put the flours and salt in the food processor and pulse until combined. Add the butter all at once and pulse 30 to 35 times, until it's cut down to lumpy morsels about the size of peas. Add 2 tablespoons of the water and pulse a few times. Watching for the mixture to come together, add additional water, pulsing it in 1 tablespoon at a time. Stop processing as soon as the mixture is uniformly moistened and a handful holds together without crumbling. Spread a piece of plastic wrap on a work surface and pour the mixture into the middle of it. Lift the wrap by its corners and, working from outside the wrap, gently compact the dough into a squat disk about 4 inches (10 cm) in diameter. Wrap it tightly and refrigerate for at least 30 minutes and up to 24 hours.

   If making the dough by hand, put the flours and salt in a bowl and whisk to combine. Working quickly with a pastry blender, cut the butter into the flour until it's broken into lumpy morsels about the size of peas. Sprinkle 2 tablespoons of the water over the mixture and incorporate it using a spatula or your hands. Add more water, 1 tablespoon at a time, until the mixture just begins to gather into a mass. Using your hands, shape the mixture into a disk about 4 inches (10 cm) in diameter. Wrap it tightly with plastic wrap and refrigerate for at least 30 minutes and up to 24 hours.

2. Preheat the oven as instructed in the recipe for the galette you're making.

3. Lightly dust a rolling pin and a work surface with flour and place the chilled dough in the center. Roll the disk into a circle about 12 inches in diameter and between ⅛ and ¼ inch (5 mm) thick, rolling outward from the center of the dough and rotating the dough 90 degrees after each roll. If the dough sticks to the work surface, use a dough scraper to lift it up and toss a bit of flour underneath. Don't fret if the dough begins to tear at the edges.

4. Evenly spread your fillings over the crust, leaving a 1½-inch (4 cm) border. Fold the edge over the filling, pleating as needed. This is a rustic tart, so enjoy the imperfections. Proceed with the recipe.

RED CABBAGE GALETTE

HERE'S A WINTRY galette that makes a terrific centerpiece for a dinner party. Red cabbage strikes me as a maligned vegetable, overlooked in favor of its green counterparts or the smaller heads of radicchio. (Radicchio belongs to the chicory family, not the cabbage family, but I find its flavor and appearance similar enough that I think of the two as related.) Red cabbage is snappier than green and tastes less cabbagey— there's less of that distinctive smell

that I associate with fermentation—but it shares its nutritional perks. In this recipe, the apple fully dissolves into the filling, leaving behind just an orchard perfume. And my favorite cheese to use here is Forme d'Ambert, but any blue cheese you like will do. And because it's easy to operate on autopilot when following a recipe, here's a heads-up: When preparing the galette dough, you need to add a teaspoon of caraway seeds to the dry ingredients.

▶ SERVES 4

2 tablespoons butter

½ medium white onion, diced

5 cups thinly sliced red cabbage (about 10 ounces, 280 g, or half a large head)

1 crisp, sweet-tart apple, such as Gala or Honeycrisp, peeled and coarsely chopped

1 teaspoon salt

¼ teaspoon freshly ground black pepper

½ cup (120 ml) full-bodied red wine

1 teaspoon red wine vinegar

1 recipe Galette Dough (page 218), with 1 teaspoon caraway seeds added to the dry ingredients

2 ounces (60 g) pungent, crumbly blue cheese

1 egg plus 1 tablespoon milk for egg wash, optional

1. Preheat oven to 375°F (190°C).
2. Melt the butter in a saucepan or deep sauté pan over medium heat. When the foaming sub-sides, add the onion and sauté until softened, about 10 minutes. Add the cabbage, apple, salt, and pepper, tossing with tongs to evenly distribute the ingredients. Pour in the wine. Bring to a boil, then lower the heat, cover, and

simmer until the cabbage is very tender, 15 to 20 minutes. Add the vinegar and continue to simmer, uncovered, until most of the liquid has cooked off, another 10 minutes or so. Let the mixture come to room temperature.

3. Line a baking sheet with parchment paper. Roll out the dough as directed. Drape it over a rolling pin and transfer to the lined baking sheet. Pile the cabbage mixture in the center of the dough, leaving a 1½-inch (4 cm) border. Crumble the blue cheese over the cabbage. Fold the edges of the dough over the mixture, pleating as needed. If desired, whisk together the egg and the milk to make an egg wash, and brush it over the pastry.

4. Bake, turning the pan halfway through the cooking time, for about 25 minutes, until the crust is browned. Serve hot or warm.

▶ LEFTOVERS: Wrapped tightly, this galette will keep for up to 2 days in the refrigerator.

▶ PREPARATION AND COOKING TIME:
1 hour and 15 minutes

BUTTERNUT SQUASH AND BRUSSELS SPROUTS GALETTE

ROASTED BUTTERNUT SQUASH and Brussels sprouts are surprisingly compatible, and this is especially fortuitous because stalks of Brussels sprouts turn up at farmers' markets just when tables are overflowing with winter squash of all shapes and sizes. The butternut squash has a brightness that's tamed by caramel notes imbued during roasting, and its flavor neutralizes the brazen taste of Brussels sprouts, which many people take exception to. I tried this galette with creamier cheeses, like Roquefort and ricotta, and decided that the cheese here needs to be assertive but essentially aromatic, so I settled on Gruyère. A drizzle of olive oil and a spritz of lemon at the end give it a fresh, barely lingering tang for a perfect balance of flavors.

▶ SERVES 4

1 small butternut squash (about 12 ounces, 325 g)

2 cups quartered Brussels sprouts (about 8 ounces, 230 g)

2 tablespoons olive oil

A few grinds of black pepper

Pinch of salt

1 tablespoon fresh thyme leaves, or 1 teaspoon dried thyme

Pinch of cayenne pepper

3 ounces (85 g) Gruyère cheese, grated (¾ cup)

1 recipe Galette Dough (page 218)

Squeeze of lemon juice

1. Preheat the oven to 425°F (220°C).
2. Trim the ends of the squash and cut the squash in half where the narrow neck transitions into the bulbous bottom. With the flat surface on the cutting board, carefully cut the skin off in thin strips from top to bottom. Cut each piece of squash in half lengthwise, scoop out the seeds, then cut it crosswise into ½-inch (1 cm) slices. Put the squash in a mixing bowl, and add the Brussels sprouts, 1 tablespoon of the olive oil, the pepper, and a pinch of salt. Toss to combine. Spread in an even layer on a rimmed baking sheet and roast for 15 to 20 minutes, until the squash and Brussels sprouts are tender but not mushy. Reduce the oven temperature to 375° (190°C).

3. Return the squash and Brussels sprouts to the mixing bowl. Add the thyme and cayenne. Taste for seasonings and add additional salt or pepper if necessary.

4. Line a baking sheet with parchment paper. Roll out the dough as directed. Drape it over a rolling pin and transfer to the lined baking sheet. Sprinkle the cheese over the center of the dough, leaving a 1½-inch (4 cm) border. Pile the squash mixture on top of the cheese. Fold the edges of the dough over the filling, pleating as needed.

5. Bake, turning the pan halfway through the cooking time, for about 25 minutes, until the crust is browned. Drizzle with the remaining 1 tablespoon of olive oil and the squeeze of lemon juice just before serving. Serve hot or warm.

▶ LEFTOVERS: This galette is best eaten on the day it's made, but wrapped tightly, it will keep for up to 2 days in the refrigerator.

▶ PREPARATION AND COOKING TIME: 1 hour

CREPES

I'VE ONLY recently begun to get familiar with crepes. A first step is learning the pronunciation: Is it "crape" or is it "crepp"? According to the Merriam-Webster dictionary, it's the former, but when I worked as a server at a French bistro, I'd be corrected no matter which way I said it. However you pronounce it, you'll be pleased to discover what easy, versatile little vessels for vegetables they are. If you're unfamiliar with crepes, the best way to describe them is as very thin pancakes folded or rolled around sweet or savory fillings. In Paris there are crepe carts parked throughout the city, the way that falafel and hot dog stands are scattered around Manhattan, and the crepes they offer are impossibly thin and filled with delicious things like Nutella, fruit, vegetables, cheese, or whatever you think to ask for.

One thing I love about crepes is that they can transform odds and ends lingering in the crisper into an impressive meal. In fact, my best dinnertime crepes have been inspired by leftovers. The crepes themselves can be used as a base, like a flat pancake, with sautéed vegetables scattered on top and a sauce drizzled over the top. Or you can fill them and then bake or panfry until crisp. They can also stand in for noodles in lasagna or tortillas in enchiladas. They can also double as dessert. (See page 165 for some guidelines on dessert crepes.) As you can see, once you have crepes in your repertoire, an easy, elegant meal will always be close at hand.

Some of my favorite dinner parties have revolved around crepes. Make the crepes in advance, stack them up on a plate, and, once they're cool, cover tightly with plastic wrap. Then prepare a few fillings: caramelized onions (page 22) or Onion Marmalade (page 23); a platter of perfectly steamed or sautéed vegetables, such as asparagus, zucchini, mushrooms, or greens; and a couple of different cheeses, like feta, a nutty Gruyère or Gouda, or fresh goat cheese, which I like to pick up at the farmers' market. Make a batch of Twenty-Minute Tomato Sauce (page 24) for topping, and prepare to fry or poach a few eggs. Let your guests assemble their own crepes, placing the filled ones on a baking sheet to be heated in the oven.

Crepe pans, which are simply very shallow sauté pans, are relatively inexpensive and are widely available if you intend to make crepes often, but I've never owned them for the same reason that I don't own pie weights: I don't have room for single-use kitchen tools. If you have a nonstick skillet, you'll have no problem making crepes.

CREPES

Basic Crepes ✦

THIS RECIPE IS suitable for savory as well as sweet crepes (see page 165). For dessert crepes, just add two teaspoons of sugar along with the dry ingredients (and, of course, don't use vegetable stock in the batter). I recommend using a blender to make crepe batter because it turns the job into a one-minute task. You can whisk by hand if you wish, but do so vigorously and thoroughly, being sure to break up every lump of flour. Cooked vegetables, like spinach, sweet potatoes, or pumpkin, can be added to crepe batter, which makes for plumper crepes. Recipes for these variations appear after the main recipe, as do recipes for several savory fillings. The filling combinations I provide are engineered as weeknight dishes, cooked on the stovetop, folded into crepes, and served right away. But after assembling the filled crepes, you can certainly cook them in the oven if you like. Simply place them on a very lightly greased baking sheet and bake at 325°F oven for about 15 minutes, just until the crepe is crisp and the fillings are heated through.

▶ MAKES 8 CREPES

½ cup (120 ml) water, vegetable stock (page15), or milk

½ cup (120 ml) reduced-fat milk (1% or 2%)

2 eggs

2 tablespoons olive oil or melted butter

½ cup (60 g) all-purpose flour

¼ cup (30 g) buckwheat, spelt, or whole wheat flour, or more all-purpose flour

½ teaspoon salt

Butter or oil for cooking

Fillings of your choice (see page 225)

1. Put the water, milk, eggs, olive oil, flours, and salt in a blender in that order, with the wet ingredients on the bottom. Puree for 30 seconds to 1 minute, scraping down the sides of the chamber with a spatula once or twice along the way. Refrigerate for at least 30 minutes and up to overnight. The batter should have the consistency of heavy cream. If it's any thicker, stir in a additional milk or water 1 tablespoon at a time.

2. Heat a 10-inch (25 cm) nonstick sauté pan or seasoned skillet over medium heat and melt a very small amount of butter. Use a paper towel to spread it around and soak up the excess so the sauté pan is covered with only a very thin film of grease. Tilt the pan away from you and, using a ¼-cup (60 ml) ladle or measuring cup, quickly pour in a ladleful of batter, swirling the pan as you pour; the goal is to uniformly distribute the batter as quickly as possible. Cook until the edges begin to curl up, the bottom is slightly browned but still pliable, and the top side is set, 2 to 3 minutes. Flip the crepe over (I do this with my fingers, but you can also use a thin spatula) and cook the other side until lightly browned, 1 to 2 minutes. Stack the cooked crepes on a plate until ready for use. If the crepes begin to stick to the pan as you

continue cooking them, rub the pan with the paper towel used to soak up the excess grease.

▶ **LEFTOVERS:** Wrapped tightly, cooked crepes will keep for up to 1 day in the refrigerator. Stored in an airtight container, leftover batter will keep for up to 2 days.

▶ **PREPARATION AND COOKING TIME:** 45 minutes

variations

SPINACH CREPES: Blanch, steam, or sauté 1 bunch of spinach (about 12 ounces, 325 g; see page 10), then squeeze dry. Or, to use frozen spinach, cook it in the microwave at 2-minute intervals on medium heat, stirring at each interval with a fork. Continue cooking until thawed, then drain and, once cool enough to handle, squeeze out as much liquid as possible. If using whole frozen spinach, finely chop it. Add the spinach to the blender with the rest of the ingredients and proceed with the recipe.

SWEET POTATO OR PUMPKIN CREPES: Add ½ cup sweet potato or pumpkin puree to the blender along with the eggs and milk. Proceed with the recipe.

FILLINGS

SAUTÉED MUSHROOMS, CARAMELIZED ONIONS, AND GRUYÈRE CREPES, TOPPED WITH FRIED EGG: Sauté 8 ounces (230 g) of sliced cremini or white button mushrooms in 2 tablespoons butter until browned and the liquid released by the mushrooms has cooked off. Divide mushrooms among 8 crepes (preferably made with buckwheat or spelt flour), and add 2 heaping tablespoons caramelized onions (page 22) and 2 tablespoons grated Gruyère cheese per crepe. Fold or roll the crepes around the filling. Panfry the filled crepes in batches in a very small amount of butter or oil until the cheese is melted and the crepes are just crisp. Top with 1 fried egg per every 2 crepes and a sprinkling of salt and freshly ground black pepper.

ASPARAGUS CREPES WITH GOAT CHEESE: Steam 8 ounces (230 g) of asparagus until just tender, 3 to 4 minutes. Plunge into an ice bath to halt the cooking and preserve the color. Halve any fat spears lengthwise, then chop the asparagus into 1-inch (3 cm) pieces. Divide the asparagus among 8 spinach crepes (see left), then top with 2 tablespoons fresh goat cheese and 1 teaspoon minced fresh parsley per crepe. Season with salt and freshly ground black pepper. Fold or roll the crepes around the filling. Panfry the filled crepes in batches in a very small amount of butter or oil until the cheese is melted and the crepes are just crisp.

SPINACH, FETA, AND SCALLION CREPES WITH TOMATO SAUCE

Sauté 1 bunch of spinach (see page 10), then chop it finely. Divide the spinach among 8 crepes (preferably made with whole wheat or additional all-purpose flour), then top with ½ scallion, thinly sliced, per crepe, salt, and freshly ground black pepper. Fold or roll the crepes around the filling. Panfry the filled crepes in batches in a very small amount of butter or oil until the fillings are heated through and the crepe is just crisp. Top each crepe with about 2 tablespoons warm tomato sauce, preferably Twenty-Minute Tomato Sauce (page 24).

CURRIED POTATO CREPE STACK

THIS IS AN easy, three-part dish: make the crepes, prepare the filling (which requires minimal prep and is a one-pot job), and then assemble. The sweet potato combined with the heat from the curry spices makes for a very nuanced, filling dish that is a gorgeous centerpiece for the table. Using buckwheat flour in the crepes here makes for a slightly nutty contrast, whereas the sweet potato variation reinforces the sweet elements of the dish. This is also a great dish for buffets, because it's excellent whether served warm or at room temperature.

▶ SERVES 5

1 large russet potato (about 12 ounces, 325 g)

1 medium sweet potato (about 12 ounces, 325 g)

2 tablespoons neutral oil (canola, grapeseed, peanut, or vegetable oil)

1 medium red onion, diced

1½ teaspoons curry powder, preferably homemade (page 229)

1 teaspoon garam masala

½ teaspoon ground coriander

Pinch of cayenne pepper

1 teaspoon salt

1 tablespoon all-purpose flour

1 cup (240 ml) water

3 tablespoons chopped fresh cilantro

3 scallions, white and green parts, thinly sliced

6 crepes, made with ¼ cup (30 g) buckwheat flour (page 224) or sweet potato puree (see page 225)

1. Using a mandoline or a steady hand with a knife, cut the potatoes and sweet potatoes into ⅛-inch (3 mm) thick rounds.

2. Heat the oil in a deep sauté pan over medium heat. Add the onion and cook until it just begins to soften and caramelize, 10 to 12 minutes, turning down the heat if the onion starts to burn. Stir in the curry powder, garam masala, coriander, cayenne, and salt. Add the potatoes, tossing to evenly coat them with the spices, then sprinkle the flour over the potatoes and again toss until evenly coated. Pour in the water and bring to a boil. Turn the heat down to low, give the dish a stir, then cover and cook until the potatoes are tender, 15 to 20 minutes. Remove from heat, allow the mixture to cool slightly, then stir in the cilantro and scallions.

3. When ready to serve, set aside the prettiest crepe to top the stack. Then choose the least attractive crepe and place it in the center of a serving platter or, if you plan to warm the dish, on a rimless baking sheet. Scoop up a heaping ½ cup, or rougly a fifth, of the potato mixture and spread it over the crepe, leaving about a ½-inch (1 cm) border. Place a crepe on top of the potatoes and press with your hands to level it off. Spread another ½ cup of the potato mixture over the crepe, and continue in this way until you have five layers of potatoes. Place your last, most beautiful crepe on top.

4. You can serve the crepe stack warm or at room temperature. If serving it warm, cover the assembled crepe stack with foil and place it in a 300°F (150°C) oven for 20 minutes. Carefully transfer to a serving platter and serve.

▶ LEFTOVERS: Wrapped tightly, this dish will keep for 1 day in the refrigerator.

▶ PREPARATION AND COOKING TIME: 35 minutes

CURRIED POTATO CREPE STACK

Homemade Curry Powder

CURRY POWDER is simply a spice blend. This may be an obvious thing to state, but it can be confusing when you see curry lined up alongside jars of bay leaves and dill in the spice section of the grocery store. Not only is it a blend, its composition varies greatly by country and region (and by kitchen within those countries and regions). What you buy at the store is usually a blend of warm spices like cinnamon and cardamom, chili for heat, and cumin and turmeric for earthiness (and color). It's often bulked up with coriander, because it's such an inexpensive spice. There are many good store-bought curry blends, and it's worth sampling a few to find which you prefer or which might work best for certain dishes. Or even better, you could make your own! Spending an afternoon making a couple different spice blends is a fun group activity, at least for a food nerd like me. The following recipe is my basic curry blend.

▶ **MAKES ABOUT ¼ CUP**

10 black peppercorns

5 cloves

2 dried hot chile peppers (chile de arbol for hot curry; ancho chilies for mild curry)

1 cinnamon stick

1 star anise

1 tablespoon cumin seeds

1 tablespoon coriander seeds

1 teaspoon mustard seeds

2 tablespoons turmeric

Combine the peppercorns, cloves, chiles, cinnamon, star anise, and cumin seeds in a dry skillet over low heat. Toast, swirling the pan frequently, until very aromatic, 1 to 2 minutes. Transfer to a spice grinder or mortar and pestle, add the mustard seeds, and grind until powdered; this may take several minutes. Sift out the larger pieces, then stir in the turmeric. Store in an airtight container until ready to use.

ResouRces

Spices
The Spice House
Phone: 847-328-3711
www.thespicehouse.com

Fleur de Sel
SaltWorks
Phone: 800-353-7158
www.saltworks.us

Beans
Jansal Valley Beans
(Exclusively sold through Sid Wainer & Son)
Phone: 888-743-9246
www.sidwainer.com

Rancho Gordo Beans
Phone: 707-259-1935
www.ranchogordo.com

Middle Eastern Foods
Sahadi's Specialty and Fine Foods
Phone: 718-624-4550
www.sahadis.com

Korean and Japanese Foods
Koamart
www.koamart.com

Bakeware and Kitchen Supplies
Fishs Eddy
Phone: 877-347-4733
www.fishseddy.com

Broadway Panhandler
Phone: 866-266-5927
www.broadwaypanhandler.com

ACKNOWLEDGMENTS

EVEN IN THE most stressful times of working on this project, I paused to wonder what my mom would have thought of me writing cookbooks. A few days before completing this manuscript I needed to look something up. I reached for *Food Lover's Companion* and remembered all of a sudden that it had been a Christmas present from my mom. She gave it to me over a decade before I found myself in the midst of an actual career in food. It was a reassuring thing to discover—proof of her foresight—though also a bittersweet reminder that she would have relished the opportunity to take a front-seat role. This book, and everything else I do, is fueled and inspired by her.

Extreme thanks as always to my family: To my dad Ron Volger for his all-encompassing support (and especially for letting me make a mess of his kitchen over and over and over again) and to Pam Robinson; to my brother Max and sister-in-law Casady and the new Volger, Zoe Jaenene(!); and also to my grandfather Glen Scott and to Ruth Keeth.

Thank you to everyone at The Experiment, especially Matthew Lore, my publisher, editor, and wonderful friend, who shaped this book in countless, invaluable ways, as well as Peter Burri, Rose Carrano, Richard Gallen, Karen Giangreco, Pauline Neuwirth, Susi Oberhelman, and Jasmine Star. Special thanks to Christina Heaston, photographer extraordinaire.

Thanks also to all who helped to make *Veggie Burgers Every Which Way* such a fun success: Grant Butler, Bob Carroll, Cathy Erway, Jeff Gordinier, Lynn Rossetto Kasper, Alina Larson, Deborah Madison, Rebecca Flint Marx, Gretchen McKay, Patrick Murphy, Gina Salamone, Martha Rose Schulman, Susan Schwartz, and Sean Smith.

Thank you friends, family, colleagues, and recipe testing volunteers: James Atlas, Peter Desrochers, Ariel Kouvaras, and Nataša Lekić of Atlas & Co.; Ashley Bouldin; Calista Brill; Sean Dougherty and Sidney Prawatyotin; Paula Forman; Katie Gilligan; Mary Holden, Anne Grant Anderson, and Erin Ferguson; Peter Joseph and Katy Hershberger; Wendy Mielke; Ann Pappert; Bevin Strand; Nicole Turney; Brian Ulicky; and Jim and Cinda Volger. A special nod to my cookbook-themed dinner party friends Ruth Curry, Emily Gould (also of *Cooking the Books* fame—thank you!), and Sadie Stein.

For keeping me sane, entertaining my meals and my recipes, and being such good friends and exemplary human beings, thank you to Meghan Best, Lesley Enston, Izzy Forman, Kathryn Hunt, and Ilsa Jule.

And a final, special thank-you to Matt Rebula, whose curiosity, patience, and support is thumbprinted on every page.

INDEX

Page numbers in **bold** indicate a photograph.

ABOUT THE AUTHOR

LUKAS VOLGER began to garner fans, readers, and media attention with his first book, *Veggie Burgers Every Which Way*. He has worked at food establishments in New York City and in his native Idaho as a baker, caterer, prep cook, server, and occasional dishwasher. He lives in Brooklyn, New York.

www.lukasvolger.com